Praise for

A Siege on Her Heart

This is an unforgettable story of courage and love! One that will stick with you and change you for the better.

-Brooke Hampton, author of *The Perfect Rose* and other titles

A Siege on Her Heart reads like a cinematic wartime drama in that moment after the smoke begins to clear. I fell in love with the steadfast captain bearing the weight of war and the spirited Spanish heroine whose heart aches to heal. This story has everything I love - gripping conflict, stand-out history, and an irresistibly sweet romance.

-Sara Cardon, author of *The Captain's Lady* and other titles

Brousseau's stunning debut takes us through the horrors of war and the beauty of healing. Against the backdrop of the atrocities at the siege of San Sebastian, we encounter the resilience of a passionate Spanish woman, the quiet determination of a British soldier, and their unlikely love that bridges cultural divides and heals broken hearts.

—Rachel Grow Law, author of *Heart of Snow*

Lyrical writing and vivid imagery take the stage in Jessica Brousseau's debut novel, *A Siege on Her Heart*. Historical details, particularly regarding the siege of San Sebastián and its aftermath, give the story depth and make this regency tale unique. Readers will be swept into the past and taken on an emotional journey, one not soon forgotten.

-Rachel Kelley Stones, author of *A Love Unseen* and other titles

Intriguing from the first page, Brousseau's debut promises a rich story with vibrant characters, vivid imagery, and deep history sure to captivate historical romance readers.

-Karen Thornell, author of *Edward and Amelia* and other titles

JESSICA BROUSSEAU

a Siege ON HER Heart

SWEETWATER BOOKS
An imprint of Cedar Fort, Inc.
Springville, Utah

Paperback ISBN 13: 978-1-4621-5079-3
eBook ISBN 13: 978-1-4621-5080-9

Published by Sweetwater Books, an imprint of Cedar Fort, Inc.
2373 W. 700 S., Suite 100, Springville, UT 84663
Distributed by Cedar Fort, Inc., www.cedarfort.com

Library of Congress Cataloging Number:

Cover design by Shawnda Craig

Edited and Typeset by Liz Kazandzhy

Printed in the United States of America

10 9 8 7 6 5 4 3 2 1

Printed on acid-free paper

For my husband. Thank you for holding me together in difficult moments and for believing in me even when I find it hard to believe in myself. And for my children, the most precious gifts I have ever received. I love you all more than words can say.

Families are forever!

Contents

Foreword

Dear Reader,

Thank you for choosing to read *A Siege on Her Heart*. The historical background of this story came to be when I was researching about Spain in 1813–15 and stumbled upon the debated Siege of San Sebastián. These events intrigued me increasingly as I learned about them. (More about this in the author's note at the end of the book!) But the heart of the story, including some of the emotional challenges that Ana María endures, resonated deeply with me as I became a mother for the first time and struggled with postpartum depression. I feel it is important to see portrayals of these types of challenges to remind ourselves that we have the strength to ask for help and choose to trust others when it means improving our lives and increasing our happiness. Most importantly, I wanted to share how my faith in God was at the heart of my healing, just as my main character's experience. It is my hope that this story and the healing that these two characters found in Christ and in each other will inspire you to seek similar healing in your life.

As Ana is from Spain, please note that there will be some Spanish scattered throughout the story, and her English will be intentionally imperfect. There is a Spanish glossary at the end of the book for your convenience.

I hope you grow to love these characters as much as I do.

Much love,
Jessica

Content Warning

Please note that this story tastefully and sensitively recalls the aftermath of a sexual assault as well as memories of physical and emotional abuse. Neither the assault nor the abuse is actually portrayed on paper. This book explores the intricacies of mental health following traumatic events with the hope of portraying healing. Please read with care given this content warning.

Chapter 1

October 19, 1813, London, England

PETER NEVER INTENDED TO MARRY. AND HE CERTAINLY NEVER INtended to marry like this.

He stood rigidly, at perfect attention. But the way his hands fisted and his heart pounded as if he was running from enemy fire revealed that this wedding day was anything but normal. His back was framed by the large windows of the Heathridge Chapel. Light streamed around him, painting the stone floor and wooden benches in radiant colors. The vibrancy almost made him feel as if he were back in Spain. But before Peter could appreciate the beauty of the moment, the red light filtering through the stained glass looked a little too physical, like a seeping, staining pool of blood. And it certainly did not help that he was wearing his finest uniform, freshly starched and gleaming in shades of scarlet and cream. The very sensation of the fabric took him back to the battlefield in an instant, try as he might to avoid it.

Not now, soldier. It's Ana's wedding day as well. This is not about you.

Mother nodded at him reassuringly from the wooden pew, but the tapping of her foot revealed an anxiety she would not confess to.

She had used all her connections to speedily arrange this day, had procured the special license and permissions for the couple to be married at the small chapel on the Heathridge Hall lands. Surely writing to her to ask for help after years of distance had implied a great deal of urgency, although she had likely not expected to receive word that he was to be married, and as quickly as possible. The familiar setting should have brought Peter some portion of comfort. It did not. He felt every muscle in his body tensing, bracing for attack.

Golden autumn light from a door opening at the back splashed over the floor, fading the red colors of the stained window to pink, and a shadowed silhouette appeared. Peter's eyes jumped upward, meeting the dark gaze of Ana María, and his hurried breathing stilled. He would not deny it; his bride was beautiful. Of course, she had always been beautiful. He would have to be a fool to be blind to her. But at the war camp, hers was a rough, intimidating sort of beauty. Today, this type of beauty was soft, romantic, and entirely enthralling. Her dark brown eyes shone with a hope that he had not seen in months. Her generous lips were rounded into a smile. Most bridegrooms would be thrilled at such an irresistible sight. Peter was made nervous by it. Theirs was not intended to be that sort of marriage. He was to be her protector, not her lover. She had a secret to be kept. He tried to swallow, but his throat was entirely dry.

The high waistline of her gown floated over her figure. The gown's rich pink shade set off her deep black hair and olive skin at a most stunning advantage. If one looked closely enough, it was clear that the fit of her gown was imperfect, even if very slightly so. Mother's seamstress had done her best to adjust one of Mother's gowns for Ana María in only a few short hours. A small bunch of red flowers was pinned in her tight curls along with a small veil of black lace, a nod to the traditions of her Spanish heritage, implying that they would be connected as spouses until death parted them. However, for Peter, death could come much sooner than expected—it could come at any moment once he returned to the battlefield.

Again, he mentally shook himself, rolling his shoulders back and squeezing his eyes shut. He would not lose this moment to powder-strewn memories and visions of the blood-soaked battlefield. This was one of the few moments of his life that Peter would want to remember. He needed to be present.

When he opened his eyes again, Ana María reached his side. He held out his arm for her, but she reached for his hand instead.

"How do you fare?" he whispered.

"*Estoy bien*," she responded, although the shadow beneath her eyes hinted at another restless night. She was putting on a brave face, as she was so apt at doing.

Peter squeezed her hand, looking down. Her wrists were no longer bruised, something he was glad for. Any visible injuries would draw too many questions, which would be most unwelcome when he was already doing his best to protect her from danger, even of the social sort. Their fingers interlaced, a strange sensation as they had never had such closeness before. Her fingers were cold and trembling, and his were flushed with heat from the adrenaline coursing through him. The juxtaposition was strangely comforting.

"Friends, we welcome you here today to celebrate a felicitous union," the vicar began in a droning voice. It was to be an Anglican service, typical of the Church, although Ana surely had always dreamed of being married in a Catholic service in one of Spain's glorious cathedrals. But they were in England, so it would have to do.

Ana María's lips curved into a confident, endearing smile, but he did not miss the tear that escaped down her cheek. And yet her shadowed eyes reflected an understanding he felt echo through him. This marriage was a necessary action, a way to protect her past and future. Prying questions into her past could put them both at risk, considering the ongoing unrest related to the war with Napoleon. Society was not kind to foreigners, and even less to unmarried women in her condition. It was, in a way, a marriage of convenience, though it would surely have repercussions that were most inconvenient indeed.

But they had known it would be this way, hadn't they?

And here he was, preparing himself to repeat vows that would alter their lives forever. He was to be a husband. A husband and a father in one act, and not a soul knew as much.

* * *

Oh, but *El Capitán* was handsome as a bridegroom.

Ana found she could no longer look away from her betrothed of mere days—and now soon-to-be husband. Peter's posture suggested rapt attention, his face carved in solemnity, his dark brown hair tied securely at the nape of his neck, leaving him looking every bit the soldier he was. And when his crystal blue gaze met hers, Ana María suddenly found herself robbed of breath. But what was this feeling? This arrangement was by no means a romantic one, yet she could not ignore the squeezing of her ribs. She certainly preferred it to the nausea plaguing her otherwise . . . but perhaps it was just nerves. After all, she had never intended to marry an Englishman.

Still, Ana clung to the warmth of his grasp. She needed the strength of his touch more than anything right now.

"Is there anyone here to give this woman away?" the vicar asked, his voice echoing not only through the room but also through the chambers of Ana's aching heart.

She dipped her chin, unable to hide her tears as she shook her head. Peter squeezed her hand, but it did not offer her the strength it normally had. "No," he whispered, his tone mournful and apologetic.

Papá had been meant to give her away.

And yet *Papá* had been left bleeding and buried on the shore of San Sebastián. Perhaps if God was as understanding and merciful as she hoped He was, her father would be able to look down from above on this day. Even so, he would undoubtedly be displeased. She was not marrying a Catholic, was not marrying for love. Worst of all, she was marrying an Englishman.

It was the strangest sensation to be married without one's family. She was dressed as a bride but didn't feel like one in the least bit. *Papá* should be here, as should *Mamá*. Unable to stave off a wave of emotion any longer, she felt silent tears slipping down her cheeks. Peter pressed her hand, a slight squeeze that made her want to launch herself into his arms and soak his cravat with her tears. But of course, such a thing would not be appropriate in the current setting, even as they were about to be man and wife, not to mention Peter's entirely unaffectionate nature. Of course, he did not intend to be cold; he was merely poised and practiced in every possible way. He was comforting in his rational-mindedness and eagerness to provide protection. Still, there were certainly times when Ana María wished he would embrace her, if only for a moment, to provide the stability she needed.

"Dearly beloved . . ." The short, old vicar with kind eyes began to warble the traditional words of the marriage ceremony.

Ana's heart twinged with longing at some understanding of the proceedings. At least in Catholicism she would have been able to follow the ceremony, even if it was held in English. This vicar was more difficult to understand. His voice sounded as if his nose was incurably stuffy, although a quick glance revealed he was not sick in the slightest. It left his tone sounding swallowed, flat, and so very English. Despite Ana's increasing grasp of English, many of the large, intricate words eluded her mind. Instead of being filled with tenderness at the moment, she was filled with confusion and quickly became overwhelmed. Even if she was being married under the most unexpected of circumstances, she should understand her own marriage vows, should she not?

But perhaps it was best that she did not understand everything. Words such as "children," "sin," and "fornication" stuck in her mind amid the muddle of flat English words, reminding her that their marriage was not a typical one. She resisted the urge to wrap her arms across her middle, as if she could protect herself from the disapproving comments that would surely come if any of those present knew of her condition. Peter had saved her in more ways than one. He rescued her from her attacker, shielded her from harmful accusations, and was now providing her and her child with a future, saving them from a number of unsavory fates. How could she ever repay him?

Her breathing quickened, and tears wet her eyes again. Peter's clothing rustled at her side as he glanced at her and squeezed her hand, twice this time. It was their secret way of saying, "*Estás bien?*" *Are you well?* She was tempted to squeeze once—"no"—instead of twice—"*estoy bien*"—but she didn't want to distract or worry him. This day was already filled with enough pressure.

Still, it was difficult to stay quiet. Surely Peter could see the emotions painting her face, threatening to overwhelm her. Unlike him, and many other people in England for that matter, she could not hide how she was feeling. It was not how she had been raised. Perhaps that was also why so many deemed her overly excitable or uncontrollable, even hysterical. Ana preferred "passionate." She was not afraid to feel, and she felt everything intensely.

Finally, the vicar pronounced words she could understand most clearly: "husband and wife." She looked expectantly at her now-husband, who seemed to be momentarily frozen. Ana stepped toward him, pulling slightly at his hand, not wanting to seem too forward but even more fearful of appearing cold and unfeeling. As if emerging from a heavy night's sleep, he blinked a few times and his tongue edged his lips, revealing the depth of his nervousness. She needed to kiss him, and *now*, even though the thought of kissing anyone made her stomach turn.

In a quick motion, Ana rose to her toes, puckered her lips, squeezed her eyes shut, and met his lips for a brief moment. She would not let her mind stray to the memory of another man pinning his rough, alcohol-saturated mouth against hers. Ana peeked one eye open and breathed readily again. Yes, it was Peter she had kissed—Peter she had married. She was safe here so long as she was with him. Meeting his gaze and mirroring his crooked, nervous smile, Ana walked back down the aisle as his family cheered modestly.

After a short, stunned-silent carriage ride back to Heathridge Hall, the Ashmores' estate, Ana was led into the breakfast room, its tall windows and intricate paneling reminding her that she was no longer in her beloved *España*. Everything seemed unnecessarily ornate, although that much could be expected at an earl's estate. On the table, an elaborate wedding breakfast was on display, as detailed as an oil painting. From the chilled butter to the golden breads to the jeweled jellies, everything was vibrantly and delicately arranged. But it did not instill any sort of hunger in Ana.

The bumpy carriage ride had only intensified Ana's nausea. She had planned to dash for the water closet upon her arrival, but in the company of others, such a move would be most unseemly, not to mention suspicious. Now she would have to push through the discomfort of her upset stomach while playing the part of the blissful bride.

Somehow Lady Ashmore, now her mother-in-law, had arrived ahead of them. "We are so very pleased to welcome you to the family, dear," Lady Ashmore said, her voice all velvet and warmth.

"Thank you, my lady," Ana said. She pressed her lips together as her stomach roiled and her heart pounded. Ana desperately wanted the approval of this woman. She would give anything to have the advice and warmth of a mother in her present circumstances. "And thank you much for this dress. *Muy* beautiful," she added.

"Not at all, my dear. I daresay it complements you much more than it ever would me."

Ana blushed. The dowager was stunning. She had maintained every bit of poise and grace from her younger years, and surely many men still thought her quite beautiful.

Ana watched as Peter's brother, Matthew, the current Lord Ashmore, stepped up to the pair, giving Peter a somewhat hesitant embrace. She eased herself down into an overly cushioned chair and pressed a hand to her uneasy stomach. She had heard much of Matthew during their weeks crossing the sea, and Peter's feelings regarding his brother were quite complicated. From what she could understand, they had been the best of friends as children, but complexities in their family drove them apart as they grew older, particularly when Peter chose to join the army. The tense history between the two was evident as a muscle pulsed on Peter's jaw and he blinked rapidly as his brother released him from his grip.

The family resemblances were obvious as Ana looked at both men. Peter's frame was a great deal broader than Matthew's, despite the lack of nutrition that the war could often bring to its soldiers. Matthew's hair was a touch lighter than Peter's and much wavier. Dimples dotted his cheeks, and his green eyes seemed much more carefree than his brother's blue ones, even given the awkwardness of their meeting after so many years. The wide, genuine smile that lit up Matthew's face when attending to his mother made Ana ache to see similar happiness on Peter's face. Lord Ashmore was clearly without many of the scars, physical and otherwise, that Peter bore.

"The ceremony was a tad bit long," Matthew joked to his mother. "However, this impressive wedding breakfast should make up for it." He rubbed his hands together in mock anticipation. Ana could sense he was trying to put them all at ease through his good-naturedness. But why didn't it dispel the sadness in her husband's eyes?

"Matthew, darling, don't be silly," Lady Ashmore said, concern puckering her brow as her eyes darted to Ana's. "It was an entirely conventional ceremony. It has simply been a few years since you've attended a wedding."

"I suppose I will believe you, Mother, although I nearly fell asleep in the pews," Matthew said with a smile as he bent down to kiss his mother's cheek.

"Clearly you have never been a bridegroom, as it is anything but sleep-inducing," Peter muttered, nervous hands straightening his cravat, but then he looked at his brother and his voice lightened, attempting a jest. "I never imagined I would be a bridegroom before the desirable Earl Ashmore."

"You wound me, brother!" Matthew exclaimed.

The brothers chuckled at that, and some of the awkwardness that bound Peter seemed to ease away. The ache of longing Ana felt only pounded deeper into her heart. When was the last time she had heard Peter laugh? Not since before San Sebastián.

Lady Ashmore rolled her eyes, but her smile remained. It was clear enough to Ana María that she was delighted to see her sons together again. It had been years, as far as she was aware.

"Peter, do assist your wife in filling a plate. Please be generous in your portions, as there is much to share," Lady Ashmore said before turning to greet the few other relations in attendance.

"Yes, my lady," Peter said, snapping his heels together and nodding a salute to his mother.

Ana María joined Peter at the sideboard. Scents of butter and cinnamon perfumed the air as she approached the food. But one small whiff of the fired fish at the center of it all made her grip the table—and her stomach—more tightly.

"Is there anything here that you believe will maintain its place in your stomach?" Peter asked, his voice quiet and careful.

"A bread? And a boiled egg, *por favor*." Simple foods would have to do. Any flavor or smell too strong would send Ana María running to the water closet. She averted her eyes as Peter repeated her requests to the servant standing by, waiting with an empty plate.

Despite the sickness roiling in her stomach, Ana María had to admit the spread looked impressive. Hot rolls, sweet lemon cakes, sliced ham, boiled eggs, and fresh fruit were piled high. But she would eat carefully, if at all. She did not wish to spend the rest of the day bent over a basin, casting up her accounts.

"Truly, you must give my compliments to the kitchens, Mother. This is an astounding collection, particularly after all the dry meat and potatoes I've faced over the past years," Peter said as he pulled out a chair for Ana next to his mother before sitting down as well.

"Indeed, darling," Lady Ashmore replied. "This fine array looks almost as beautiful and appealing as your new wife. Almost." She smiled knowingly.

At the words, both Peter and Ana María's faces flamed.

"When will you leave for your wedding trip?" Matthew asked.

"We've had our fill of traveling as of late," Peter said, his fists balling beneath the table. Ana pried at his fingers, trying to calm him, but was unsuccessful in calming herself. At the thought of the rocking boat, Ana felt a burning rising in her throat. She pinned her lips together even more tightly and clenched her hands in her skirts. The strong smell of the fish seemed to overtake the entire room.

"Then where will you be staying tonight?" Lady Ashmore questioned.

"We'll be settling in at Abbeygate and look forward to enjoying the peaceful environment of Surrey Hills," Peter said, squeezing Ana's hand briefly under the table.

"Oh, the ride to Abbeygate only lasts a few hours, does it not, Mother?" Matthew said.

A *few* hours? Ana would not endure it. Her stable, wooden chair seemed to transform into the bumping, jolting bench of a carriage, and her stomach could no longer contain its contents. She burst from the table, spinning to face the door, and ran as quickly as her feet would carry her. *Por favor!* She begged her stomach to wait. Almost there . . .

She heard Peter's voice growing louder as he trailed after her. "She still feels a bit uneasy from our long journey. Surely, you understand. Please continue without us."

Chapter 2

August 31, 1813, San Sebastián, Basque Country, Spain

A few months prior . . .

The first time Peter had met Ana María Bailon, he'd been truly astonished by her boldness. She had a commanding presence, just like her father, and did not seem out of place in the slightest as she conversed with and translated for other military leaders. Peter's officer rank, and undoubtedly the rank of his family, had earned him a seat in such meetings, where he made her acquaintance. She was not from Basque Country but was from Southern Spain, so he attempted to communicate with her with the measly Spanish he knew, the few times he had gathered his courage enough to do so.

Her father was aware of all the ongoings of San Sebastián, no matter the camp. The city was a small one, but it was currently overrun with armies from four different countries, including the native Spanish. It was a critical location for French war supply and strategy, being on the border of the sea, and needed to be reclaimed from the French, requiring the aid of the British and the Portuguese. Ana María's father, a Spanish captain, had played an essential role outside the city, doing everything possible to keep peace between the Allied forces at play during the siege.

Ana, it seemed, was just as invested in the experience. Even though Major Bailon was a dominating figure, he clearly doted on his daughter. But instead of spoiling her with material goods and causing her to become soft and selfish, like some young ladies in London, he had sharpened her and made her into a valuable tool. Her mother's unexplained and seemingly permanent absence likely intensified Ana's education as well. She was incredibly well-learned and was not afraid to speak her mind, even among numerous military leaders who were visibly shocked to see a woman present in their meetings. Although her official role was a translator for Basque, Spanish, and Portuguese relations, she had often contributed to the communicative stratagem that was so critical in a siege that had dragged on for months on end.

Most of all, she was a captivating communicator, but not in the way that many ladies of English society would deem themselves to be captivating. Instead of making herself seem simple or subservient in mock humility or silly flirtations, she was assertive and audacious. Her command over Portuguese and Basque, even with the struggle that translations brought, silenced even the haughtiest of men in those upper circles. Her father had positioned her as a translator, as none of the British knew Basque, but it was clear that her role was more of an ambassador. She managed to keep the peace amid the heated conversations that occurred between Spanish, Portuguese, and British armies while they were waiting out the French.

Still, amid her responsibilities, it was evident that she was a lady, and a very beautiful one at that. Lucious, black curls streamed down her back, escaping her carved Spanish hair comb and coiling tightly in the humidity of the coast. A scarlet fabric rose was pinned just behind her ear, brightening the structured design and muted color of her military-inspired gown. Shorter tendrils bounced about her forehead, framing her heart-shaped face, rose-colored cheeks, and full lips that were continuously curved upward. But her eyes were the most captivating of all. Framed by thick eyelashes, her irises were a dramatic shade of brown, so dark they were almost black. When Peter caught Ana's gaze, he found it more than difficult to escape their depths. They almost made him forget they were in the middle of a war.

As the siege continued, Peter found himself increasingly curious about Ana, this rose among the thorns in the intensity of the siege. He'd ascertained that she was twenty-one, so he was three years her senior. But the wisdom she exuded made her seem far older. He'd been so flustered when he first spoke to her that he destroyed even the most basic of Spanish phrases. When he should have said "*Cómo te llamas?*" to ask what her name was, he instead said "*Cómo te amo,*" which, embarrassingly enough, meant "How I love you." She had laughed heartily, and he had turned positively crimson and choked with embarrassment. The discomfort evident in his ramrod-straight posture did little to stave off her laughter. Then, much to his horror, she had approached him, greeted him with the customary Spanish *besos*, or kisses, on each cheek, and responded by saying, "*No te preocupes, Capitán, te amo también.*" *Don't worry, Capitán, I love you too.* Her response, reciprocating his accidental confession of love, had embarrassed him more than anything. His effort to impress her with his Spanish was a failure, one that his comrades teased him mercilessly for. Every time she had seen him in the weeks that followed, she had called out with great gusto, "*Hola, Capitán! Cómo te amo!*" His regiment had even started to refer to her as his *prometida,* or betrothed.

All the tension of the previous months had come to a point on the 31st of August. What had started as a moment of relief and jubilation—as they received news of France's surrender after eight days of bombardment and months of siege warfare—had turned into a living nightmare. When the message that the French were giving up the city had rolled through camp, Peter had expected his fellow soldiers to celebrate in their usual manner, with a bit of boisterous singing and a little too much to drink, activities he was not remotely interested in, so he had spent the evening tending to his injured men in the medical tents. But instead of celebrating in their typical way, British soldiers stormed down the narrow peninsula and went on a reckless rampage in San Sebastián, the city they had been fighting so hard to recover from France. It seemed they decided it was their right to pillage and terrorize the town.

Much to Peter's horror, the men ran amok in their wine cellars and left destruction and tragedy in their wake after robbing the people of their valuables. Precious gold crucifixes splashed with blood or wine dangled from their hands. After becoming a deadly mob of drunken fools, they began destroying all they could touch in riotous fashion. Yes, they fought off the fleeing French, but they didn't stop at that. They turned on their leaders, fighting against their own countrymen, and then they began to set fire to the homes of San Sebastián with large, dripping candles stolen from the town's own convent. Smoke cast a haze on the sky, shimmering orange and red as flames conquered house after house. By the end of the first night, the dead British, Portuguese, and French soldiers lay in piles, stripped naked and robbed by their own.

But it had worsened still. The Basque women and children who had been trapped in the city were dragged from their shelters and injured or worse. Soldiers forced themselves upon countless women in a violent and cruel manner. Horror and disgust reigned in Peter's heart as he saw what was happening, driving bile to his throat and tears to his eyes. Peter would never be able to shake the ringing screams of the women and children of San Sebastián from his ears. It had driven him to fight his own, an act he never imagined he would be required to do. But how could he have acted otherwise? He had tried to defend a group of helpless women, throwing himself at his countrymen, fighting more viciously than he had the French. A single defender in a sea of attackers. Not seeking to kill but to defend. Only once the women had escaped had he stopped his pleading, cursing, and slashing. He'd raced back to camp, hoping to find other leaders to help him stop the drunken rampage. Instead, he found their abandoned posts or their dead bodies, killed by their allies with their own swords.

And then he saw Ana María.

She had been stumbling about the outside of the city's crumbling wall, her dress ripped, face bruised, and arms smeared with blood. Bewilderment and fury laced the stream of Spanish that flowed from her. Pain was evident in her every move as her hands clutched her waist and her face contorted at each step. Yet somehow she had recognized him, clinging to his arms for support. The great sobs that shattered through her body only grew in a crescendo to desperate wails when he told her that her father had not survived the drunken attack on the resisting leaders at camp. She had collapsed into his arms. He had witnessed much bloodshed during his time as a soldier, but the stain of her blood on his uniform, the feel of it on his hands, had scarred him irreparably. Roaring, desperate anger exploded inside him like a great keg of gunpowder exposed to a careless spark. But Ana was at his side, and quickly losing consciousness, which was the only thing keeping him from storming back into San Sebastián to cut down his own.

They had escaped the city together, hesitating only momentarily to glance at the smoldering hill rising out of the ocean, then stumbled off into the shroud of the surrounding forest. Surely the devout faith of Ana and the earnest prayers of Peter's mother were the reason they survived that day.

The events of a few hours had altered Ana forever. Even though she was still as intrepid and forthright as ever, she had been robbed of something precious. He could see it in her eyes. Where once there was a fire of confidence and ambition, there was now a smolder of grief and pain.

Peter could not have left her in San Sebastián. He owed that much to her father, who, for all the effort he had given to the Allied forces, had not been able to prevent this disaster. And he had given his life, and his daughter's future, as payment. It was not fair. And it seemed that life for Ana María would never be fair again.

Chapter 3

September 1, 1813, San Sebastián, Basque Country, Spain

SMOKE SEEPED THROUGH THE TREES, RISING FROM THE VALLEY BElow, and stung Peter's eyes. Entangled branches overhead filtered out some of the smoke and shielded them from the ashfall that followed. Still, the suffering of the past day was heavy, sticking to them like an ever-persistent shadow.

Peter and Ana María had walked far into the forest until she had practically collapsed. He had his pack and a few materials to tie up a makeshift tent for her under a weeping fig tree, camouflaging the entrance with fallen branches. He slept across the campfire on his blankets. The space between them, he hoped, would provide a sense of propriety and security for her. Luckily, as an officer, he had known where to find supplies. He even shot down a few birds and cooked them to give them strength to continue. The aching in Peter's head and ringing in his ears were slowly subsiding, but he doubted that the guilt that split his heart ever would. How could he have allowed such a thing to happen to her?

Every time Peter looked at Ana and saw the scrape marring her cheek and the lesion encircling her throat, he nearly lost himself to outrage. Her dress was pockmarked with tears and burns, and her wrists were a painting of purple bruises and red swelling. He wished he had an ointment or salve to provide her some sort of relief. The sight of her, the reminder of the pain she endured, made his hands shake and his stomach roil. Then his mind would spiral, questioning what would have happened if he had not found her when he did. In those soul-blackening moments, he wanted to storm through the trees and strike down as many of the soldiers as he could reach. But that would not help her. What she needed now was a protector.

She would likely say that she could have fared just as well on her own, and he knew not to doubt her resilience. But she was clearly still recovering from her attack, her movements slow and staggered, pain creasing her forehead continually. She might have found shelter, but she would likely be prey to attackers. Peter never could have left her there in San Sebastián, not after the carnage he had seen from his countrymen, not after the trust he had shared with her father. He felt a sense of responsibility for her. And he thanked God continuously that she had trusted him enough to leave with him after the unspeakable pain one of his own countrymen had caused her.

Still, he found it difficult to reach her. For once, the vibrant, passionate Ana María was silent, distant, and dazed. Even when he asked how she was faring in his cumbersome, too-flat Spanish—"*Estás bien?*"—she remained unresponsive. Only when he touched her could he bring her mind back to their present circumstances. Upon touching her shoulder, she would jerk away like a lost, young child. So he learned to communicate with her by squeezing her hand. The contact dragged her out of the horrors in her mind and grounded her back into the present, at least long enough for her to communicate a hint of her feelings. Although perhaps it was a blessing that they were not able to talk extensively of their feelings at present. The silence between them could comfort her, help her feel safe.

He was at a loss as to how to care for her injuries when they were of such a private and delicate nature. Particularly when this sort of pain was just as much emotional as it was physical. When he had suffered more invasive injuries in the war, he knew that lots of rest would be most helpful—something that was not easy to achieve in the woods. He needed to move her somewhere safer. But first, he needed to check back in with his regiment. Allowing the army to think that either he or Ana had abandoned their posts and deserted would only lead to more challenges.

Peter had known a few deserters. Many of them had been made examples of, their good names and reputations scathed forever after facing legal trials. The rest were outcasts. They were shadows, largely unnoticed by society. But that was how they had chosen to live after being publicly shamed and cast out from the country that welcomed their brothers home as heroes. The army was not for everyone. Even those who escaped unscathed without significant physical injury often had nightmares that haunted them for the rest of their days. Some people could not survive, even after deserting the army, and found their way into an unmarked grave, just like many before them. Peter would not let Ana María become one of those mounds of earth, forever uncared for, forever forgotten.

"Miss Bailon, I need to meet with my leaders. I promise I'll only be gone a short while."

Vacant eyes met his. Had she heard him?

"*Poco tiempo. Yo voy. Sí?*" he said, the words bumbling and awkward in his mouth as he tried to explain he would only be gone a short while.

She blinked, and a hint of fear rippled across her face. Her lips pressed together, her jaw clenched.

"You are safe here, I promise. Just stay covered and quiet. I will be quick. *Muy rápido.*"

Ana María nodded but didn't duck into the tent. He moved, slow and cautious, until he grasped one of her hands. He squeezed twice, questioning how she fared, as was their tradition now. She squeezed twice back. "*Estoy bien.*" She was as fine as she could be, given the circumstances. Wrapping his jacket, a makeshift blanket, around her shoulders, Ana moved into the tent.

Peter flattened his hair with one hand while wrapping a bandage around his head with the other. The coastal air, thick with humidity, made it difficult for him to rein in his curls. He needed something to imply a head injury, to account for his absence over the past day. He had plenty of bruises and soreness but needed something more visible than that. He shrugged on his red coat and straightened his uniform. Most importantly, he could not draw attention to Ana's absence—that is, if any of them remembered her.

While hiking back to the field officers' headquarters, Peter's mind was overrun with questions. He had never witnessed such devastation, such violent carelessness on the battlefield. How would the officers be disciplining the errant foot soldiers? How many of the hundred foot soldiers in his company had been involved? Would the investigation and military code involve a military court? And most importantly, how could he protect Ana? He needed to return to camp today to account for his absence over the last twenty-four hours and to divert any attention away from her absence. He would also gather more supplies.

As an officer, he assumed he would have some role in the disciplinary action that would take place among the offending soldiers, and he wanted to be fully involved. He had to ensure that the people of San Sebastián were treated with care and mercy after all they had been put through.

Finally, he broke through the forest's edge, and the charred remains of San Sebastián were revealed. Only a handful of houses remained, standing solitarily in the ash and wreckage. Pain sliced through him at the too-recent memory of the suffering he witnessed. But now all was silent. Peter jogged to the former center of the infantry camp and encountered the first snag in the carefully woven fabric of his plan. The camp had been laid waste as well. Most tents were blown over and singed. Trampled food crates and souring wine mixed with the dirt, creating a repugnant smell. Even the few adobe brick buildings that the officers had commandeered for their sleeping headquarters were in disarray, with broken window glass scattered on the ground like a mosaic. It was little wonder that Major Bailon had not been safe, even at headquarters, from his drunken allies. Disgust squeezed Peter's stomach again, and he pressed his eyes shut against the wave of nausea.

Finally, Peter located the tent where the field officers' meetings were held. The low murmuring of voices greeted him, cutting through the eerie silence. Two sergeants stood outside and stepped aside at the sight of Peter's uniform, identifying his rank. He grabbed the fabric door of the tent, ducked inside, and fell into rank among the captains gathered at the back.

"Ah, Captain Ashmore. We worried when you didn't report back to camp last night. Any injuries to report?" Captain Davies inquired.

"Some pain in the head and blurred vision after a run-in with the French. I needed to take some distance from the smoke."

The others nodded, seeming to believe him. He wasn't lying—but the head pain wasn't from any physical injury. His head hadn't stopped pulsing since the carnage he'd witnessed. It was one thing to defend innocent people against the French, but it was another thing entirely to see his own turn on those innocents and ravage them.

Peter turned to Captain Davies. "Has a camp physician been to see the women and children in the city?"

Davies stared at Peter for a moment, his brows furrowing in confusion. "They are fully occupied with our injured."

"We can't leave those innocents to suffer, not when we are partly at fault for their pain. If we merely make our way up there, we can rest assured they'll be taken care of. I can organize a group—"

"You'll do no such thing, Ashmore."

"But the women . . ."

"We've received our orders. We march at daybreak. There are ships awaiting us on the coast to carry us to England."

"So you would abandon them?" Peter thought of Ana, bruised and bleeding somewhere in the forest, and his stomach heaved in anger.

"This business is bad enough as it is, Ashmore. Leave it where it lies. It is not your decision to make, nor mine, no matter how we may wish things had turned out differently."

The soldiers eyed each other nervously, and it was as if Peter's vision finally cleared. The sacking of the city had not been the fault of overly drunk foot soldiers alone; it had also been the fault of great incompetence in command. Where had all these leaders been? Clearly not in the throes of it all, fighting against their own, like Peter. And if they wouldn't acknowledge the serious indiscipline that occurred, then who would?

"Have you no shame? No sense of decency?" Peter's voice had risen enough now to alert others. A man stood from where he had been seated at the mapping table. General Sir Thomas Graham.

"I understand that many of you may be concerned for what has occurred here," he said, speaking to the group. "It is not surprising that such destruction would occur after so many months of French occupation. We'll let Spain care for their own. I assure you all will be well."

But how could he say that with such confidence, especially when they were leaving the city in ashes?

"Wellington has been alerted to the . . . repercussions of France's surrender. Our trusted allies of Basque Country and Spain remain here. Major Bailon will make reparations on the part of the Spanish government."

"He was killed," Peter barked, his hands balled against his sides.

General Graham paused, genuine surprise freezing his features. "I am sorry to hear it. He was a great resource for us."

No mention of Miss Bailon, a fact that only heightened his anger. He clenched his hands to keep from grabbing—or hitting—his superior.

"We have done Spain a great service by forcing the French to surrender this city and its ports," Graham continued. "I am sure they will repair any damage made by the French. Rest assured, these people rejoice to be freed from the French, even if they left such great destruction behind. We can aid them by returning to our own soil, allowing them to recover in peace. There is no need to take responsibility for the evils done by the French when we were not involved."

There was no hope in helping San Sebastián if the colonel in charge of this battle would not admit the faults of his own regiment. Fury raced through Peter, flaming and insatiable, as he thought of Ana María, nursing her wounds alone and entirely undeserving of the cruelty afforded her. How many women like her had been subjected to such horrors? And the children? It made him ill. The only thought that had kept him from losing his composure entirely over the past few days was the knowledge that he'd be able to return to the city, for however briefly it may be, and try to help in whatever way he could.

"You are dismissed," Graham said curtly, his eyes finding Peter's. "Return to England and recover. There will likely be a period of respite for all involved. We will write you when we expect you to report for duty again." His tone left no room for protesting.

Graham was a hurried leader and often wavered, making contradictory decisions, but now there was a certain finality in his words. Peter made no effort to hide the rage in his gaze, fisting his hand at his side while the others saluted. He stormed away, but not before he heard muttering voices at his back.

"Ashmore's position could incriminate us in the worst of ways. Even jeopardize your career, Colonel."

"He is the least of our worries now. We have the angry Spanish to deal with."

It was clear that Peter had no place here in San Sebastián. He had no power to provide comfort, no authority to help the many injured. Even if he tried, the people of the city would likely reject him. The reality of that made his head throb even harder. He had not been able to discipline his men enough to prevent this grave crime, and he had not been able to save their victims. Guilt wrapped about his throat, choking him as he turned his back on San Sebastián. If only the ocean waves could wash over the city and cleanse it of the great pain that had been caused there.

The only thing he could do now was take Ana María away from this place, if she was willing. Surely she could not remain in Spain, not when she could possibly be incriminated in the vile misdeeds that had occurred here. Whether she was framed as a guilty party for her role as an ally translator or forced to be a witness of harm done against her, she would suffer immensely. Peter simply could not allow it. They too would have to leave for London. Ana had no one left for her here. She had attested as much in her heaving sobs as they buried the body of her father.

By the next morning, Peter and Ana had reached the border of Basque Country and were staring across the sea toward England as they left a burning, bleeding Spain. Other soldiers gathered and boarded various ships to return home after the siege for a temporary so-called "period of recuperation." To Peter, this respite indicated that their leaders, the Marquess of Wellington included, were scrambling to cover the damage their troops had done. Repercussions, including legal trials, had already started in San Sebastián and other parts of Basque Country, and the British were no longer safe in the area. Peter decided to travel back to London without his comrades. Before the siege, the brotherhood of his division had brought him a great sense of strength and comfort. But now he was glad to be separated from them, both for his sake and for Ana's. He would not be able to bear their company at present, not after witnessing what they had done. And he would not force such a thing upon Ana, when her physical and emotional wounds were so fresh. It was nothing short of miraculous that she would trust him, when his uniform and his language surely reminded her of her attackers at every turn.

Peter could not say what the future held for either of them. But the only aim in his mind was to provide Ana a place of refuge.

Chapter 4

October 19, 1813, Abbeygate, Surrey Hills, England

So far, the two-hour journey to Surrey Hills had been surprisingly calm. Despite having traveled alone with Ana María for more than a month, Peter had noticed a shift in their company since the wedding ceremony. He had always been able to read her emotions as easily as the large writing in a young child's book. But now he could see that there was something bothering her. Her incessant chewing of her lip was enough to tell him that her mind was scrambling. And he suspected the cause of her worry.

There was one topic that Peter had been avoiding—their wedding night. All their staff would expect them to act like an affectionate, freshly wed couple on their wedding trip, despite the fact that they wouldn't be traveling due to Ana María's current sickness and condition. Undoubtedly, there would be talk below stairs regarding their relationship. And while he wanted to act the part of the happily married couple to prevent any embarrassment to his new wife, he also didn't want to begin their married life with any confusion surrounding his expectations for their relationship. He needed to be clear on the subject, particularly after the violence that Ana María had endured.

"I did wish to say one more thing regarding our marriage," Peter stated, shifting uncomfortably in his seat.

"*Sí*?"

"I have no illusions about the nature of our relationship, particularly considering your health and condition. Our marriage will be in name only, and I hope that will bring you some measure of comfort."

"Name . . . only? I take your name, *no*?"

Oh dear. This incredibly awkward conversation just became even more difficult. Peter breathed out heavily. How could he make her understand?

"Yes, that is . . . I mean to say that we will likely have adjoining rooms and all sorts of well-intentioned preparations on the part of our staff. But I will not be visiting your room tonight. My only intention in marrying you was to provide you with a safe place to bring your child into this world, not to pay you a visit on our wedding night—or any other night, for that matter."

It was not a typical marriage arrangement. But Peter couldn't ever imagine her being comfortable with such familiarity after the horrors she endured.

"Wedding night? But our wedding was during *el día*, not *la noche. No entiendo.* And what means *adjoining*?"

A heated flush crept up Peter's neck, making sweat bead on his forehead. Why was he still wearing this blasted cravat?

"Our rooms will be close. Connected, even." He motioned with his hands, placing his two palms together to signify his words. "As your husband, I normally would have certain responsibilities that I would be expected to fulfill . . ." Her lips were scrunched to one side, her brows quirked in obvious confusion. He was certainly making a grand mess of this, wasn't he? He hardly knew how to broach the topic in English, much less Spanish. All the polite vocabulary that could explain the situation was currently beyond her understanding. He would not embarrass her or dredge up recent traumatic experiences by spelling it out in frank words or common language. So he decided on the next best thing.

He reached out and grasped her hand. "You will be safe with me, Ana. I promise."

The stiffness slid from Ana María's posture like rain on a glass windowpane. Her shoulders fell and she pressed her eyes closed, resting her head against the back of the bench.

"I had not planned to marry. But I hope I can be the sort of husband you deserve. I will protect you, just as I vowed. And I will protect your child."

"*Gracias, Capitán.*" Her large, dark eyes glistened with emotion. "*Muchísimas gracias* for everything."

"I could not simply sit by and watch you suffer."

She nodded as tears trickled down her cheeks. Peter's heart squeezed in his chest. He had softened in the months prior to the rambunctious Ana María and was no longer totally mortified by her teasing. But he could not bear the sight of her crying. Tears would not do.

Peter fumbled in his pockets for a handkerchief, offering it up. He settled back into his chair, staring out the window to give Ana María some privacy as she calmed her emotions.

"Do you mind, *Pedro*?"

Surprised, he saw Ana María patting the bench next to her and motioning for him to join her.

"Do you feel ill?"

Sometimes it had helped her to lie down to ease her stomach. He had been happy to provide his lap for her to rest on to help stave off her nausea. As intimate as it might have seemed, Peter had merely felt he was fulfilling a responsibility.

"A little, *pero estoy bien*. I want that you sit here."

He would not refuse her. Peter nimbly shifted to the forward-facing bench. He settled in next to her, an appropriate distance between them, and waited. She scooted closer to him until their knees and arms touched. Then she snuggled up against his shoulder, the movement accompanied by a series of hiccupping breaths and sniffles.

Peter found himself unable to move. He was frozen, as if he were carefully hidden from the French in the underbrush of the Spanish countryside. But this felt entirely different. Instead of bracing himself for attack, he was trying not to scare off a very frightened and fragile creature. Indeed, he would not complain if this moment continued for a great while.

They were married, but this was a closeness he was not accustomed to. It was also not the reaction he had necessarily expected after telling his new bride that he would not be fulfilling all of his husbandly responsibilities.

"I do have one request," he said.

"*Sí?*"

"Could you perhaps call me Peter? Or *Pedro* at least?" he said, chuckling.

"You no like *el capitán*?"

"Perhaps something a little more . . . personal would help keep up appearances."

"I understand. *No hay problema, Pedro.*"

Finally, their carriage was pulling up the long gravel drive of the Ashmore family's summer estate and country seat, Abbeygate. Towering trees were splashed in vibrant autumn colors, blurring Peter's vision into shades of gold, scarlet, and rust. Arching branches swayed as the jewel-like leaves dripped onto their carriage. A rush of nostalgia flooded Peter's senses, his chest aching suddenly. How had he stepped away from this place, his family, for so long?

He turned from the window to see Ana María, similarly smitten by the sight. The ache faded somewhat. She deserved to bask in this moment of awe. He would do anything to prolong this breath of reprieve from her pain. What a blessing he could share such a beautiful place with her . . . and her child.

"Mother has been generous enough to grant us Abbeygate as our home, at least for the time being. And I must tell you it is one of my favorite places in the world," he said.

"I much prefer this *vista* to London. Everything is so . . . *hermoso*."

It was indeed beautiful. Even more so than he remembered. "There is a lovely pond out beyond the house and a walking path in the gardens. There have always been singing birds about, as you will hear very soon. A wonderful sound, it is. I have so many memories here."

He hoped it would bring him as much happiness as it had before. If so, this place had the potential to help—and heal—them both.

The carriage pulled to a stop, the crunch of the gravel quieting. Peter hopped out and savored the freshness of the air. No smoke, like San Sebastián. No fog, like London. This air was pure. He held out both hands, helping Ana down slowly. It may have been a bumpier journey than she had expected, but he would think that she would prefer the carriage to the incessant rocking of the ship they had endured for weeks on end.

"Are you all right?"

She grabbed his arm, steadying herself, while her other arm pressed against her stomach. "Better *ahora*. How good to stand on the ground!"

He chuckled. "Indeed." They approached the tall wooden doors that split the stone exterior of the building. Glints of small, glass windows shone from the high walls, almost like a Spanish mosaic. It was a historic structure, built years before more modern, large windowpanes had been invented. On the stone steps waited the staff, their numbers minimal but their talents immense. Peter was thrilled to see Mr. Burnsey, the butler. His short frame had rounded out slightly over the years, but his smile-lined face and impeccably combed white hair were unchanged.

"Ah, Mr. Ashmore, wha' a delight to see you after all this time."

"Indeed, Burnsey, it has been a number of years."

"More than that, at least by my count. We've missed you 'ere."

"And I have missed this place as well."

Abbeygate had been like a small haven in Peter's childhood—a place where Mother, Matthew, and he could escape Father's furies and play carefree, just the three of them. But he hadn't been here since the summer of his seventeenth year. Oh, how he had missed it.

* * *

Ana had not felt any great emotion at the sight of London. It was dirty and stuffy and altogether too gray. How she had missed the intricacies of Spanish architecture and tradition! But at her first glimpses of Abbeygate and the Surrey Hill community that surrounded it, she was *completamente enamorada*. How could she not be in love with it all? Still, she could hardly believe she would be the mistress of such a house. She never would have guessed that shy, stoic Captain Ashmore had ownership of such a grand estate. She would be somewhat unnerved and intimidated by it all if it weren't for their arrangement affording them both great privacy and anonymity. This would be a place for her to heal. To heal and to hide.

While the house was stately, its tall exterior dotted with windows and parted by a large wooden door at the entrance, it did not make Ana feel small and insignificant like the Ashmore estate had in London. Instead, it felt just large enough to be inviting but not so large as to eliminate any feelings of coziness or comfort. Ivy curled up the gold-brown brick, covering nearly half the exterior and framing a good portion of the windows as well. The remnants of fall blooms were scattered about the gardens, their faded colors peeking about the curving paths. Ana had also spotted a small hewn stone chapel through the trees that she would surely be visiting each week. It was almost enough to distract her from the squeamishness of her stomach.

The staff was just as lovely as the estate, although they were quite pointed in their behavior toward the couple, just as Peter had expected.

"We have prepared your mother's rooms for your wife and the adjoining rooms for yourself, my lord. I believe such arrangements should be pleasing to you."

Burnsey, the butler, had bowed his head, but Ana didn't miss the teasing glint in his eye or the twitching smile that played at his lips. For all he knew, they would be like any other recently married couple, eager to spend every moment in each other's company, waking and sleeping. And while the two had experienced proximity while they were escaping San Sebastián, they had never done so with carefully listening ears and watchful eyes all about.

"Thank you, Burnsey. Those arrangements will be perfect indeed," Peter said. "Allow me to present the Honorable Mrs. Ana María Ashmore, my wife."

Widened eyes and a gaping mouth made it clear that this Mr. Burnsey had not expected Peter to attach himself to a foreigner. But as Ana scanned his features, she did not see any hints of fear or hatred, only surprise. For that, she was entirely grateful.

Still, Ana would not permit any sort of anxiousness about her country of origin. She would make herself familiar with the staff here, and in doing so, fully intended to continue with her traditional greeting of *besos,* as it would help her feel more comfortable as well. So she stepped forward, kissing Burnsey on each cheek, much to his immediate embarrassment. When she stepped back, his face was flushed, and his words were stammering. "Welcome to Abbeygate, Mrs. Ashmore," he managed to say with a slight smile.

Her new title could not feel more foreign or ill-fitting. If she was to have some degree of safety and comfort here at Abbeygate, she wished the staff would address her as a friend.

"Ana," she corrected, her Spanish pronunciation tall and bright.

"Of course," he replied with a nod. "Mrs. Ana Ashmore."

"No, just Ana."

Burnsey locked eyes with Peter, who chuckled slightly. Then he placed a hand on her back and leaned in to whisper in her ear.

"I know you prefer to be called Ana, but here, you must allow them to use a title. It's their way of showing love and respect for you."

He could certainly choose to be called by a title of sorts, but Ana would go by the name her mother and father had given her. She had inherited every bit of fire and stubbornness that her father had possessed and would not give up a fight easily.

"Because I marry you. Not because *soy una* lady. I no want to separate me from they." Ana would not pretend to love an identity she felt wasn't true. It felt like a lie, a secret.

Peter cleared his throat, betraying his discomfort. "Please, Ana. It's not about separation. It is merely about maintaining a standard that has been normal for years. This is our way of life here—our tradition, you might say."

Tradition. He would know this word held such power over her. Peter had always respected the traditions of *España* and her *familia*. In this matter, she would have to do the same for him.

"*Bueno.* Mrs. Ana. I no understand why we have to be so formal, *pero bueno.*"

Peter's eyebrows raised ever higher, but he pressed her hand and nodded to Burnsey.

"Please alert me or Mrs. Thompson, the housekeeper, if there is anything we can help you with," Burnsey said.

"I will do that. *Gracias.*" Ana María nodded, stretching her smile as bright and as wide as the sky.

A faint redness tinged Burnsey's cheeks and, much to Ana's surprise, his face parted in a wavering smile. And with it, any tightness in her shoulders relaxed. If she could put the staff at ease, she could be certain that she would be happy here. Even though she and Peter both had a great deal to learn in their marriage and their new responsibilities, surely this was a good indication of their hopeful future.

"It is a pleasure to meet you, Mrs. Ana. We are so pleased to serve you."

"Gracias, Mrs. Tom-som." Ana stumbled over the name as she pressed quick *besos* to the woman's round cheeks.

"Can I favor you with a tour of the estate?" Mrs. Thompson asked as she stepped forward. Her flat, swallowed accent was even more foreign than Burnsey's. The short lady was quite petite and struck more of a wiry figure than a motherly one. But her cheeks were flushed with color and her eyes were bright with genuine happiness. This may not be Ana's own *mamá*, but she surely was a kind and trusted figure here.

However, Ana's condition would not allow for a tour at present. Even now, her legs trembled with exhaustion and her stomach throbbed with pain. Ana wanted to see every room in the house, explore the place that her child would come to love someday. But for now, her sickness could not be ignored.

"*Lo siento*, but I no feel very well. I need *un poco* rest, I believe." Her hands jumped to her midsection before she could pull them downward again. Would Mrs. Thompson guess at the real cause for her maladies? Not wanting to give the impression of her condition, Ana rubbed a hand across her forehead, feigning a headache. How difficult it was already proving to keep such a sensitive secret from these people who would be caring for her and working alongside her.

Ana tried not to tremble with exhaustion as Mrs. Thompson assisted her in changing into a more comfortable day gown. They would have to find a maid, at least according to Peter. Ana was happy to care for such responsibilities on her own, but he insisted that it would get increasingly difficult with her pregnancy.

"Are you nervous, little dove?" Mrs. Thompson asked. "Not to worry, my lady. Mr. Peter Ashmore has always been a most gentle soul. And I can tell he cares greatly for you."

"*Gracias, Señora.* I am well."

"How did the two of you find each other, if you mind me asking?"

"We know each other *en España* for the first time. He is very good soldier, and very pretty." Mrs. Thompson laughed. Ana blushed; she would not lie about that. After all, he was her husband now. Thankfully, there were some small slivers of their history that could make it sound like a believable love story.

"He try so much to speak Spanish to me. And very soon after, he says he loves me. I could not believe. I laugh so much." She had great difficulty expressing such things in English, but apparently the meaning was not lost on Mrs. Thompson, who laughed heartily.

"That does sound like Peter. Always a sweet little pup, he was."

"He was very good and kind to me and my father." Ana's voice broke at that, her heart constricting. How had she endured this day without *Papá*? The pain wrapped thick arms around her, squeezing the breath from her lungs.

"Oh, my dear. You must miss your family, sweetling." Mrs. Thompson's gentle hands combed through her hair.

"*Sí. Mucho.*"

Ana had always imagined her father and her husband would get along delightfully. Now, *Papá* had a son-in-law and a *nieta* on the way that he would never get to see.

"I may not speak your Spanish, but I'll do me best to help you. Whatever you need, you hear?" Mrs. Thompson gave her back a gentle rub as she tucked Ana's freshly plaited hair over her shoulder. "And as for Mr. Ashmore, trust me that all will be well. He loves you, I'm sure, and he'll take great and tender care of you. I'll let him know that you're ailing, and I'll send up a tray from the kitchens. Now you come 'ere and rest on your bed. There's a dear."

And with that, Ana was left alone, her bed far too soft and far too large, and her room entirely too quiet. It was incredibly unnerving to be waiting in such a state, even knowing, as she did, that her husband would pay her no company tonight. After a long time ruminating over his attempted conversation on the topic earlier, she finally understood what he had been trying to say. As both of them had intended from the start, their marriage would remain an arrangement of protection, not affection. There was to be no expectation of intimacy between them, which filled her with relief. Still, her mind teemed with nearly every emotion imaginable, and her body filled to the brim with tension as she heard occasional footsteps in the hallway.

How could she feel so peaceful, so nervous, and so devastated all within the same day? The gratitude that she felt for Peter had no bounds. He had saved her in every way imaginable. But still, she felt her heart would split open with pain at the thought of beginning a new life with a husband and child in a country so entirely different than her home. And she had no concept of knowing if she would see her mother ever again, although that particular worry was not a new one.

A quiet, vibrating knock sounded on the main door to her rooms, interrupting her thoughts. Ana jumped, instinctively pulling her knees to her chest and wrapping her arms around her legs. Her heart was thundering, nearly blocking out the whispered words that floated toward her from the wooden door.

"May I open the door?"

She knitted her fingers into the folds of her gown, trying to breathe down a wave of panic. It was just Peter. He would not harm her.

"Yes,"

"*Estás bien*, Ana?"

"*Si*," she whispered.

Peter eased the door open and practically tiptoed to her side. His cautious demeanor would have been humorous if Ana did not feel so entirely overwhelmed.

"Mrs. Thompson said you were ailing. How fares your stomach? Did you . . ." He motioned to the water closet.

She shook her head. "No, I feel *mejor* now I rest here. But I feel very tired."

A maid ducked through the door behind Peter and placed a tray of food on the desk next to Ana's bed. She then tutted about the room, fussing with the drapes and arranging the blankets at the foot of the bed.

Would Ana never be afforded a minute of privacy here? She almost laughed at the irony. She had never been one to long for isolation before. She sent a pleading look Peter's way, who nodded and quietly dismissed the maid.

"How I live here, Peter? I no understand how to live *así* in England. *Mi vida en España* is so *diferente*."

When Ana's emotions were particularly strong, it became more taxing to express herself in English. Some things could be felt better in Spanish, it seemed.

"Are you unhappy with our decision?" Real concern creased Peter's brow, and he approached, sitting on the edge of her bed.

"No. It is just *difícil*. So much change all today. All the people are so very nice to me, and you are so good to me, *como siempre*. But I feel . . ." She shook her head, pressing her hands into her temples.

Peter reached and squeezed her hand between his. "I promise you will become accustomed to your way of life here. And I will always be by your side to make it easier in whatever way I can. I promise. We will experience this journey together. You remember, I have never been a husband or a father, so there is quite a great deal I will be learning as well. But I am your servant in whatever you may need." He strode to the wooden door across the room. "I am just through this door here if you need anything in the night, no matter the hour. And I believe you are already acquainted with the water closet . . ."

"*Claro*."

"Well, good then." He rubbed his hands together. "Please do try to eat at least a small portion of this food. It will do you good. I hope you rest well."

"You too, *Capi . . . Pedro*."

"*Gracias*. Oh, Ana?"

"*Sí?*"

"*Cómo te amo!*" he stated, raising a hand in a dramatic pose, like a great theatrical actor. His expression, which had been quite somber as of late, warmed into an endearing smile. Ana could not help but laugh at that, just as her heart started beating strange patterns in her chest.

Yes, *she* would be safe with him *siempre*. But would her heart?

Chapter 5

October 31, 1813, Abbeygate, Surrey Hills, England

"Mr. Ashmore, a . . . newspaper of sorts has arrived for Mrs. Ashmore," Burnsey said as he stood in the doorway of Peter's study.

"For Ana? Are you certain?" Peter asked, reaching out his hand. "From whom, I wonder."

"I haven't the foggiest. But it be in Spanish, so it must be for your lady."

"I see. Thank you, Burnsey, I'll show it to her myself."

Peter's hands trembled as he grasped the folded paper. The print was disorderly, rushed. It didn't seem like a product of a regular print shop but rather an individually constructed manifesto. Who had delivered this item to them? How had they known that Ana was here? Nobody knew of her existence, her origin. Fear clenched in his stomach as he reached Ana's door and knocked.

"*Pasa*," she called, indicating to him to come in.

"Ana, a newspaper has arrived in Spanish. I wondered if you might take a look at it." He placed the paper into her outstretched hands. "I suspect it is some sort of report. The length and form of it indicate as much."

"It is from San Sebastián." Ana's face was shadowed with fear in an instant; the lightness in her eyes that had welcomed his arrival had disappeared entirely.

"You know that my Spanish is absolutely horrid. Would you just translate a bit of it, please?" Peter stood tall and firm, but he could not stop the nervous tapping of his foot. What would the paper contain? Perhaps some proof of the fault of the British and Portuguese armies?

"I no want to read this." Her eyes widened pleadingly.

"But this report very well could be a blessing to us. It could provide a way for me . . . for *us* to make right all that was done in San Sebastián." All that was done to *her*. A twinge of pain settled in Peter's chest, his breathing increasing in excitement and desperation.

"Very well. I translate *un poco, sí*?"

"*Gracias*, Ana." Peter reached for her hand and squeezed firmly. He smiled, harboring the hope that this newspaper would bring them good news and save them from the memories that haunted them both.

"The town of San Sebastián was put on fire by the Allies," Ana began, her voice trembling and halting. "After, these troops started an attack very horrible . . ." Ana begun, her voice trembling. She was much more practiced in translating from text, Peter realized, than in forming English sentences on her own. It must have been part of her education and role as a translator.

"The people of San Sebastián were controlled for so long time by the French," Ana continued. "So they welcome the Allies with much gratitude, but these soldiers responded to them with gunfire at their doors, and many people die." Ana's voice cracked with emotion, as faces of the Basque and Spanish victims, young and old, paraded through Peter's mind.

"When it became dark and the French retreated, there was much horror. All around could be heard the sound of crying women who were being attacked." Tears soaked Ana's face now, but her voice continued in an automatic, learned fashion. "No matter their age, wives were hurt in the view of their husbands, girls attacked in front of their parents . . ."

Peter pulled the paper from her hands as bile rose high in his throat. "Forgive me, this was a grave mistake. I should not have you read such things. Not after what you endured."

"*Por favor, Pedro.* I no want to remember these things *terribles.*"

"I am sorrier than I can say. I hadn't the faintest idea that it would be such a . . . descriptive account. I merely hoped it would give us some names or remind us of specifics to help bring to punishment those who were at fault."

"San Sebastián is *siempre* in my mind. I no need to be reminded of this."

"I know," Peter said, squeezing Ana's hand.

Her brow was furrowed, her jaw set with concern. If he could not somehow take away the pain inside that caused this reaction, he wished he could at least reach over and smooth the lines himself. Even worse, Peter had caused her distress without gaining any of the evidence that he had been hoping for. And he had forced his tender wife to relive such terrible events. He was not rescuing her from her fate in the slightest when he requested she read such things. It appeared Peter would have to continue his efforts on his own.

But first he needed to comfort his wife.

"It is nearly time for your *siesta*, correct?"

Ana nodded mutely as she wiped at her tears. Peter helped her over to the bed, pulling back the bedclothes and preparing the pillows for her.

Peter experienced an actual physical pain at seeing his wife cry. It seized and squeezed his chest. "Deuced fool," he muttered, cursing himself and shaking his head. Never again would he be the cause of his wife's tears.

"Please allow me to fetch you some drinking chocolate. That would take your mind off these horrid things, would it not?"

"I hope yes," Ana whispered as she climbed into bed and collapsed onto the pillows.

Peter eased the door open, started down the hallway, then raised the paper to his view, squinting. He strained to understand and caught bits of each sentence.

"*The sack endured for days. . . . They appeared to be authorized by the commanders. . . . The stolen items were sold by the English, and right beside their military headquarters.*"

That was a bit of information Peter had not witnessed himself. Perhaps that had occurred after he and Ana had already started fleeing to the coast. The words came easier now, context aiding him.

"*When we thought it had finished, the Allied troops threw our precious belongings into the fire, a fire which grew so fast . . . it appeared deliberate.*"

"*Of the hundreds of houses . . . there were less than forty left. . . . Fifteen hundred families were abandoned without food and shelter.*"

"*Everything had fallen to violence or flame. . . . San Sebastián exists no more.*"

Then the manifesto ended in the most heartbreaking of manners. The language was too simple, too straightforward, too devastating for Peter to miss its meaning.

"*When, on 25 July, we saw Allied armies arrive, we wanted to help them; the women ran to the camps and hospital to give them clothes, food, and care. Our loyalty has been repaid with the destruction of our home.*"

"Mr. Ashmore, is something the matter?" Mrs. Thompson hovered in front of him, concern marring her normally happy features. Peter felt the tension hunched in his shoulders and the anger bunching his brow. Even his jaw was clenched. Little wonder she assumed something was the matter.

"Oh, Mrs. Thompson. I was just seeking you out."

"You look to 'ave seen a great fright indeed."

"No great fright at all. Only a bit of bad news." He tapped the paper and then folded it, shoving it into a pocket. "An unwanted reminder of difficult days."

"Aye, 'tis how it be when you're a soldier. My own father often had night haunts of the battlefield, again and again. Wake the whole house with his screaming, he would."

"I am so sorry, Mrs. Thompson. I never knew your family bore such a difficult past, particularly one I am well familiar with."

"No matter, dear. Pop be in his grave, sleeping peacefully now. And we are safe here in England, isn't we? No cause for this kind of concern."

"Indeed," Peter said, wishing his mind would agree with his words. If there would ever be a time he was free from the guilt and pain of San Sebastián, he would be more than glad for it. But he would never forget the sight of seeing Ana, dress torn, stumbling toward him through the flames.

"Now, what were you seeking me about?"

"Mrs. Ashmore requires some drinking chocolate."

"Feeling ill, is she?"

"I don't believe so, at least not physically. She is quite tired and a bit emotional."

Mrs. Thompson cast a knowing glance at the pocket where Peter had stored the newspaper. "I see. I'll have drinking chocolate to her in just a moment."

"Thank you," Peter said, squeezing Mrs. Thompson's hand.

It was more likely than not that this mysterious paper had arrived at their house through someone who knew that Peter had spent many months in Spain and wanted him to read the report. It testified of truth, despite the misinformation that was already spreading through England regarding the events. Now that he knew the contents of it, he doubted that any of the few individuals who knew Ana would intentionally cause her grief by alerting her to such horrid events. And besides that, none of them knew that his wife had been at San Sebastián. That was a secret well-locked away by Peter alone. Still, remembering the pain of the trauma so many innocents had endured there made anger boil in his stomach. He had never been so affected before by a war event, but he had also never witnessed such atrocities for himself. Worst of all, the woman he cared for would be scarred forever by its injustices.

Chapter 6

November 2, 1813, Abbeygate, Surrey Hills, England

Ana lay on her back, cushioned on all sides by thick bedclothes and feather-stuffed pillows. Her eyes followed the small, web-like cracks in the whitewash on the ceiling above as her fingers traced her midsection. How strange it was that there was life, ever-growing inside her, even though she could feel no swelling of the womb, no shape of motherhood. The only evidence she had was the abnormal ways her body was acting as of late.

Hiding her ever-progressing condition from others at Abbeygate was proving more difficult than Ana María expected. Her body had yet to curve and grow in the telltale shape of motherhood, but her sickness could not be prevented. She had learned to spring from the water closet, where she was retching, back to her bed at the slightest noise outside her door, for fear Mrs. Thompson would be coming to dress her for the day. Fortunately for her, the flooring just outside their rooms was awfully creaky and would always reveal the presence of a member of the staff. It seemed that the floors had been well-worn, likely from years of rambunctious boys running to and from their parents' rooms.

The exhaustion that weighed her down seemed to reveal that her tiny, growing child was already quite demanding of her attention and energy. She chuckled. So insistent, her little one. Just as she had been to her own parents as a young child. Despite having a strained relationship with her own *mamá*, Ana María had always desired to be a mother, had always adored the sight and smell of a freshly bathed babe. Perhaps her own lack of siblings made that desire even stronger. She longed to create a safe and joyous home for her children, with attentive parents who were besotted with one another. A home that was not at all like her own. She had always dreamed that discovering she was expecting a child would be accompanied by feelings of joy, hope, and happy anticipation.

How wrong she had been.

Deep down, Ana had suspected she was with child while they were still aboard the ship headed for England, but she hadn't said anything of it to Peter. She had been violently ill, something she had attributed to her lack of "sea legs," as Peter called it. But then her monthly bleedings had not occurred, despite her body's dependable predictability in years previous. She had counted each day of that intended week, hardly breathing for the nerves she was feeling. And then the suspicion had slowly started to settle upon her, like a misting fall rain—that she was with child by a wicked man she did not know and did not wish to remember. Of course, it was difficult to be certain. Mother had never told her of such things. She had not been present to do so. Ana had discovered her monthly courses on her own and hadn't the faintest idea of how one's body reacted to carrying a child.

Once their ship landed in London, the seasickness had not retreated. Feelings of nausea still plagued her, squeezing her stomach with extra force during the morning and evening. And she was no longer able to lie to herself, no longer able to deny her condition. She was with child. And completely and entirely on her own.

The realization of her condition had filled her with panic, fear, and desperation. She had lost her appetite and cried herself to sleep, retreating into that unfamiliar place inside herself where she drowned in her nervousness and hopelessness while she was frozen silent on the outside. She would bring a poor soul into the world, entirely dependent upon her, without a father to speak of. There would be no safe home, no loving parents. Worse still, Ana had no understanding of how to be a mother, at least not the kind she had dreamed of being. She could not be a calm or wise or confident mother when she had no way of surviving alone. All of her carefully laid plans were shattering around her, and it was all Ana could do not to fall apart alongside them.

The heaviest burden to bear was the guilt that threatened to pound her into the ground. So many other women had suffered the same fate as her that wretched night, and still she carried the burden of her condition as if it were the weight of the world. In her heart, she knew she was not at fault for what had occurred, but her religion taught her that having a child out of wedlock was a grave sin indeed. Would God ever forgive her?

Would she ever forgive herself?

How Ana had sobbed that night, releasing all the pent-up mourning for her father, her mother, and herself. Yet another secret burdened their family, even in their absence and death, and it was a secret she felt might break her if she had to carry it alone. She had cried until it was difficult to breathe, until her side had cramped with sorrow, until finally, mercifully, her exhaustion dragged her into a fitful sleep.

But amid her distress, Ana had convinced herself that her child had to be a sign of mercy or grace. Somehow God knew. He knew that she would need an *ángel* to pull her from the darkness that she had been subjected to in San Sebastián. That *ángel* would be her precious *bebé*. God would give her the strength sufficient to carry and care for this child. He had to.

Ana pressed her hand more firmly to her stomach, as if embracing her child, the motion bringing her back to the present. She looked at the door separating her rooms from Peter's. Perhaps God knew she needed Peter too. She chuckled. He did have a sort of angelic look about him. Particularly when his brows were drawn together with concern on her behalf or when one of her comments made him laugh in a rare, relished moment. Yes, he was one of Ana's angels, to be sure. He had saved her. And also managed to make her feel comfortable without causing her guilt for feeling so. Still, their little haven of conspicuity could not last forever.

Peter had arranged for their marriage as quickly as possible, but Ana still feared that some member of the staff or the community would be adept enough at calculations to discover their secret. She had not been in England long, but she already understood quite well the expanse of his family's reputation, and she would not let any rumor of impropriety mar it. Perhaps she should even consider shrinking the staff of Abbeygate, as minimal as it was.

A knock sounded at the adjoining door. Peter had only entered her rooms through that door when she had been noisily heaving the contents of her stomach in the middle of the night. But she was resting quietly now. What could he be needing?

"*Pedro*?"

"*Sí*," Peter said. "May I come in?" His voice was rough from sleep and lack of use.

"*Un momento*." Ana shrugged on a silk wrapper that she had found in his mother's wardrobe, which Peter had ordered to be moved into her room. The wrapper's gold and red floral pattern made her yearn for the intricate designs and unique fashion plates of her home. How quickly she tired of the subdued colors of the dresses that were popular here. She didn't require any fanciful styles. She just needed to feel more like herself. Once she felt presentable, she walked to the door and opened it.

There stood Peter, with a breakfast tray in his hands that was piled high with more than enough food for them both. He stepped over the threshold into her room and busied himself preparing a plate for her at her desk. It was a new sight, seeing him without his uniform. This new version of Peter still revealed the same precision, with a neat knot at the base of his throat and orderly buttons lining the front of his waistcoat. But compared to the patterns and colors she saw on the clothing of many gentlemen in London, it seemed that Peter preferred earthy tones. She would not complain about this brownish-red color he wore today. It reminded her of the clay earth on the borders of Spain and set off his tanned skin and dark hair quite handsomely. And she much preferred to see his sun-darkened hands stirring her herbal tea than handling a musket.

A flood of emotion suddenly overwhelmed her. Tears blurred her vision, and she blinked hard, slapping her cheeks. She almost laughed at the silliness of it. Was she truly crying over a mere breakfast tray?

"I know mornings are most difficult for you . . ." he stumbled. "I only mean I have observed that it is challenging to sit in the breakfast room when your stomach could heave itself up at any moment."

"*Lo siento*, I do not know why I cry!"

But it wasn't a mere breakfast tray. It was a symbol of thoughtful kindness brought to her by her husband. It represented the attentive way that he would minister to her needs, down to the most minute of details. He was already showing her that he was everything Ana had hoped for in a husband.

Peter merely smiled and straightened into a pose that was somehow perfectly disciplined, stiff, and comfortable, all at the same time. He wasn't affected in the least by her outburst, as if he had been surrounded for years by overly emotional expectant mothers instead of rough and hardened soldiers. The thought transformed her sniffles into giggles. What was happening to her?

"Come, sit here and do try to eat," he said. "I may not know of the mysteries of carrying a child, but I have at least heard that having a bit of food in the morning can stave off the sickness somewhat."

How strange it was to have to eat to keep down the sickness when eating was the very thing that seemed to cause her sickness to worsen. Ana rubbed a hand down her temple.

"Yes, I will do that, *gracias*. Will you eat too?"

"I already took my breakfast, thank you. I simply wasn't sure how hungry you would be and didn't want your food to be scarce." He scratched at his head, a wobbling smile on his lips.

After devouring more of the bread and preserves than she had been anticipating, Ana finally settled back into her chair and sighed. The desperation of her nausea was already beginning to diminish, and it was a most welcome relief.

* * *

Peter watched with no small amount of pride as Ana—his *wife*—ate a larger amount of food than she had managed in many weeks. She then settled back into bed with a sigh of relief and contentment. Her spiraling hair was somehow contained in a braid that looped over her shoulder. He found the arrangement to be most becoming, particularly when the depth of her black hair contrasted with the deep scarlet of the wrapper she wore.

"I'm proud of you," he said.

"*Por qué?*"

He tilted his head at her breakfast tray. "You've managed to eat a great deal of food this morning."

"Ha! It is like I am a little child. You are so proud that I eat all my food!" she laughed, the sound bouncing musically about the room.

Peter could not help but chuckle along until she suddenly doubled over, clutching at her stomach and covering her mouth with a hand. He sprang into action, scooping up a clean chamber pot from beneath her bed.

"It proves *difícil* to hide my . . ." her hands went to her midsection.

"I know. I understand it is somewhat of a delicate business . . . Perhaps I can ask Cook if she knows of any remedies."

"I would love to have some . . . remedies." She sounded out the new word slowly, rolling the *r* in a telltale sign of her accent. "But it would tell of my condition, no?"

Peter's eyes darted to her hands, and his neck heated. "Of course. I understand it is somewhat of a delicate matter. Particularly when your 'temporary illness' will not subside. But I can assure you that you have no need to be worried about any of the staff. And as for the timing of it all, I feel confident they will believe that we have . . . that you are . . . that the child is mine," his voice finally finished, his cheeks reddening further. "And properly so."

"*Entiendo.*"

"Right, good."

Peter's gaze brushed back to her midsection, trying to imagine the tiny miracle of life growing there. He was still coming to terms with the fact that he was a husband and also a soon-to-be father. He had never anticipated becoming a father, not when he was given such a horrible example by his own father. The reality of his impending fatherhood still felt entirely fictitious, just as it had felt when the words had come racing out of his mouth, claiming responsibility for Ana and the child.

When Ana had revealed to him her condition, they had just recently landed on the border of England, with soldiers, travelers, and immigrants swelling around the coast. Peter had felt relieved to have his feet on English soil again, but Ana had looked more distressed as the day went on. Then she had revealed to him the reality of her situation. They had argued fiercely that night as they scoured their minds for solutions.

"You do not deserve the fate of the other women in San Sebastián," he had protested, a very real panic searing his mind.

"But I am no better than they. I going to fight for *mí*, and *mi bebé*, how these women do."

"That is not what I meant to imply." How could he make her understand? "I only wished to say that . . . well, you know the complicated nature of being an unwed mother. It could put you in a position of grave danger, particularly given the . . . history of the events we have just survived. If we can make an arrangement for the babe . . ."

"I will not leave *mi bebé* without a mother. I cannot."

"She would have a mother, just not . . ."

"Not *her* mother. It would be a *gran error*."

Her gaze was fiery, her jaw set, and her nose scrunched in disgust at the suggestion. But beneath her firm facade, Peter did not miss how her lip trembled. Some other women would consider it a welcome solution to give up their child to a wet nurse or to a family in want of a baby so that they could return to society and their life before. Clearly it was not so for Ana María.

He blew out a sigh and ran his fingers through his hair. "Very well. Then what do you suggest we do?"

"I come to London. You say there are good physicians there, no?"

"Yes, true, but you cannot simply come . . ."

"*¿Y por qué no?*"

Because it was entirely unacceptable and improper for him to arrive at home with an unmarried woman, particularly one who would begin to show signs of pregnancy in the coming months. And then there was the issue of their countries being tangled in war. How would his friends and neighbors view her heritage after news of the battle reached them? What would his family think of her? He shook his head. This was all much more complicated than he had imagined it would be.

"I'm sorry, it simply wouldn't do . . ."

But how could he rescue Ana María from San Sebastián and then turn her out to survive on her own in even worse circumstances? Doing so when he had every reason and every resource to be able to rescue her would be a sin. He would be no better a man than his father had been.

Peter rotated toward Ana María until he faced her completely. "Look at me." Reaching out a finger, he lifted her chin, raising her gaze from where it had been trained on the floor. Apprehension coursed through him, tightening the muscles in his shoulders and neck. He would protect her in the only way he knew how. It had to be done.

"I know that you likely have no desire to be involved with an Englishman ever again after what they did," he said, unable to meet her eyes. "But I hope that you would harbor some measure of trust in me for coming with me this far. And now I only see one way to continue to protect you *and* your child. If you would accept, I would make you my wife."

As the words left him, all breath likewise abandoned him. What sort of future was he submitting himself to?

"*Ay que romántico!*" she exclaimed, rolling her eyes and tossing her head. "Why marry?" Her theatrics did not hide the worry that laced tension through her features.

He should have known she would fight it. Peter's rational mind started whirring, creating detailed plans as to why this was the solution with the greatest chance of success and safety.

"Because I cannot bring you to London, to my home in your . . . current delicate state without some kind of arrangement between us. It would not seem proper."

"But the people, they know that *mi bebé* is not yours, *verdad*?"

"That's just it. If we did marry, we would act as if the child were mine. To protect you. And the child."

Ana María had gone quiet for a moment, something that was most irregular for her. Then she whispered, "*Sí*, this will work. I will marry you."

He had always imagined that a proposal of marriage would incur some kind of emotion in the gentleman proposing, even if he hadn't ever imagined being married himself. But instead of being swept away by a whirlwind of affection, he felt empty and uneasy. Instead of grasping her hand, embracing her, or even kissing her, he merely bowed his head in resignation.

Things had certainly gotten complicated very quickly.

He had felt so frightened then, and he hadn't even been the one to be carrying a child or suffering from the sickness that child brought. A long yawn sounded from his side. His eyes again focused on Ana—his wife—relaxed against the pillows, her eyelids low in exhaustion and relief. Now he had to do all he could to ensure that she was safe and protected.

"How are you settling into things here?" Peter asked.

"*Muy bien*. It is so beautiful here. I so much love the gardens and the church. I miss *España*. I miss *mi familia*. But I feel safe here." Ana's delicate hands went to her abdomen, her brow relaxing, its creases slowly disappearing. "*Mi bebé* will be safe here. I hope she no will feel lonely."

A memory splashed through Peter's mind. His own mother had married and settled into a comfortable life but had been abandoned in every other way possible. She had been left with the boys to rely on her own devices while her husband was off entertaining himself with every carnal pleasure he could conceive. Raising one child alone was difficult enough, but raising two rowdy boys? It had been nearly impossible for her in those early days. Even her large staff was loyal to her husband, leaving her emotionally isolated. Peter remembered well how she would sit next to his bed and silently cry for hours after she had supposed him asleep. The image of his mother, her beautiful face sucked thin by worry and fatigue, her cheeks doused with tears, gave Peter pause. But she had always felt a special, heaven-sent peace here, hadn't she? Indeed, there was a special spirit in Abbeygate for the mothers of his family, one that would bless Ana María as well.

The path ahead of them was not an easy one. He still had no certainty of his standing with the army and could not guarantee that Ana's identity and life here would remain secret forever. But he would protect her—and her child—with his life. If he had not been able to protect his own mother, he owed it to her and himself to protect his wife.

Chapter 7

November 9, 1813, Abbeygate, Surrey Hills, England

Ana had been living a few weeks at Abbeygate already and had started to become quite familiar with Peter's daily schedule. He rose incredibly early and spent some time in his rooms reciting prayers of some sort. At least she had gathered as much by the ritualistic murmuring she heard at precisely the same hour each morning. He then took out Warrior, his horse, for a ride before breakfast. He had also made a habit of bringing up Ana's breakfast tray himself, something she would never complain about. She found it rather endearing to see him at the beginning of her day. After that, he'd usually spend a few hours in the office taking care of bookkeeping and other estate responsibilities. In the afternoon, he would meet with the staff, visit the tenants, or make connections and conversation in town with neighbors. He then spent the remainder of the evening in her company.

They liked to take their dinner together on the back balcony just off the dining room. Although she had gathered that it was not a traditional or customary practice in England, it was one she appreciated greatly. They would often spend some hours conversing and practicing English until it was time to retire for the night.

Indeed, he made such an obvious practice of having such a strict routine that she could predict his responsibilities and activities at nearly any hour of the day, although she was still struggling to discern her own place in the house, particularly when he seemed to bustle about with such busyness and purpose.

In comparison, it seemed that she had become a statue. His movements in the house, particularly in his rooms that were so close to hers, were the only indication of the passing of time. In the moments of silence, she sat, still frozen by the shock of the events of the past months. Her pain, both physical and internal, seemed to still be echoing through her, no matter how hard she tried to close her mind to the memories. The weight of it all left her in an empty stillness that seemed never-ending. She would lay in her bed for hours, or kneel, unmoving with her rosary dangling between her hands until her legs were tingling and pricking with numbness. Often, Mrs. Thompson would interrupt her silence to remind her that she might feel better if she bathed or took a walk outside. Or Peter would bring her food, and she would eat, if she managed to keep it down, while he spent time with her for a short while. Mrs. Thompson had brought her a number of Lady Ashmore's gowns from her wardrobe, but Ana had only rotated between the same few simple dresses with colors similar to those of mourning. She lacked black options, so deep violet, rusted brown, and silver-gray would have to do.

The only thing that would break her out of her pain-induced trance was an awareness that she was not alone in her suffering. Peter was suffering too, even if she only got small glimpses of it. Perhaps that was why he had occupied himself so quickly with so many tasks, to help in sorting through the disaster that San Sebastián had left in their minds.

Tonight, however, he was much more solemn than she had seen him in previous days. Such silence hadn't enveloped him since their time on the ship crossing the Bay of Biscay and the English Channel. He sat, stirring his lemonade while he stared, unseeing, at the bloodred sunset. He did not drink any type of alcohol, a fact that Ana appreciated greatly, even without knowing his reasoning for such a choice. Port, ale, and other drinks seemed quite popular among the British soldiers, particularly among the upper ranks. A shiver of fear traveled up her spine as she remembered the drunken rampage of the men during her last night in San Sebastián. Was that why he avoided drink? The enduring respect that she fostered for her husband grew even greater at that, accompanied by a sharp stab of sorrow. That night had taken so much from her. From them both.

"Would you care for any more lemonade, my dear?" Peter's voice was automatic and methodical, but his eyes were so distant that he looked nearly blind to her.

"*No, gracias.*"

"Very well."

His face was a glided statue, all but for the pulsing muscle deep in his jaw that indicated to her that her assumptions were in some measure correct. He was troubled . . . but about what, she wasn't sure. Her time spent with him over the past few months had taught her to read the subtle signs of his moods, which he normally kept so orderly, disciplined, and hidden. It was not so difficult; she had done similar things when learning to translate from languages that were not as familiar to her. The movements of one's face, eyes, and body could tell her a great deal about the ongoings of one's mind. Still, she was not perfectly attuned to Peter's and had yet to discern the cause for his concern.

Ana reached a hand to him, squeezing twice. He jolted from his reverie, blinking rapidly and rolling his shoulders backward, as if trying to shrug off some weighty pack.

"I am well, Ana. *Estoy bien.*"

Ana watched as Peter rubbed at his eyes, further emphasizing the dark shadows underneath them. Had he been sleeping just as poorly as she was?

She often found herself waking at many hours of the night, not from nausea but from terror. She could feel clawing hands at her arms, her waist, her face. Could feel a wild panic that was insatiable. Could smell hot, rum-saturated breath. Then she would rub at her eyes and heave panting breaths as she clutched her soft bedclothes and stared into the dark. No glimpses of fire and smoke, no cruel, drunken fools could reach her. Only the quiet peace surrounded her. She was safe and protected, more than she had ever been, thanks to the man who slept alone in the room next to hers.

Did he ever wake from night terrors like she did? Ana was beginning to feel calmer during the day, but at night, fear enveloped her. She often found sleep so impossible to claim until the early hours of the night. Was it possible that memories burdened him just as much as they did her? And if they did, how sad to think that they should suffer, side by side, but still divided by a thick, wooden door. In moments like these, it felt they were farther apart than ever, a fact that Ana mourned.

Her gaze returned to Peter's face, lit by the fading sun. The exhaustion evident in his face and the knitting of his brow testified that he was not faring as well as he insisted.

"Truly, I am well," he repeated.

Ana huffed her disbelief, shaking her head and pursing her lips. "*No te creo.*" *I don't believe you.*

"I am trying to find order and peace here in this new way of living," he said, at last meeting her eyes.

"*Yo también.*" Ana nodded, gesturing to herself. Didn't he know she was working through many of the same issues? She moved her chair closer to him and left her hand clasping his. But what was he thinking about? "*Piensas en* San Sebastián?"

"I find I am always thinking of . . . it. I find I almost cannot escape it all."

She nodded. "I think of other things in the day, but the night . . . it is full of *terrores.*" Unwilling, Ana pulled her hands from his grasp and twisted them about in her skirts, bunching them up terribly as her mind spun into darker memories.

"I don't wish to carry on in this way. I wish to be a better father than my own, a better example for your child. And I fear I cannot do so in my current state."

Ana nearly laughed. He was not alone in feeling so. She was entirely unprepared to be a parent. But if their marriage was going to be strong enough to endure the challenges that were coming, they needed to be able to speak plainly about such things. She knew such open communication was not customary for many Englishmen, and gentlemen soldiers even less. But speaking her mind was the way that Ana understood the world. And if he was to be half of her world, he would need to learn to speak his mind too. Perhaps he just needed a little assistance.

"Can I help you, *Pedro*, when you feel *así*?"

"That is just the issue." He pressed his hands together in a learned, methodical movement, popping his knuckles and stretching out the tension in his fingers. "I am seeking to discover how I need to be helped myself. For so many years, the army was a place of order. I could expect how things would be carried on. But now . . . I find I have lost all faith in them."

"*Quizás* . . . it helps that you talk about these things."

Ana managed to unlace her fingers from the fabric of her skirts long enough to reach for Peter. He took her hand and squeezed it. Ana's breath caught in her throat, and she felt her heartbeat thud in her chest.

"I can certainly try. But would you mind if we walk as we talk?"

* * *

Peter's eyes scoured the faded evening skies as if he would find a script written there. But instead of words, he only spotted a few last birds darting about, the dregs of a bloody sunset, and the faintest glimmer of stars. He sighed. Clearly Mother Nature would be no help to him tonight. But at least she serenaded them with the quiet song of the night singers. His own mother would have liked to pick out the different songs, identifying the nightingale, robin, and blackbird. She had always appreciated that sort of thing. Peter was just grateful there was something to break up the silence so Ana would not be so entirely bored at his lack of communication.

How did one talk about the most vulnerable parts of one's life? Peter was accustomed to running from these types of conversations. He'd build fortifications as high as the sky and arm himself with a practiced, silent, uncaring air if only to convince himself that the war in his mind was simply that—in his mind. But something about being around Ana seemed to bring all these dangerous, conflicted feelings to the surface. He could not ignore them as he used to. And if Ana was to thrive in this marriage, he supposed he should probably share the defenses of his mind with her.

Peter started them on a slow march through the gardens, Ana's arm laced through his. Years of drills and training had cemented into him a minimalistic routine that did not exactly translate well to life at home. However, the precision, discipline, and restraint he had gained would benefit him somewhat. Moving about always seemed to clear his mind. At the mere motion of walking, he found that the memories that he had fought to hold captive began to loosen their hold on his tongue.

"You said the *armada* was a place of order. You joined the army for this?" Ana asked.

"More or less." The day Peter enlisted in the army flashed before his eyes. Oh, how his hand had trembled as he signed his name on the papers, just as it had trembled as he wrote a note to his mother that he had left behind on his bed. He had prayed so desperately that she would forgive him for enlisting without consulting her first. He had, essentially, run away. But he found he could not abide his father's company any longer. If Mother would not leave, then he would. And he would return when he was strong enough to protect her from her husband.

But she had not allowed him to remain in that grueling role of foot soldier for long. Their position in society and her assistance had elevated him much more quickly than any of the men who surrounded him.

"Mother purchased my commission to be an officer after I spent a year in the army. Four years I have served as a captain since then. And I would not allow her to purchase a commission that was higher yet. I was content with my lot. But my peers were not."

That having been acknowledged, his subsequent rise to the position of captain could only be attributed to his strict efforts, bravery, and ungrudging obedience. Such things had become a rarity, particularly during the siege.

"It gave my fellow soldiers great reason to treat me with contempt. They did not know I was the second son of an earl, but they did know I was a gentleman and, as a result, treated me with great disrespect. What an irony, I know. However, the officer position did provide me with additional safety, which was Mother's intention. It is likely because of my position that I survived San Sebastián. Hundreds of our men were killed. And that was before the burnings."

"I am most *agradecida* you are safe. I do not know what I would do without you there."

"But only God knows how undeserving I am of such responsibility. What did it matter at all if I could not keep my men from performing such unspeakable things?" Peter pounded a fist against his leg, trying in some way to ease the agonizing regret that he could not shake from his mind.

"But you rescued me, *Pedro*. And *mi bebé*. Is that not enough?"

No. "Yes, of course. I am immensely grateful for you. For you both."

In reality, Peter didn't know if it—or anything—would ever feel enough to redeem him from the weight of it all. Yes, he was eternally grateful to God that he had stumbled upon her and managed to get her out of Spain. Every day, he woke in a panic after seeing her bloodied face and hearing her pained cry in her dreams. If it had been one of his men to touch her, he would have killed the man himself. And if Peter felt so strongly, how must the fathers and husbands feel who had seen their wives and daughters suffer in the most horrifying of ways? *That* was the weight that threatened to crush him each day. They had left behind so many shattered souls and broken families, and the British army had no intentions of taking any sort of responsibility for it. Fury burned through him at the injustice. The beautiful woman at his side was a constant reminder of the undeserving cruelty so many had suffered at the hands of British soldiers. It was not right. And Peter felt an insatiable urge to fight back against the injustice, just as he had desired to fight back against his father.

But how could he do so without putting their future at risk?

"I try very much to discover how to live a life of faith, not a life of fear," Ana said. "I have *muchas problemas* still and much to change. But I want to believe God will bless us to have a life of faith, as it say in *la Biblia . . . 'Porque no nos ha dado Dios espíritu de cobardía, sino de poder, de amor, y de dominio propio.'*"

"Ah, yes, Second Timothy, is it not?" Peter repeated in English, "'For God hath not given us the spirit of fear; but of power, and of love, and of a sound mind.'"

Peter did not have a large Spanish vocabulary, but he had memorized some Bible verses during his time in Spain, as there had only been a Spanish pastor in camp. And this was one that he knew by heart. How often the words had flowed through his mind as his body was tensing against enemy fire, or as his mind was fighting an onslaught of dangerous memories. It had brought him peace, even if he hadn't understood it completely.

"*Precisamente.* We need to have the faith in God to find this spirit. The spirit of power and love. And that will bring us the peace of a mind . . . how you say?"

"A sound mind."

"Yes, a sound mind. I know God promises this to us."

Slowly, the tension that pinned Peter's shoulders upward started to melt away.

"If I might speak candidly, I do not understand many things of God. But I have a great desire to understand. I want to be healed by this faith and power, as you say."

"I want this too." Tears glazed Ana's eyes, and Peter glimpsed the pain that was still very real there. She needed healing as much as he did, and he could not forget it. God would have to mend her heart and protect her in ways that Peter would never be able to. They would seek Him together.

"I am grateful to have such a wise and faithful wife at my side. *Gracias*, Ana."

Ana's hand slid down his arm until her fingers laced through his. He squeezed her hand and pulled her closer to his side. He was truly most fortunate to be married to such a woman.

Chapter 8

November 14, 1813, Abbeygate, Surrey Hills, England

November 8, 1813—The House of Lords

Notations from Matthew Ashmore, Earl of Heathridge Hall

A politician named Bathurst came to the House of Lords today to present on recent issues that occurred in a certain city in Spain named San Sebastián. Apparently, the British army was accused of robbing churches in the area, which was certainly true of the French, according to their reports. But Bathurst claims that the only charge that the British should be guilty of is saving French lives—nearly 600 of them—even after the danger of the siege and some burnings that occurred in the city. He reiterated his trust in British leaders, including Wellington and a General Sir Thomas Graham, and finished with a speech of optimism about the successful crossing at a place called Bidassoa. Wellington was lauded, and Graham was given thanks for his efforts.

I admittedly do not understand a great deal of what occurred here. Peter would, of course. But it does seem as though they have not presented us with the whole and entire truth today. Perhaps Peter and David would like to know.

Matthew

Peter placed Matthew's notes down on his desk, sighed, and rubbed a hand across his forehead. It was infuriating, to say the least, to discover how the disgusting tragedy of San Sebastián was being completely and entirely swept under the rug. Once again, anger and guilt married in Peter's heart as he wished for some ally in testifying about the truth of what occurred there. An ally that was not his wife, who would be placed in danger, at very least of the social sort, if the truth of her attack and subsequent condition were ever revealed. Surely he was not the only soldier who had seen the horrors of that night and wished he could have saved even one more soul from suffering.

Yearning for a break from the weightiness of Matthew's notes and the thoughts that accompanied them, he reached for the larger piece of feminine stationery that he had already read through numerous times.

Dear Peter,

On November 8, Matthew attended a session in the House of Lords and heard some reports on the battles in Spain that he thought might prove interesting to you. I've enclosed his notes, written to you, on the matter.

My dear boy, I am sorry I do not bear more uplifting news, but I knew that you would want to know of it. But I must tell you that it brought me so much joy to see you again. I hoped for that day for many years, and never dreamed that not only would I see you but would also be witness to your wedding to such a beautiful and kind woman. I pray that you are well and that Ana is enjoying our beautiful Abbeygate. Do write and tell me how you are faring. I hope to see you again soon.

I love you, dear.

Mother

Peter's heart constricted and he rubbed at the spot as he reread those last five words over and over. Is this how his correspondence with Mother might have been if he had chosen to maintain any sort of consistency in his letter-writing with her throughout his years of service? How often had she waited for his letters with an anxious, aching heart only to receive silence?

Peter reached for a length of paper and a fresh quill. He had best start making up for lost time—and letters—now.

"Mr. Ashmore?"

Peter shook his quill, surprised at the interruption, splattering ink across the page.

"Yes, Burnsey?"

"Mr. and Mrs. Clarke have come to welcome you back to Surrey Hills."

"Shouldn't they have left a calling card or something to announce themselves in some way?"

"Perhaps they disregarded such things due to their familiarity with the family in your youth."

Peter sighed. The Clarkes were a very well-meaning family, and friends of his mother's, but they certainly had a tendency of being nosy. What could he expect from this visit?

"Very well. Will Mrs. Ashmore be welcoming them with me?"

"Mrs. Ashmore is taking her *siesta*, which you have instructed me to never interrupt. I am afraid you will be facing off this . . . battle, shall we say . . . on your own."

"You are correct. Never disturb the lady's *siesta*." Peter sighed again. It appeared his fate was sealed. "And Burnsey? That is quite enough talk of war."

"Very well," Burnsey replied with a chuckle.

Peter straightened his shoulders, snapped his heels together, and practically marched into the drawing room where his neighbors were awaiting him.

"Ah, Peter! That is, Mr. Peter Ashmore! What a pleasure to see you again!"

"And you, Mr. Clarke, Mrs. Clarke." He bowed before Mrs. Clarke wiggled her way into his arms in an insistent, too-familiar embrace. "Please, do sit. How do you like your tea?"

Peter waved to Mrs. Thompson, who was waiting at the door, for a tea tray to be brought in. After pouring two cups, spooning in a shocking amount of requested sugar into the tea, and relinquishing the teacups to his neighbors, Peter settled back into his seat.

"Now, to what do I owe this pleasure?"

"Of course, we were anxious to see you when we heard tell that you had returned to Abbeygate," Mr. Clarke said, holding his hand out to his wife. Whether he was attempting to stay her tongue or reach for her hand, Peter wasn't sure. If it was the first option, it did little to silence Mrs. Clarke.

"I simply cannot wait to meet your wife," she said exuberantly. "A number of neighbors in town have mentioned that she is foreign, correct? Is she French?"

Curiosity was apparent in the lightness of her tone, but a certain criticism and fear caused creases in her brow and around her mouth. Anger began to boil in Peter's stomach at the assumptions she was surely making solely because of his wife's birthplace. He opened and closed his mouth, shock making him entirely incapable of finding the words to respond to her question. Luckily, or perhaps unluckily, Mrs. Clarke continued.

"I also am most curious about your time in the army. You were abroad in Spain, were you not? There have been whisperings about a number of misdeeds that have occurred recently in Spain. A city called San Sebastián. Can you tell us what occurred there?"

The words crashed through the illusion of peaceful conversation that Peter had created.

"She is correct," Mr. Clarke grumbled. "There is quite a bit of talk about this San Sebastián in the game rooms in London. I heard tell there was quite an uprising in the army, even some soldiers fighting against their superiors and the sort. And something about the city burning."

"Although it could have been made up entirely by those French," Mrs. Clarke interjected. "You can never be sure what is gossip and what is truth."

Blood roared in Peter's ears, almost too loud for him to hear the Clarkes' continued prying, and he had to clutch the arms of his chair to keep from bursting from his seat.

"Mr. and Mrs. Clarke, I would be delighted to visit further with you at another date, but I have some very pressing responsibilities that I really must be taking care of."

"Has the army called for you?"

Peter stood, motioning for them to do the same, regardless of how Mother would scold him for the rudeness of such actions.

"I truly apologize. I will write to you and invite you another day. For tea, shall we say? And we will see you at the services on Sunday, I am positive."

"But we were not able to meet your new wife! I so looked forward to meeting her!" Mrs. Clarke pouted, her bottom lip puffed out dramatically.

"I promise you will have the pleasure another day. But for now, I must wish you good day."

Peter practically shoved the couple out the door after assisting Burnsey in fetching their coats, then nearly collapsed against the door as it was shut behind him, silence finally enveloping him. His heart was pounding as if he had just been running across a battlefield. Once again, the need to provide Ana with safety and privacy overwhelmed him, just as physically and literally as the need to breathe. He had to protect her. And for now, the way to protect them both was to protect their secrets.

Chapter 9

December 1, 1813, Abbeygate, Surrey Hills, England

Ana's personal dressing room was a haven now that it was not entirely white and cold. She had gathered certain colors and textures to remind her of her beloved homeland, creating a vibrant, comforting room that made her feel more secure, more like herself. Each morning, she knelt to recite her prayers, and the stabbing guilt at the origins of the growing babe inside her had slowly dulled to an ache. Although the holy experience of praying for and creating that spirit together with a husband had been viciously, selfishly stolen from her, Ana was still responsible for her child. God had somehow entrusted this little spirit to her, to care for and to love. That her condition was progressing had to be a sign of His blessing, His forgiveness. That was her prayer. And she would cling to the shred of peace that came at the thought.

Ana fingered the vibrant, woven fabric that she had wrapped around the back of her chair. It was a strangely bittersweet sensation to reflect on her heritage and culture, as it always brought painful memories of her parents to her mind. She had nothing physical to remember her father by. She had not been able to bury her father, had not been able to mourn him traditionally in the manner of *luto riguroso*. She would never be afforded the privilege of decorating his grave with a *rosario*. But she vowed to remember that day each year. She would mourn San Sebastián, mourn her father, and celebrate his life.

For now, she found that the sweet, early memories of her childhood were the only happy things grounding her, besides the quiet comfort of her husband. She was painting an illustrative map of her hometown in Valencia when Peter knocked on the door, interrupting her work. She froze, startled, carefully lowering her paintbrush so as not to mar her painstaking work.

"*Sí*?"

"May I come in?"

"*Por supuesto*." Of course. He was her husband, was he not? Did he truly need to ask permission to enter?

"How are you today, Ana?"

"*Muy bien, gracias*."

"And how fares everything with Mrs. Thompson?"

"*Todo bien*." In reality, Ana felt that many of the traditional responsibilities she was being taught were frivolous or ridiculously stiff. She did not understand the careful arrangement of calling cards and visiting hours. Perhaps she was fortunate that she managed to marry Peter without the complexities of a regular English courtship. She was not certain she could have survived one. Her lips blew out a huff of amusement.

"Is she proving helpful in teaching you about the responsibilities of your role as the lady of the house?

"Mrs. Thompson is good to me. So very kind. But our *casa* here is so private. Do I need to know all these things of hosting *y eso*?"

"I can't honestly say I enjoy all of England's traditions, but I'm afraid they'll be expected of us."

But she couldn't so easily adopt such foreign traditions.

"While Abbeygate is not a particularly vast estate," Peter continued, "there is still quite a lot that needs to be done to ensure that the property is well cared for. I'll care for the tenants and the land, and I was hoping that you would take charge of caring for the house, including much of the day-to-day happenings as well as any needed decoration changes or guest parties, things of that sort. At least, this is what Mother has explained to me would traditionally be done."

"Traditionally?" Ana María raised a brow in his direction, rolling the *r* for emphasis.

"I understand that things may be different in Spain, particularly on the part of your family, but we have been allowed to live at this wonderful place and need to do our part to take care of it, you see. And that includes calling on our neighbors, hosting events in our home, and maintaining our standing in society."

Peter seemed to tick off his words like a great list of tasks to be completed, but Ana could see that he'd gone into that practiced, methodical form of himself that came out when he was on assignment or instructing soldiers. Notably absent were the melodic passion in his voice or the emotion-filled crinkling of his eyes. Clearly he did not feel a great personal connection to all their new responsibilities, not like he felt for their missions on the battlefield. He had to comprehend why such a life felt so foreign to her. Ana's chest tightened with emotion as English words fled.

"*But the traditions of Spain are important to me too,*" she rambled in her native tongue. "*I cannot abandon the culture of my heart.*"

Peter's eyes remained distant; his brow furrowed in concentration. He truly wasn't understanding a thing she said to him.

"*You have no idea what I'm saying to you,*" she rattled off freely, her pronunciation sharp and precise. It was so much easier to speak Spanish than English!

"That is precisely right," he said with a smile.

She had to at least acknowledge that his acting was rather good. But she could say all sorts of nonsense, and he would never realize what she was speaking about. It seemed that the responsibility would be hers to learn *his* language better.

"*Bueno*, there are many things to do, I see. But can we not choose to live how we like? Perhaps I want *una siesta* to rest during the day, like in *España*, but always there are guests that come visit. What do I do?" Ana tried to lighten her voice as if jesting, but it cracked with emotion, betraying the weight of the issue on her mind. She rested her hands at her waist, her eyebrows raised.

"I'm afraid it would not be proper." Peter bit his lip, rubbing one hand across his brow. "While this is somewhat of an isolated estate, it is well known in Surrey Hills that Abbeygate is an earl's country seat. There would be talk, you see."

This Ana could not understand. In Spain, the position of *hidalgo,* or gentleman, was often determined by those who possessed land or money, instead of it being a lineage or royalty-bequeathed title. Certainly, there was a layer of the lower nobility that fit under the name of *hidalgo* through inheritance, but one could also become a *hidalgo* through their responsibilities, accomplishments, ownership, and more. The broad inclusion that this caused in their culture blurred the lines between nobility and middle class, and there was a greater sense of comfort and flow between people of differing birth and origin.

This was why Ana felt so bothered, so uncomfortable, at the thought of being constrained in who she could and could not interact with in public solely because of who she married. Couldn't she receive a little bit of help from whoever was willing to offer it? It seemed that settling into life here would be more difficult than she had hoped, particularly if she was trying to put the house in order while also preparing for the birth of her child. A prickle of frustration cut at her throat. She spun on her heel, pacing the room.

"But I cannot do all. *Entiendes*?"

In moments like these, she longed for Spain. Longed for her house, the lively banter of her family, the cooking of *Mamá*. Why must everything be so different here in England?

"We must find you a maid. That will help you a great deal, I'm sure. A Spanish maid, even better. I'll write to Mother. Surely she has heard of something among the ladies of the Ton. That will help you feel more comfortable."

"*Sí*, a maid would be nice, but I need that I feel comfortable!" Ana said, her voice rising as she strode about the room, emphasizing her words as she cast her hands into the air. "I need that I feel safe to live my culture here. I cannot have *una bebé* and live a different life than I always dream of. It would not be true. I will not feel safe."

Pain splashed across Peter's features as he nodded. "I know very well how it feels to be an outcast, a stranger in one's own home. But this is *our* home now. And I wish to do whatever is necessary to ensure that we are both comfortable, happy, and safe here."

"But I cannot feel *segura aquí*!"

That was just it—Ana didn't feel secure here, so far away from family and familiarity. She desperately wished to, but she doubted if she would ever feel safe again after the events of San Sebastián. One hand pressed against her abdomen, feeling the tiniest hint of rounding hardness there. How could she bring a child into such a world?

"This isn't merely about Spain, is it?"

Ana sank down to the floor, sobs finally shuddering their way out of her.

"No."

Firm, strong hands grasped her upper arms, then softened, circling around her.

"Everything is wrong. I always wanted a child, and now I have a child but not from my husband. I always want a home, and now I have a home but not in *España*. I am so far *de mi familia* and I *no entiendo nada* of mine responsibilities here. It is all wrong. *Todo.* And I no feel comfortable like this is my home." Ana wiped at her doused cheeks. "But I no want to be ungrateful, *Pedro.* You are so kind. You saved me and my child. I feel so mad to be ungrateful."

"I know it's difficult, Ana. I also know I cannot understand how you are feeling. I have not passed through the . . . pain you have experienced. I am also not carrying a child and enduring the sickness and changes you are enduring. But when I asked you to marry me, I was entirely serious that I would support you in whatever way necessary. Not simply out of responsibility or honor, but also because I know what it is to feel unsafe and alone in the world. I do not desire the same for you or your child."

Ana blinked hard, trying to clear her eyes, and looked up at Peter. His face was before hers, creased with concern and sincerity, his eyes dark with pain and understanding.

"I will help you, Ana María. You will not be alone, I promise. *Te lo prometo.*"

The racing of Ana's heart began to slow as the faintest glimmer of hope broke through on the horizon of her mind. She had experienced some of life's most painful changes in the last few months, but she did not have to move forward alone. Peter would help her, just as he had in listening to her concerns. That was surely an indication of safety in their relationship, was it not?

Chapter 10

December 11, 1813, Abbeygate, Surrey Hills, England

PETER JOGGED UP TO WHERE THE OLD STONE CHAPEL SAT NESTLED among thick oak trees. Cool, winter sunlight sifted through the criss-crossing branches, tracing the building in highlights and shadows. He had paid many visits to this chapel throughout his childhood, not many of which involved actually going inside it, much to his mother's dismay. It was a fact that he swore to change. He knew that Ana was a devout Catholic, or at least she was before the war. He was not very familiar with that religion, but he would support his wife in practicing it. Her murmured prayers had carried her through many dark days. She would likely want her child baptized and christened and anything else that particular faith required. Perhaps it was for the best that he was seeking to make amends with God and find forgiveness and peace, even if the Church of England was the only place he knew to do so.

The aching in his soul begged that such a thing could really be done.

He eased the chapel door open and started down the aisle. The broad form of the vicar, Mr. Smith, rose from a pew and turned toward him. He was a tall, muscle-bound man, a sight that Peter was sure wasn't entirely common among men of the cloth. A thick, gold-edged Bible was clasped carefully in his strong hands, its corners visibly well-worn.

"Why, Mr. Peter Ashmore. What a delight! Happy Christmas," he said with a bow.

"Happy Christmas, Pastor," Peter said.

"I heard of your return and am anxious to see you and meet your new wife. I apologize that Mrs. Smith and I have not yet paid you a visit."

"Well, I have also failed to pay *you* a visit, both in your home and here."

"Both can be remedied, beginning today." Mr. Smith gestured to the open pew next to him, and they took their seats together. "How are you faring? I know that life at war can be quite difficult to endure, even after one has returned from the site of conflict."

Mr. Smith always had a way of spearing the point on its head. Peter found his rehearsed, polite answers were quickly overtaken by brutal honesty.

"I'm afraid I've gotten myself into quite a lump of trouble."

"Oh, surely no more trouble than all the mischief that you and Matthew used to manage," Mr. Smith replied with a chuckle. "Why, I remember one time when you climbed onto the chapel roof just to escape the service your mother seemed so insistent upon."

Peter laughed bitterly. "Times were simple then. If only I were speaking of something so lighthearted. I'm afraid that the issue that seems to haunt me is a great deal more serious than that."

"And is that why you have come here? To rid yourself of the guilt that comes from a mistake?"

Peter's cheeks burned at the thought. "No, not guilt in the way you might imagine. Only memories I wish I could rid myself of." He was not the one who had done the great sin in San Sebastián, but it seemed he was still carrying the weight of it.

"Do you have anything you wish to discuss?"

"Yes . . . No?" Peter shook his head, his gaze darting around the room. He had come searching for answers, for peace, but it was difficult to divulge the pain he'd been carrying. "Clearly I'm not quite certain."

"Would you care to share what happened?"

Peter stood from the wooden pew, rolling his shoulders. He began to speak, slowly putting to words the nightmarish occurrences of San Sebastián, from the slow torture of the long months of siege, to the heart-stopping explosions that rocked the city, to the agony of finding Ana's father, Major Bailon, killed by the men he had called friends. He paced in the small stone aisle so firmly he was sure he would wear a path in it.

"It doesn't matter that I was not the one to light the city aflame. It matters even less that I laid not a hand on a woman or child. I was in a position of leadership over the men who performed these horrors, and for that I can never forgive myself. I'm afraid I'll take this sin—that these things were permitted—to my grave."

Words gushed from him like the blood from a wound, and a physical, visceral pain accompanied it. He pounded a fist into his leg as he walked.

"The very worst of all is that I just today received a letter from one of our contacts in Northern Spain. There was a trial held in San Sebastián just recently, at the beginning of November, in an effort to bring to justice the soldiers who did so much harm there. They sent out notices and questionnaires to try to gather those who had been treated with such brutality. Only two women attended. Two! Even worse, Wellington denied all claims that were put up against him, against us, instead blaming it all on the French. It's infuriating."

Peter buried his face in his hands as a rare tear of anguish escaped his eye.

"My, you are brave, to speak against the prized Wellington."

"And now you understand why I feel so trapped by it all. Wellington has made many excellent decisions in this war and many others and has brought victories that bring us all hope. But this was too intimate a mistake. To turn around, raze San Sebastián, and then abandon those poor people after we camped for months in hope of freeing them and their city? It disgusts me."

"This is quite a complicated issue, Mr. Ashmore. I wish to speak to you first as your vicar and then as your friend. I can't promise I will know quite the right thing to share, as I don't usually deal with matters on such a large scale . . ."

"Please, share your thoughts freely. I am past helping myself and appreciate any wisdom you'll give me."

"First, all the pain, both of the mind and body, that you have described is entirely real. There is a great amount of suffering that has been inflicted on the people of that city. But you are not responsible for carrying that suffering." Mr. Smith paused for a moment, allowing those words to sink deeper. "You need to allow Christ our Lord to carry it for them, to save them in this manner. Only He can do such a thing."

Mr. Smith flipped deftly through the Bible in his hands, landing upon a well-worn page, and quoted from Isaiah chapter 53: "Surely, he hath borne our griefs, and carried our sorrows; yet we did esteem him stricken, smitten of God, and afflicted. But he was wounded for our transgressions, he was bruised for our iniquities; the chastisement of our peace was upon him; and with his stripes we are healed."

He continued, placing a hand on Peter's shoulder and meeting him with an emotional gaze. "Only the Lord can take them under the healing of his wings and provide them with safety in this life and peace in the life to come. You must allow Him to save them in this way by letting go of the guilt and pain that you carry for them."

Peter sighed deeply as guilt began to painfully, slowly ebb from his body and tears began to leak more freely now from his eyes. He grunted and swiped at the unfamiliar sensation.

"But how do I let Him carry it all for me?" he whispered. In recent years, the tragedies of wartime had weighed upon him. He had taken to reciting prayers and meditating on the feelings of peace he believed the Lord had sent him in an effort to help. On occasion it did seem to alleviate him, but as of late, it had not made as great a difference as he hoped.

"It would help to start learning from His word. To come to know the Lord, you need to know His word. You can read how He helped His children by working miracles and see how He can work miracles in your life and heart as well."

Peter nodded. Surely Ana would have a Bible he could study, although it might be in Spanish. He vowed to search the library for an English copy he could keep at his bedside to add to his morning routine of reciting prayers.

"Now, speaking as your friend, please allow me to be frank."

"I would expect nothing less."

"Surely you cannot believe that you could have stopped an entire army by yourself. I do not doubt your abilities, Mr. Ashmore, but it seems that they were an uncontrollable, rampaging group of dangerous drunkards. You likely would have put yourself and others at risk by continuing to fight them, and then you wouldn't have been able to save Miss Bailon, that is, Mrs. Ashmore. Your life would be entirely different for that, as she is now your wife."

"I know, but I cannot help but wonder if I could have saved the others."

"I seem to remember you telling me that you were not permitted to do so—that in doing so, you would have been cast out of the army."

"Yes, but . . ."

"So, in escaping Spain with Ana, you were not selfish in choosing your own safety, as you have implied. Instead, you allowed the truth of these events to survive, in yourself and Ana. Surely they will live on in your family. Even if the army sins in hiding the desperate pain that was caused in San Sebastián, you have preserved the truth in preserving your family."

"Still, it feels that someone should be responsible for what transpired."

"You cannot be responsible for the joined armies of Britain and Portugal. You are only one man, albeit a great one."

Peter bowed his head, the truth of the words slicing through his heart. Still, he doubted whether God deemed him a great man. He certainly didn't view himself in such a way. "I only wish there was a way I could testify against the guilty without risking Ana's future. She would be called to testify, her reputation and condition bared for all to see. I cannot allow it. But continuing as if nothing ever occurred tortures me. These two opposing, impossible circumstances hold me captive."

Mr. Smith nodded slowly and tapped a finger against the heavy Bible in his hands. "I cannot claim to understand the complexity of crimes against the law on the battlefront or the legal workings of war punishment. But I think you are wise in wanting to protect your wife. She is your future."

He was right, Peter knew. Ana was his greatest priority. But perhaps there was still a peaceful way for him to be a voice of truth. Perhaps he could ascertain if the leadership's feelings regarding the battle had changed in any way. Matthew had a friend, Sir David Huntington, who had also been a captain in the army, although he had sold his commission and now played some sort of administrative role in London. Perhaps he would have some unbiased information on the topic.

"The truth of the battle will always weigh upon me, I think, even when the pain and guilt have passed on," Peter said. "I will accept, someday, that I could not have saved everyone. I could not have prevented the sacking by myself. But for now, it lives with me."

"Truth tends to act in such a manner, although some people are adept at ignoring its pressure. But truth will always remain, weighing you to the things that are most important, like the gravity that keeps your feet grounded to the earth."

There was great wisdom to that. How could Peter rid himself of the guilt he felt without forgetting what had happened? The pain in his heart lessened after speaking with Mr. Smith, but he still felt he had a role to play. Was there something yet he could do for the people of San Sebastián without harming them or Ana?

Peter thanked Mr. Smith and sent a silent plea to the heavens before leaving the chapel in long, swift strides. Maybe he could not travel back to Spain, but he could write to London and inquire about the trial. Perhaps then his soul would find a measure of rest.

Chapter 11

December 20, 1813, Abbeygate, Surrey Hills, England

PETER AND ANA HAD TAKEN THE CARRIAGE INTO TOWN IN SEARCH of warmer clothing. Mother's discarded wardrobe only contained clothes that were fit for warm weather, as Abbeygate had usually been a summer destination for their family. It was to be Peter's first Christmas here, along with Ana's, and while it seemed a bit frivolous to focus on Christmas celebrations when weightier matters were at hand, he still wanted her to enjoy the holiday. And to do so, they needed warmer clothes.

They each selected fine wool cloaks, and Peter ensured that Ana also had a variety of warmer day dresses with long sleeves or matching spencer jackets as well as thicker dressing gowns for the chilly nights. He had, however, left her to speak to the seamstress about the underthings that she would require.

Heat rose on his cheeks now just thinking of it. While Ana was his wife, it was better that he did not have the image of her in her underthings in his mind, whatever said underthings might entail. He would likely never recover from such an intimate sight—although it would be a welcome replacement for the nightmares that currently occupied his mind. He fought to repress a chuckle.

"*Qué*?" Ana questioned, having rejoined him outside the shop.

"Oh, nothing, my dear, just something Burnsey said," he lied, his words desperate.

"What did he say?"

Peter rubbed a hand over the back of his neck. He was in trouble now. Burnsey definitely did not say anything about the enticing nature of a woman's unmentionables. His mind scrambled.

"He simply reflected on my deviousness as a child. Have I ever told you about the time that I turned the corner of the gardens into a great mudhole?"

"No, but I am not surprised. It does sound like an *actividad* that a little boy would love so much."

"Indeed, it was. I will have to show you the very spot. Matthew and I spent many a happy afternoon playing in that mudhole. And Mother spent many a frustrating evening washing us off afterward. She ought to have thrown us in the lake."

Ana laughed as he helped her up into the carriage. Peter breathed out a relieved sigh. Ana need never know that he had ever imagined anything so familiar about her. But when had his thoughts about her strayed from being overprotective to curiously romantic anyway? That was just as distressing as the whole undergarments plight itself. He had promised Ana—and himself, for that matter—that this arrangement would be a marriage in name only. Physical affection of any sort was not to be trifled with. He could not make her feel endangered in any way, not after her attack.

And yet there were some actions they had grown accustomed to that could be seen as affectionate. Like when Peter settled down onto the front-facing bench next to Ana, she sidled up near him and looped her arm through his. Her closeness spread warmth through him, but it was also expected, nearly habitual at this point. He wanted to provide her with comfort when she needed it. But he would never forgive himself for allowing friendly affection to become too overbearing. How could he draw a very clean line between what was proper and what was protective?

Their carriage started to move, cold air whooshing past outside. Ana broke the silence.

"We may need to tell everyone *en la casa* about my condition soon."

Peter's heart resumed its errant pounding, but now for an entirely different reason. He pulled at his cravat as he tried to maintain his calm, confident smile.

"Oh, I'm certain we can wait a little while longer. You needn't be worried about such things yet, Ana."

Peter felt a great deal of peace at the ignorance of everyone around them. Of course, it was not because he intended to keep them in the dark about the truth of Ana's condition, but rather he wanted to prolong Ana's safety for as long as possible. The longer her condition was a secret between the two of them, the longer the origins of their relationship would go unquestioned.

"But I would prefer that they know before it is very much obvious," Ana said, indicating at her midsection. "They may be more suspicious if I start to appear as if I am . . . oh, how do you say in English?"

Peter flushed. "I believe one of the phrases commonly used is 'in the way.'"

There were not many polite ways to refer to the condition of carrying a child. Peter knew that Ana was more comfortable speaking about these things than he was. Admittedly, any mention of the terms made him feel heated in embarrassment.

"*Sí, eso.* I will feel so much happier to know that everyone knows when my *bebé* starts to grow bigger and I need more help. I think today. We can tell them of the *bebé* today."

Peter tapped his feet against the floor of the carriage. He was not prepared to announce his imminent fatherhood to the household. Such an announcement would normally require days of careful planning to decide how he would describe their situation, as complex and delicate as it was. But if Ana was carrying the weight of their secret and the weight of her child, he needed to ensure that she was comfortable.

He sighed in submission. "Very well. When will you feel comfortable telling them?"

"When we return to the *casa*?"

So soon? Peter had no time to think of all the possible questions he would be bombarded with, no time to build defenses for Ana's reputation if it happened to be called into question. He breathed deeply as the faces of his household flashed before his eyes. He could trust them; he had told Ana as much. They would surely be happy to know their news and would not have any untoward thoughts about the timing of Ana's condition. After all, that timing would not truly be revealed until the child was born, as far as Peter understood.

"Yes, I believe that would be ideal," Peter smiled. "I'll ask Burnsey to gather the household together after we've returned indoors."

"*Perfecto.*"

"And you are certain you are truly ready? Everything will change upon them knowing."

Ana nodded as she nestled into Peter's side, leaning her head on his shoulder.

"I know it will be *muy diferente*. But I realize now that I feel so much safe when I talk to you about all I feel in my mind. And perhaps it will help to not keep a secret in the house too. I feel much better to be more honest this way."

Peter nodded. He had noticed a change in Ana, aside from the sickness that had been improving as of late. She did not need to be reminded to eat, and she slept much more easily. It seemed she was more motivated to care for herself. While he knew she was far from recovering from the mental repercussions of San Sebastián, he was encouraged to see her progress. And perhaps telling the staff their secret was a step along the path of healing.

"I need their help, as I do yours," Ana continued. "They will help to prepare everything for the *bebé* when she arrives. They will help to ensure I am healthy and well. *Sí*, I am ready. *Estoy lista*. Still, I no wish that anyone else know."

"Even Mother?" Peter rubbed a hand over his jaw. He wanted to respect Ana's wishes. But surely Mother would provide them both with a great deal of wisdom as they were preparing to be parents. "I confess I would feel a great deal of comfort upon telling her that I am going to be a father. I will not divulge the truth of your condition, of course. That secret will forever remain between the two of us."

"Soon. We will tell her soon, *sí*?"

"Very well."

The ride back to Abbeygate passed by quickly. He hardly had a chance to slow his heart rate before he was placed in front of his staff, a nervous Ana at his side. His mouth was as dry as gunpowder. His eyes darted to Burnsey, wanting to ask for a glass of water to drink but thinking better of it.

"Dear friends, we have gathered you together to share with you a bit of joyous news. Mrs. Ashmore and I . . . that is, we are . . . I mean to say . . ."

"I am 'in de way'!" Ana burst out, a smile spreading across her face as she placed her hands on her middle. The trembling of her frame revealed she was much more nervous than her exuberant display let on.

"Yes," Peter chuckled nervously. "Mrs. Ashmore is with child."

A silent, surprised pause lasted only a few beats, until a crescendo of applause swelled. Happiness echoed throughout the hall in the form of laughter and exclamations. Peter scanned the group, noting no suspicion. There were no fingers being counted in calculating the months, no hands being raised to cover accusatory whispers. Only open smiles and fond embraces, signs of genuine happiness.

Peter could see those same signs in his wife. Her shoulders were loose, rather than the tense posture she often adopted. Her face was smooth, devoid of worry lines, and her smile had a serene light that he wasn't sure he'd ever seen before. She had been quite insistent upon telling the staff today, so much so that he had not paused to consider whether she could be feeling anxious about such a revelation. After all, she had taken to a rather quiet, solitary lifestyle in the house so far. But now that he saw the physical transformation in her after announcing the imminent birth of their child, he knew it had been troubling her. Perhaps this would provide the perfect opportunity for her to trust more in those staff members and friends around her, just as much as Peter trusted them. She would require their help more and more as the months progressed.

Peter stepped closer to Ana and wrapped an arm around her waist. Her hand crossed her belly to lace her fingers through his.

"They are delighted," he whispered, "And they will be a great support to us."

He saw bright tears of contentment in her eyes. It had been so long since he had seen her so happy, so carefree. Too long.

"When are we to expect the arrival of the dear babe, Mr. Ashmore?" Mrs. Thompson called from across the room, clapping her hands eagerly as she approached Ana.

"She expects to be confined in July, according to the physician's knowledge."

About a week prior, Peter had taken great pains to have a discreet physician with great expertise who would confirm her condition while still maintaining their secret. It had not been an easy task to find such a physician, particularly when trying to be aware of the discomfort that being alone with a man could incite when Ana had undergone such violence only months ago. But she had endured the appointment well and had emerged with a peaceful smile on her face as the physician confirmed her condition. A spark of pride had lit in Peter's heart. And he would permit himself such a feeling; although he was not physically the father of the child, he would truly be the father in every other sense of the word.

A chorus of giggling grounded Peter back into the present as Mrs. Thompson released a tearful Ana at last and then approached him, her arms open and expecting an embrace.

"Aye, Mr. Ashmore!" Mrs. Thompson said as she wrapped her arms around him, tears sparkling in her eyes. "A lil' babe in the house! How delightful 'twill be! I'm simply tickled, meself."

"Thank you, Mrs. Thompson. We are quite delighted ourselves."

"Our sincerest congratulations are in order, Mr. Ashmore," Burnsey said. "We couldn't be more thrilled for you and Mrs. Ashmore. You certainly wasted no time, just as should be done, if you ask me. No wedding trip necessary!" A jolly chuckle shook his frame, the buttons on his uniform wiggling humorously.

Peter's cheeks flamed red hot. He glanced at Ana, glad that she had not overheard. He had only imagined his role in claiming the child as his own once he or she was born. But he had not anticipated the insinuations that would come beforehand. Perhaps his staff was too bold for making such comments. But they had known him for the entirety of his life. They were just as much family as Mother was. Perhaps it was better this way, as Peter would become accustomed to the suggestive comments and hinting jokes before they became all too blatant in the company of his brother, friends, or fellow soldiers.

He lifted his arms, waving to address the exuberant crowd. "We thank you for your excitement and congratulations and thank you in advance for the additional measures of support you'll undoubtedly bring to Mrs. Ashmore during this time. Please do all you can to ensure that she is comfortable and cared for, and I vow to do the same. We share this news in confidence, knowing that you will respect Ana's privacy as she adjusts to this new stage of life."

"And soon we will meet our little *bebé*!" Ana exclaimed.

Chapter 12

December 24, 1813, Abbeygate, Surrey Hills, England

ANA STIRRED HER TEA AND PICKED DISTRACTEDLY AT HER SLICE OF bread, trying to think of some way to drive away the loneliness that stabbed through her at realizing she would spend today, *Noche Buena*, without her family—this Christmas Eve and every one after that. The pain of *Papá's* passing had dulled, but his absence felt as though some part of her soul was missing. Even in future years, she suspected she would never feel the same again. And the holidays were particularly hard to experience without one's family, she had learned. Even though it had been years since she had spent a holiday with both her parents present, the loneliness still stung.

And Peter, it seemed, had noticed. He had already finished his breakfast, cleared away his dishes, and was now staring intently at her.

"I am glad to spend this day with you, Ana," he said, leaning in to squeeze Ana's shoulder. The fact that he did not seem to relish physical closeness in the past made the touch even more tender and sentimental. A rush warmed over Ana's skin.

"I thought we might go out for an excursion this afternoon," he continued.

"*De verdad*?" Ana scooted forward in her seat; her hands pressed against her heart in excitement. "Truly?"

"Yes, truly. Mickleham, a nearby village, has a lovely Christmas festival arranged. I thought we could participate in the festivities in town. Perhaps that will help to make up for my lacking any and all knowledge on how to prepare a house for the Christmas holidays."

The anticipation that lit his eyes dimmed momentarily, and Ana mirrored him, her heart slowing, her excitement dampening. Something was the matter.

"It sounds so lovely. But did you never celebrate *la Navidad* with your *familia* before you joined the *armada*? Surely you remember some traditions or preparations, no?"

"Society would have you believe that the Christmas season is all about spending time together as a family. But our celebrations were not typical of many other households. My father chose to spend his time outside of the home instead of inside it, where his family was, where he perhaps should have been. Mother did her best to encourage our enthusiasm and anticipation, but I could always sense that something was not quite right."

Ana had likewise not had an idyllic holiday in many years, at least not in the family-strengthening, traditional sense. She recognized all too well the long-buried pain that simmered in Peter's eyes. That same pain wrenched at her heart each December and January at the absence of *Mamá*. And now with *Papá* having passed on, it was even more acute. She rubbed a hand on her chest, as if that could diminish the very real ache that dwelled there. "I know how you mean."

Peter rubbed a hand over his neck as a muscle pulsed in his jaw. It seemed he was truly bothered by this memory. Ana's heart ached. She wished she could smooth the lines of frustration that creased his forehead. How could she make this better?

"*Quizás* we can celebrate together. We are a family, *tú y yo*, and soon to be a bigger family *aún*." She rubbed a hand over her middle. "It is important that we make our own traditions, no?" Ana spread her lips in her brightest, most encouraging smile.

The pain in Peter's eyes and the tension in his face melted away, and he could not seem to avoid the reluctant grin that curved the corner of his smile.

"I suppose you're right," he said. "Perhaps this is a great blessing for us both, to start the holiday season and the new year afresh. I would love to make more traditions with you, Ana."

Butterflies erupted in her belly at the thought of spending this Christmas and all the Christmases after that with Peter. And slowly that longing ache in her chest started to dull. It appeared it would be a much-needed season of healing for them both.

"*Ay Pedro, muchísimas gracias!*" Ana jumped from her chair and pressed an unrelenting kiss to Peter's cheek, despite his gentle resistance. But this was no mere *beso* of greeting. Her lips had lingered on his cheek. She had wanted him to feel her closeness, her appreciation. She had wanted to kiss him. That reality filled her with a shocking excitement just as much as the prospect of a Christmas celebration did.

"It is Christmas Eve, after all—we must celebrate somehow," he said with a crooked smile.

Ana hurried upstairs to dress for the day, breakfast abandoned and forgotten. Finally, her sickness was beginning to abate, and she was anxious to get outside of the house. Even though Surrey Hills likely had drastically different Christmas traditions than Valencia, she would jump at any excuse to be freed of her chamber. It was still a beautiful, peaceful space, but her enduring nausea had begun to make it feel more confining than comforting. How freeing it would be to be outside. And she was quite curious about the Christmas traditions the day would bring.

Once they were prepared, Peter helped Ana into the carriage, handing her a basket of food for their midday meal.

"Mrs. Thompson has certainly ensured that we won't starve, although I assured her we would only be gone a few hours."

"*Perfecto*. You know how with the *bebé* I have so much hunger."

He chuckled, "Yes, I know. And we shall have to sample some of the traditional foods in town as well. They may not be Spanish, but I can attest they will be delicious."

Sometime later, the carriage rocked to a stop in front of the charming Mickleham village square, and Ana had to fight back a sigh of brief disappointment. It was nothing like Spain. Even though she understood quite well that she was in an entirely different country and climate, she had still found herself imagining the cobblestone-lined square in Valencia, doused in golden afternoon sunlight and full of countless booths, each sporting porcelain toys, decorated instruments, delicately constructed cakes, and countless stacks of vibrant fruit. Ana could smell the sea's salt in the air, could hear the strumming of strings, like waves of music. How she longed for the *Navidad* in Valencia of her childhood. Instead, the scene in front of her was completely engulfed in evergreen boughs, red winter berries, and spindly candles.

No, it was nothing like Spain. But it still was magical.

The next few hours were full of new and exciting entertainment. Music trilled through the air, and the freeing country dances were enjoyed by all. Ana had feasted upon all the roast boar, berries, gingerbread, and bread pudding she could possibly eat. How blissful it felt to enjoy food without the restraints of a nauseated stomach! Peter had even joined the men in a feat of strength that consisted of sitting on the ground across from each other, the bottoms of their feet touching as they both grasped the same thick, wooden stick and pulled. Peter easily pulled over man after man, to the great amusement of the crowd, until they finally allowed him to take a rest. Ana cheered louder than anyone in the crowd, laughing alongside them each time Peter pulled over another man at an increasing rate. Laughing did seem to help tamp down the growing rush of attraction that made her want to march over to her husband and wrap him in her arms. That is what she told herself, at the very least.

Peter sat heavily on the wooden bench next to Ana and chuckled. "They are quite the rowdy group tonight. I do apologize."

"It is perfect. I love to see this happiness and celebration."

"I do as well," Peter said, his shoulder rubbing against hers, sending delightful tingles running down her arm. "How do you celebrate *Navidad* in Valencia?"

Again, that familiar pain speared Ana's heart, but she steered her mind elsewhere. Instead of focusing on the lonely, too-quiet evenings at home or camp with *Papá*, she recalled the enchanting scene set each December in the town square.

"Oh, it was so *especial*. Like here, we eat so much delicious food and many sweets as well. In Valencia, we also enjoyed a lot of fish. It was rather warm there during *la Navidad*. There are always many *luces* with candles in the windows of the buildings, and it looks like the sparkling stars of the night."

"I'm sure it is a marvelous sight to behold."

"Indeed. One of the traditions *más favoritas* of my *Papá* was *el Día de los Inocentes.* On this day, everyone celebrates the baby Jesus and the Mother Mary, how they trick King Herod and escape to Egypt. The people *en España* celebrate this day with play tricks and telling *chistes* or jokes. *Mi Papá* wore a funny wig and coat and acted like a *policía* to scare the children. It was so amusing!"

"Perhaps we should hold our own Día de los Inocentes. It sounds quite hilarious."

"It is. But I do not think you be prepared for the jokes I play on you!" Ana chuckled and wiggled her eyebrows at Peter, who laughed in return. "But the *celebraciones* do not end in December. In January, the *Reyes* come to bring gifts and *dulces* to the little ones."

"The *Reyes* . . . the king of Spain?" Peter's eyebrows raised into his hairline.

"No," Ana said with a laugh, placing a hand on the slight roundness of her growing belly. "The three wise kings of the time of *Jesús*."

"Ah. That does seem much more likely." Their laughs mingled. How Ana loved the ease that laughter set loose in his eyes, his face.

"We also have a *Roscón de Reyes,* a cake for the kings with a tiny *bebé Jesus* inside. It has sweet cream and dried fruit and is so *delicioso.* But the most delightful part of all is if you happen to find the *bebé Jesús* inside your slice of cake, you get to have all the luck for the new coming year. I miss so much these *tradiciones*."

"They sound quite special indeed. If you wish, I suspect we could teach Cook to create one of these cakes for us. We could share it with the staff. Or we could keep it for ourselves. Perhaps I would have the greater chance of becoming lucky," he chuckled.

"Truly, *Pedro*? I would be so delighted if we were to make one!" Ana could already imagine tasting the softness of the brioche cake, the sweetness of the cream, adorned with the gummy, tart fruit. Delighted indeed!

Peter wrapped his arm around Ana's shoulders and pulled her toward a building echoing with light and laughter. "Come inside. Let's warm ourselves for a minute with some drinking chocolate before we journey back to Abbeygate."

Delightful tingles spread down Ana's spine at his touch, and she did little to subdue them. They heated her chest delightfully and made her fingers ache to reach out for Peter and pull him closer. If his touching her had such irresistible results, Ana would begin finding every opportunity to invite such attentions. She ducked inside the doorway of the cozy tavern. Small tables were scattered about the room, each bustling with joyful guests. In the middle of the space hung a lovely sphere of evergreens, twisted twigs, bright berries, and shining, pink apples. What could it be?

She turned to Peter, "*Qué es eso*?"

"This is a kissing bough," Peter said as amusement and embarrassment married on his face.

"Kissing . . . *como un beso*?"

"Precisely." His lips were pursed as his eyes scanned the room, and his hands stayed hidden, deep in his pockets.

"Aye, Mr. Peter Ashmore!" a man called from the other side of the counter. "Ye ought to give yer sweet bride a kiss beneath the kissing bough. 'Tis tradition."

"Aye!" the townspeople agreed with hearty cheers and whistles.

Ana chuckled at the crowd's reaction, but then her gaze slid over to Peter. His eyes were darting about nervously, his cheeks abnormally reddened, and not merely because of the crisp winter air. Clearly he was not comfortable with the prospect of kissing his wife.

"*Estoy bien, Pedro*," she whispered. "You do not need to."

But he waved a hand to the crowd and stepped closer to Ana, grabbing her hand and pulling her beneath the kissing bough. His face lowered closer and closer until she could nearly count the rough whiskers already budding on his jaw. Those light, *celeste* eyes met hers and then darted down to her lips. Ana's breath choked in her throat and her shoulders jerked involuntarily as another man, another kiss, suddenly flashed in front of her. A whimper squeezed out of her, and she wobbled.

Peter's eyes flashed, his brow folding in a familiar look of concern. But instead of pulling away, his ever-approaching lips darted to the side and brushed ever-so-slightly against her cheekbone. Ana's heart ached but not with relief—with disappointment.

The pair waved to the crowd, quelling their laughter. Ana bowed her head and patted her chest, as if to signal that she was the shy one, that Peter was acquiescing to her wishes. Ana stepped away from the scene, but not before noticing Peter pluck a round, red berry from the bough and slip it into his pocket in a disguised, discreet manner. Whatever could he be saving a single berry for?

Soon another couple was beneath the kissing bough, and the crowd was caught up in its reverie again.

Ana's chest rose and fell with heavy breaths. Peter's hands tightened around hers, squeezing twice, and his eyes were locked on hers again.

"I'm sorry," his voice rasped.

"*No, Pedro. I* am so sorry. The people, they wanted a kiss *de verdad*."

"It likely won't surprise you to know that I don't care in the slightest what they want. I only care what *you* want." He paused, then whispered under his breath, "Or in this particular case, what you do *not* want."

But she *did* want to be kissed by Peter. He was everything warm, safe, and comforting. He made her laugh, even when she felt oddly melancholy. And he was beyond thoughtful, despite his seemingly calloused exterior. *Sí*, Ana wanted to be kissed to dispel the dreadful memories of her previous kiss by that dark, wrongful man—if she could even call it a kiss. Would that memory forever keep her from happiness with her husband?

"The hour is getting late. We should return home."

Ana sat silent for the remainder of the ride, trying to make sense of what had happened. They had enjoyed such a lovely day together, and at the end of it all, Ana had desired that closeness with Peter. She would not have protested if he had kissed her, despite her initial panicking. But how could she show him that she was beginning to heal? That she desired that entirely new type of trust and safeness between them?

Soon Abbeygate rolled into view. Once Ana stepped out of the carriage, something faintly touched her head. She turned toward the light of the house and was frozen in delight.

"*Pedro! Mira!*" she pointed, begging him to look. Small, lacy fluffs of white were meandering down from the sky in lazy patterns. "*Es nieve?* How you say?"

"Snow. Yes, that is snow, my dear," Peter said, a broad, free smile warming his face as he tilted it upward to meet the falling flurries.

"I never seen *nieve en mi vida,*" Ana exclaimed, her mouth hanging open in wonder and her eyes filling with tears.

"You have never seen snow? It can be quite magical on Christmas, so today is the perfect day to see it. Perfect indeed. But after December, it can get quite wearisome. Turns into sludgy stuff and sticks around far too long."

"Oh, I will never grow weary of this beauty. *Me encanta!* I love it!" Ana reached her hands out to catch the snowflakes. Two large, velvety flakes alighted on her hand, momentarily pressing their cold into her palm before melting into the tiniest spots of water.

"It is beautiful," Peter agreed. "And so quiet."

"This is the noise of peace," Ana whispered, her eyes closed, face still tilted upward. "No explosions. No muskets. No screams or yells. Just *todo el mundo* silent, sleeping."

When they arrived at the top steps, Ana reached for Peter's hands and pulled him close to her until her rounded midsection brushed the front of his coat. For once, he did not stiffen or pull away.

"This is the most happiest day *de mi vida* in England. I thank you so much."

Peter smiled, "I wish to bring you many more happy days. You deserve all the happiness the world can possibly offer."

Ana's heart sped rapidly, her breath puffing out in small clouds before her. She stared into his blue eyes as they gleamed in the bright winter light. Could she be so brave to try to put to words the way he had made her feel today?

"You bring me this *felicidad, Pedro.* I have all the happiness when we are together." She leaned closer to him, imagining how it would feel to have his lips pressed against hers.

A slight wave of nervous tension laced his face and then released as open honesty widened his eyes and curved his lips into a smile.

"Ana . . ." he said, his eyes traveling down her face to her mouth. Ana's heart leapt to her throat, and she bit her bottom lip. Was this to be a blessed second chance at their disastrous kiss from earlier? Would he really kiss her?

True, they had never spoken of how to navigate such a circumstance. He had been so uncomfortable with their first kiss at their wedding that Ana assumed they might never share a kiss again. And then on their way to Ivybridge, he had a very jumbled, indirect manner of telling her that there would be no physical affection shown in their marriage. At the time, Ana had felt relieved—once she managed to sort through translating in her head and understand what he'd been trying to say. But now she wondered if such an agreement had been a huge mistake.

If Peter's strict honor hadn't required him to say such things, what sort of marriage would they have had? Would they have learned to find comfort and healing in one another's arms instead of doing so much separate searching for the same conclusions? Was it too late to wish that she could change this marriage of convenience into a marriage of compassion? The warmth of Peter's hand in hers, sending tingles up her arm, told her no. But as she looked into his eyes and saw wariness, she wavered.

But why wasn't he moving? She leaned closer, hoping her posture would signify that she welcomed the moment. They were married, after all. Wasn't it a sort of responsibility of hers to kiss her husband on Christmas Eve? Ana bit her lip to quell a nervous laugh from escaping her.

A loud creaking of the front door echoed through the cushioned silence of the snow-filled yard. "Ah, Mr. Ashmore and Mrs. Ashmore, you've returned!" Mr. Burnsey said.

Ana and Peter jumped apart, their faces heated. How she wished she could press snow against her cheeks to calm their high color. But should she really be embarrassed to be caught nearly embracing Peter? He was her husband, after all.

"Please, come in and warm yourselves," Burnsey said. "Oh, and Mr. Ashmore, there's a letter come for you from London."

"Could it be your mother?" Ana asked, a friendly smile lighting her face, hoping to dispel the awkwardness lingering between them.

"No, I don't believe so." Peter's eyes met hers, but they were glazed over, his mind clearly elsewhere. "I apologize, Ana, but I must remove myself to review this letter. I'll meet you in your dressing room for spiced tea later, if you wish."

"*Sí*, that would be lovely."

And with that, Peter hurried away to his study. His shoulders were knitted together with tension, his fists clenched tight. What could be in this letter that he would anticipate with such distress?

"May I take your cloak, Mrs. Ashmore?" Burnsey asked.

"Yes, *gracias*," Ana said, shrugging the snow-watered garment off her shoulders. "And would you send for a tray with spiced tea, *por favor*? In my dressing room *está bien*." She would do just as Peter said and prepare for their nightly tradition.

A sudden chill wrapped around Ana. It seemed that she could feel Peter's absence like a warmth that was ripped from her, and not only because they had been standing so close. Only months ago, she had wondered how they would get along as virtual strangers turned spouses and then parents. And now she found she nursed a deep ache at the thought that Peter might receive a letter at any time that he would need to read in seclusion, away from her. Would they ever achieve the complete, open honesty in which husband and wife shared the entirety of their lives together? Not just their kisses and embraces but also their dreams and devastations?

She hoped so. More than she could say.

Ana had changed into her thick, white nightgown and wrapped her deep, purple dressing gown over the top, knotting it tightly. She arranged the padded chairs near her desk in their nightly positions long before Peter finally came up to the room. When he opened the door, his posture was slumped, defeated, and his eyes were trained on the floor.

Ana's heart plunged as she reached out to him. "What is it, Peter?"

"The army has called me to London."

Chapter 13

December 25, 1813, Abbeygate, Surrey Hills, England

PETER WAS SEATED IN HIS LIBRARY, REREADING HIS RECENT CORRESPONDENCE for the fourth time, willing his eyes to derive some new meaning from the words. He was anxious about his journey to London. The sweat that beaded on his brow and the nervous bouncing of his knee indicated as much. At least he had already made the necessary preparations for his journey. His knapsack was packed with his uniform and the essentials for a quick overnight stay. With any amount of luck, he could stay at the London estate, Heathridge Hall, with Mother instead of one of the barracks at the army's headquarters. His back already ached at thinking of sleeping on one of those hard, narrow beds. Peter chuckled. Had he become so soft in only a few months of sleeping on a comfortable bed here at Abbeygate? Perhaps he could become accustomed to life outside the army after all.

He had also been in contact with Sir David Huntington, whose letter had arrived alongside the summons from the army, warning him of the heightened tensions surrounding the issue of San Sebastián and the recent legal trial and counseling him to proceed honestly but cautiously. It seemed that Peter's account of the happenings of the siege had moved Sir David, at least enough to confess that he was perturbed by the army's position of feigned innocence in the trial. Peter was anxious to speak more with him. He would need all the information he could possibly obtain to give himself a chance of success in the verbal battles that surely awaited him. His last meeting in San Sebastián had certainly indicated as much. But he could not stand by such moral weakness and let it go unprotested.

Now he had but a short time to devote entirely to Ana, and he vowed to try to make her feel as comfortable as possible before he had to leave. And, he reminded himself, he needed to participate in some semblance of a Christmas Day celebration.

It had been years since Peter had spent Christmas on leave from the army. Even if he hadn't been on duty, he had found it too painful to return home for a holiday that was wrapped up in all sorts of nightmarish memories. Holidays—and any sort of celebratory day for that matter—had always turned out that way when Father was around at their London home. He had found the special day as an excuse to get tremendously intoxicated and had proceeded to terrorize his wife and children. Even at a distance, it was terrible. Peter remembered sneaking downstairs in search of a sip of spiced punch only to be greeted by the sight of Father flirting outlandishly with a young woman who looked half his age. He also remembered Father's yelling and Mother's sobbing echoing down the hallway as he and Matthew had lain awake, all thoughts of Saint Nicholas entirely abandoned. He wasn't sure which memories hurt worse.

But now Peter had a chance, even if it was a limited one, to recreate Christmas in his mind. He had his own family now, and they would be making their own traditions. The smallest flame of hope lit in his chest at the thought of mixing Spanish and English traditions together until they found the perfect sort of holiday that they would love to celebrate in their home. Finally, the moments of the year that were intended for rejoicing would regain some sort of allure for Peter. And there was nobody he would rather spend them with than Ana. He only wished he wasn't required to leave so soon. The timing was rather awful, really.

Peter stood, stretching his arms above his head and shaking out his legs one by one, as if that could dispel the nervous energy that coursed through him. It was their first Christmas. He could not permit himself to make a mess of it. He reached for the package that lay on the corner of his desk, carefully wrapped in creamy silk and green ribbon. Mrs. Thompson's help in wrapping the gift had been invaluable—it looked simply beautiful. But what lay inside had the potential of being even more beautiful. How he hoped Ana would appreciate it. But what was this nervous pounding in his chest? He had never felt so anxious to see her, not since . . . well, since before he had nearly kissed her beneath the kissing bough and then again at the front of the house. Was that truly only yesterday?

The close sight of her soft red lips had undone him entirely. Somehow, in the short span of a few months, he had gone from vowing to never touch his wife in any sort of romantic fashion to desiring more than anything to kiss her. How it had happened, he could not say. And it bewildered him to no end.

And yet to see panic widen and glaze her eyes, to feel her jump away from his touch, to hear her breathing quicken in desperation . . . it had all terrified him. He knew, deep in his heart, that her reaction had been because of the attack she had endured after the siege. But some small part of him wondered, even if it was only for a moment, if she was truly so repulsed by his touch. Surely she couldn't be, not if she had invited his touch again so soon after. But he would never want to presume, not when she had experienced such pain already. He had sworn to never do anything to make it worse.

Peter pulled open the heavy wooden door of the library and climbed the stairs leading toward their bedrooms. He knew the stairs well, knew which ones were creaky and which ones were spotted with paint or blood from the many adventures and mishaps he and Matthew had shared as young boys. Most of the summers of their childhood had been spent here in such a carefree manner, something that had only been possible when Father was not around. And as a result, they had gotten into more mischief than Peter liked to admit. But the climb to the second floor had never felt so long as it did now. With every step, his heart pounded, but not from exertion. It was only his luck that he would be called away from his new wife during the Christmas holiday, and just when they were beginning to make some progress in their relationship.

He knocked on Ana's dressing room door. "Ana?"

"*Pasa, Pedro,*" she called, bidding him to enter.

Ana had put away the conservative-colored gowns she had worn religiously the past few months, instead donning a deep maroon dress, the shade of darkened rubies. Clearly this dress was not one of his mother's; it fit Ana too perfectly. No, she must have had this dress made up for herself, and he was mighty glad she had done so. It was perfection. Delicate sleeves puffed to her elbows, emphasizing the soft, even color of her olive skin. A swooping neckline framed her form most becomingly, Peter noticed as his cravat felt suddenly much too restraining. The shining dark red fabric spilled from her waist and was embroidered with black roses at the hem, a nod to her heritage. He also noted that she had wrapped about her shoulders the black lace *mantilla* veil that she had worn on their wedding day. The combination of the dramatic hues and the wide, earnest smile on Ana's face made a strange heat boil in Peter's stomach. If he never saw her wear another color for the rest of their lives, he would be perfectly content.

"*Feliz Navidad, Pedro.*"

Peter opened and closed his mouth several times before finally managing to speak.

"*Feliz Navidad*, Ana. How are you faring?"

"*Muy bien, gracias.* And you?"

"I am well, thank you. You look . . ." Again, words escaped him.

"*Bien*, I hope?"

"More than *bien*, Ana. You are positively beautiful."

Ana's cheeks matched her dress with a rosy blush. "*Gracias, Pedro*, you look very beautiful as well."

Peter opened his mouth to correct her choice of vocabulary until he saw the twinkle in her eye. They laughed together, and Ana rose on her toes to brush a kiss against his cheek. It seemed Peter's heart would not get a break for the entirety of the day. The woman was torturing him; surely she knew as much. He needed to distract himself . . . that is, if he could remember why he had come to her rooms in the first place. Surely he had another reason other than gawking at her beauty and considering how best to kiss her. Ah yes, their plans for the day.

"I thought today we might attend the Christmas service at church and then enjoy Christmas dinner with the Smiths. They were delighted to receive our invitation." Peter knew that Mrs. Smith had stopped by on a number of occasions, but Ana had been unwell and unable to receive her. He hoped the two women could make a sort of friendship. They would have a great deal to talk about, considering Ana's devout faith.

"Would it be appropriate that we dine with the priest?" Ana's brows lifted in obvious confusion.

"Of course, dear. Mr. Smith is our friend. And he is a vicar, not a priest. It is a tad bit different compared to your Catholic church. He is perfectly welcome to dine with us if he wishes to. After all, he can make house calls and minister to his vicarage."

"Then that sounds very nice. *Me parece perfecto.*"

"Splendid."

Ana stood near enough to him that he could hear her quickened breathing and see her round eyes boring into him expectantly. Her lips curved in a smile, but there was an undeniable sadness in her gaze.

"I wish you didn't have to leave. It is *el día de la Navidad*, after all."

"I know, but I promise I will return as quickly as possible. But today I don't want to talk about London or leaving. I simply want to enjoy our first Christmas together. And to start our day off properly, I have a small gift for you."

He finally held out the gift that he had been holding behind his back with one hand. Ana's head cocked, and her mouth gaped in surprise as the sadness was banished from her eyes. She motioned to herself. "*Para mí?*"

"*Claro! Obvio!*" Peter said teasingly, as if poking fun at the situation would slow the rapid beating of his heart. He pressed the gift into her grasp, his own nervous hands sweating enough to leave several marks on the silk packaging.

"You wish that I open it now?" Ana asked, her smile widening.

"Please do."

Ana walked back to her desk and sat in her chair. Peter joined her, standing at just the right angle where he would be able to see her expression at the precise moment when she realized what he had given her. She slowly, carefully pulled at the two ends of the green ribbon, and the fabric tumbled open. Inside lay a long length of twisted, white satin cord, threaded through with small pearlescent beads and tied at the ends with bits of embroidered lace. At the bottom of the package, a handful of coins clinked together, shining brightly against the backdrop of the pure fabric.

"*Qué es eso?*" Ana asked, her eyes bright with excitement and wonder as she fingered the cord. Then she held up the coins with one hand, reaching for Peter's hand with the other. "Are they some pin moneys?" she asked, laughing.

He joined in her laughter. "Well, they could be, but I hope they'll have much more significance than that. I gather you're familiar with the Spanish wedding tradition of *arras*?"

Ana fingered the coins, looking at them more closely as shock was written across her face. "*Sí*, of course. *Ay*, but these are *reales*!"

"Indeed. Spanish coins. And there are thirteen of them, to be precise. It is my understanding that the coins represent Jesus and His twelve apostles and bring promise of wellness and happiness in our marriage."

"*Es verdad*. That is true. And my accepting the *reales* also represents my trust in you."

"And my willingness to provide for you financially. Although my future standing with the army is uncertain, Ana, I promise that I will always provide for you. We will have a prosperous life."

Ana's bottom lip trembled, and her dark eyes lightened with tears. "And Pedro, I promise that I will trust you, and I will care for our house and our family." Her hand strayed to her midsection. "We will have a life *tan feliz* together. *Muchísimas gracias* for honoring the traditions of my country and family. This is the most *precioso* gift you could ever bring for me."

"There is something more in your Christmas present, if you care to look."

Ana returned to the package, pulling out the length of cord with quiet reverence. Peter's legs trembled with nervousness. Would she think the gift too intimate? Or entirely unfestive?

"We did not have the opportunity to honor this Spanish tradition on our wedding day, as it was a bit of a rushed affair, but I wished for us to have the opportunity, as I understand the *lazo* is a ritual of great importance. I only hope I can explain all this without making a fool of myself—or the traditions—entirely."

"*Sí,*" Ana murmured as her eyes filled with tears. Peter froze for a moment, fear seizing him, but her growing smile revealed them to be happy tears.

"*Gracias, Pedro.* This thing was the most thoughtful and considerate that anyone ever do for me in my life," she laughed. "And for you, this is *muy romántico.* My stiff *Pedro. Un romántico.*"

"You deserve it all, my dear. And I would have included these traditions in our original wedding day had I . . ." *Been of an emotionally sound mind. Been prepared for a wedding that I could not have possibly anticipated . . .* "Had I made more careful plans." He cleared his throat and continued. "Now, although I have been married to you once before, I'm not entirely certain how this all is supposed to work. Traditionally, I believe we would be kneeling, but I wager it's all right if we stand here." Peter moved to the middle of the room. "So, if you will come stand beside me, please."

Ana stepped close to him, their shoulders pressing and their hands interlacing.

"Now, I believe I should wrap this about our shoulders," Peter said as he extended his arm above her head, weaving the cord about her.

"*Sí,* in the shape of an *ocho,* eight," Ana said, reaching up her hand to help Peter in intertwining the *lazo* around them, crossing at their shoulders.

"We have no pastor here, but I suppose it will have to do." He blew out a breath, hoping to calm his nerves, but the trembling in his knees was incessant. "Ana, I promise you before God that I will protect you and care for you forever, just as this cord wraps around us in a continual motion."

Ana repeated his vow-like words as tears began to drip down her cheeks. "Pedro, I promise you that I will be support for you through the *dificuldades y gozos* of life. Through the moments of difficulty and the moments of joy, the moments of pain and the moments of peace."

"And we have lived through so much already," Peter said, his chuckle tinged with sadness.

Ana nodded. "And I promise to give you a life of *felicidad y amor.*"

He repeated her words, meaning every one with sincerity, even if he was not entirely certain how he would bring them to pass.

Felicidad y amor. Happiness and love. Peter's chest constricted. How long had those feelings felt so out of reach? And yet light was breaking through years of darkness as a small hope bubbled up in him. If anyone would be capable of bringing love to his home, it was Ana. Peter leaned down and pressed a kiss to the top of Ana's head as she leaned into his shoulder, wrapping her arms around his. He wanted to linger in the warmth of her closeness, wanted to press a kiss to a number of locations other than merely the adorable curls on her head. But he would not ruin the sentimental moment by getting ahead of himself.

That is, until Ana interrupted their quiet contemplation herself by shifting to stand in front of him, their torsos pressed together, until they were helplessly wrapped in the shining white cords. "*Ay, que error!*" she said, her eyes full of laughter and her brows raised in feigned innocence. "We are tied together! Oh no!"

Peter chuckled nervously, "My dear, what will we do?"

"*Está bien,* I am sure you will get free of this . . . perhaps tomorrow." She raised her eyebrow suggestively, teasingly.

He was now entirely certain that she would be able to feel his heart pounding through his chest. It nearly drowned out her voice, it was so loud in his ears. What on earth could she be trying to accomplish?

"Pedro, you forget one thing so *importante.*"

His stomach dropped in panic, and the excitement of her nearness dampened significantly. "Oh no, do tell me what it is."

"You need to kiss your bride!"

That request was entirely surprising but not entirely unexpected. Ana certainly was one for tradition. Still, Peter found himself entirely frozen in shock, his arms not knowing how to embrace his wife, much less pull her in for a kiss. Their first kiss at their first wedding was certainly not romantic or emotional, and now that some of those feelings had developed, he hadn't the faintest idea of how to react. He searched her face for any of the wide-eyed panic that he had seen beneath the kissing bough, but her eyes were clear and bright, her smile peaceful. He had no desire to kiss Ana if it would cause her to remember such painful moments. But could it be that she had begun to leave those memories in the past?

"Are you entirely certain?"

"Yes." Her voice was firm and steady. "Pedro, we are *esposos*. You are my husband. It is right to desire to kiss you, no?"

"Well, yes." Peter's face was flaming—he could feel it. "I simply want to ensure that you are comfortable, given your . . . past experiences. I would never want to experience any discomfort in my company. And if that requires that I maintain a safe distance from you, I will willingly do so without complaint . . ."

"No. Peter, I need you. I need your touch." Ana placed her hands gently on his cheeks and stared into his eyes for a moment. "This helps me to feel safe—more safe than when you are not with me."

Still, he hesitated. He had sworn never to frighten or harm her. But had she not just given her consent, her invitation?

Luckily, Ana moved for him. She brushed her lips against his with enough tenderness to draw tears to Peter's eyes, which was not an easy feat. She pulled away for a moment and stared at him, vulnerability written in the blush on her cheeks and the brightness in her eyes. But before Peter could put to words his surprise and delight or apologize for his lack of experience, she covered his lips with hers again, this time looping her hands around his neck. Her lips were full, soft, and distractingly warm. Peace rose in Peter upon feeling closer to Ana than he had ever thought possible. For countless years, Peter had neglected every relationship of value in his life and had filled that void with an incessantly busy schedule, causing his quick rise in the army. But no victory or position compared to the deep contentedness that flooded him upon holding Ana in his arms. And upon feeling her closeness, countless memories raced through his mind. Passing Ana at camp, while fumbling to squeak out a word or two in Spanish to her. Watching her confidently and gracefully navigate complex communications in multiple languages. Seeing her walk down the aisle to marry him, her expression heartbreaking and beautiful. And kissing her for the first time as man and wife—a small, innocent peck that altered his life irrevocably.

After the initial surprise of Ana's touch and the emotion of the memories wore off, Peter realized that he was kissing his wife, a moment he had dreamed of for longer than he cared to admit to himself. And that realization seemed to blessedly thaw him. He wasted no more time in wrapping his arms around her, slightly constrained as they were by the cords that still surrounded them. He threaded one hand through her hair and cupped the other around her growing waistline. Involuntarily, he sighed into their kiss. Her lips were perfection. Ana pulled back, laughing, and he brushed a kiss against her conveniently exposed throat. It would seem her throat was also perfection. Peter tested her cheek. Again, perfection. He returned to her lips, all his resolve completely dissolved. Yes, he was startled to discover that he most thoroughly enjoyed kissing his wife. This would be a new weakness of his, it would seem.

Finally, Ana pulled back from his grasp. "Wait, I have *una pregunta*."

"Yes?"

"Why you take the berry from the kissing bough?" Her lips curved teasingly, but her eyes were genuinely curious.

Peter felt his face burn. He hadn't realized she noticed him do so. "They say that if a man kisses a woman beneath the kissing bough, that he should take a berry as a sort of proof. Or remembrance. Perhaps it shall bring us luck."

"Yes, I believe it bring us this *buena suerte*. Because you kiss me, I be so lucky, *no*?"

And Peter found it a good opportunity to pull her close again.

Feeling her nearness and tasting her sweetness was as dangerously intoxicating as any sort of liquor Peter had ever heard of. Granted, Peter had never kissed another woman, but he imagined Ana's kisses were the most delectable of all. Then he returned her kiss, moving his lips against hers slowly, gently, hoping to convey how deeply he cared for her. He laced his fingers into her hair and deepened their kiss. Ana pulled back, smiling and breathing hard, and Peter felt his knees weaken slightly, both at her reaction and at his realization that he had kissed his wife. Finally. He cupped her face with one hand and leaned down to press his forehead against hers.

"*Feliz Navidad*, Ana."

Chapter 14

December 26, 1813, Abbeygate, Surrey Hills, England

ANA HAD BEGUN TO LEARN THAT MARRIAGE WAS A PARTICULARLY chaotic business when one got emotionally involved, particularly when one's husband was in the army, was called away during the holidays, *and* spoke a different language. There were entirely too many things that were lost in translation in the chaos that ensued from all of that. Only this morning, they'd been trying to have a conversation about the future, and Ana's mind had become so worked up that she seemed to forget English entirely.

"What can I do to help you today?" Peter had asked. In days past, the question had seemed to bring them together, like the binding of a book, helping them to work in better unison. But today, the question overwhelmed her. The pages of carefully memorized English words were falling all too quickly out of the book of her mind. Learning that Peter would leave her soon for a meeting with the army caused her insurmountable worry, even if it was for a mere day. She knew that it was a routine sort of meeting—at least, that's what he had implied. But she could not shake the deep feeling of foreboding that weighed on her incessantly. This meeting could very well be a great deal more complicated than Peter believed. What if it threatened their future?

Anticipating his absence, and all the unknown that accompanied it, made even the simplest of tasks feel impossible.

"*Hay tanto por hacer para preparar la casa para recibir un bebé.*" She sat at her desk, scribbling a list of items that she needed to complete for the house to be prepared for the baby, while she rambled off as much in her native tongue. Beside her, Peter murmured to himself, apparently trying to make sense of her Spanish.

"*Preparar* . . . prepare. *Casa* . . . ah, yes, I remember that one. House."

Ana breathed deeply in an effort to calm herself. It was humorous, was it not, that he was struggling to translate? This was her experience during every conversation of every day. It was high time that he did some of the translating, particularly when she could not organize a coherent thought in his tongue at the moment.

"*Bebé* . . ." he continued. "Well, that one I will not forget. Baby. You wish to prepare the house for the baby?"

"*Claro,*" she said with a nod.

"We still have many months to prepare, Ana, I'm not certain that all this is necessary right now . . ."

"Of course it is!"

Did he truly not understand what his leaving meant? If he left to meet with the army tomorrow, he could very well get called back to Spain or France within the week or the month. Surely they would not allow him the remaining months until her confinement. He would get sucked back into that distant, stoic version of Peter, so unlike the warm, attentive, thoughtful Peter she now lived with. All the progress that they had made together in learning to confide in one another would be lost. Ana knew her affection for him would not diminish, not ever, but she did not know she could say the same about him. She knew he cared for her. He had to, did he not? To kiss her and hold her and say and do such lovely things? But could he truly care for her as deeply as she did for him if he left her now? Now, when she only had a few more months until her confinement arrived?

How would she do it all alone? Mothers were not meant to be solitary creatures. That sort of living had destroyed her own mother.

And so Ana was clinging to the only thread of hope that she had, wondering that if she could remind Peter of the child she was carrying, who would soon join her in this world, that perhaps he would remember they had an entire life to live together. Perhaps he would remember that he cared for her more than he cared for his responsibility in the army. More than he cared about gaining justice for San Sebastián. And in telling him all that there was to do to prepare for the baby, she sent prayers up to the heavens, begging God to help her husband to come back to her, at the very least for the sake of her baby.

And there *was* a great deal to prepare for. They would have to get the nursery together, not to mention find a nurserymaid if such a thing was needed. But she wasn't certain what else was necessary. She had never had a child before. She hadn't the least idea what to do to prepare for childbirth. How would she endure such a strenuous and potentially dangerous experience when she could not even communicate with the midwife or physician? A sudden anxiousness bathed her brow, and her heart quickened. Her hand scribbled even faster now.

"I worry myself that I will not be able to do *todo lo necesario para prepararnos*,"

"*Más lento, por favor?*" Peter said, his voice strained and rough.

Ana sighed, shaking her head in frustration. She could try to revert to English, but her mind was already racing. It was so much easier to express herself in her native tongue. After all, Peter had insisted he would learn Spanish. She should be practicing with him more often.

There was much that needed to be done to the house to prepare. Her bedchamber needed a small bassinet and *pañales* for changing the baby at night. Not to mention all the preparations that would need to happen when her confinement was close at hand. And Peter's impending absence seemed to rip out from under her the feeling of stability she had slowly been building. She had started to depend on him so much. And anticipating his absence made her feel all the more insecure about her own abilities.

There was much that needed to be done in *her* to prepare. But how could she tell him that she felt entirely inadequate to be a mother? How could she bring a child into a world that had been so cruel to her and her family? It was as if she had pushed off to sea all on her own in a tiny fishing boat. She was trying to row, trying to survive with the life growing inside her, but there were moments, even days, when the waves around her looked terrifying indeed. Tears filled her eyes and trickled down her cheeks as she stood, her chest heaving and her hands cupped over her midsection.

If anything, emotion would always get Peter's attention. Not that she had contrived her outburst falsely, but sure enough, Peter's eyes, cloudy with visions of Spanish translations, became clear instantly. He was at her side a moment later, grasping her hand and her waist, helping her to sit.

"Are you ill? Should I call for the physician?"

Ana shook her head. How could she make him understand? This language! This Englishman! It made this all the more frustrating and difficult.

"Then what is wrong? Should I call for the physician?"

"*Estoy bien*," she said through her tears, squeezing his hand twice for emphasis.

His fingers released hers to rub at his temples, and she felt the absence of his touch, his warmth, like a stinging wound. "This is a great deal more difficult than I imagined, I must confess. How can I help you if I cannot understand you?"

"*No me siento preparada para ser una mamá sin ti.*" *I don't feel prepared to be a mother without you.* There. She had said it. But had he understood?

"Ana, I promise I will only be gone for a day."

Ana didn't believe it.

Peter continued, "David—Sir Huntington—has implied there is some urgency in the meeting, but I do believe it will be taken care of with great efficiency."

"But what if you are gone longer than that?" *What if you are gone a great deal longer? And what happens if you never return?* Ana wrapped her arms around herself, as if that could protect her from the sky-high waves that surrounded her.

Peter ran a hand over his forehead, squinting his eyes shut in obvious frustration and confusion. Spanish words spilled haltingly from his lips. "*Ana. Estoy embarazado, pero no entiendo.*"

I am pregnant, but I don't understand.

He was pregnant?

"*Qué?*" Ana María burst into laughter, despite herself. Her tears continued but for much happier reasons this time. "*Piensas que estás embarazado?*"

"Uh . . . yes? I am embarrassed. And I see you take great pleasure in my embarrassment."

"Oh!" Ana laughed even harder upon understanding. "Embarrassed?" Ana's wide vowels and rolling tongue fought against the word. "You said you are expecting a child!"

"I what? Is that what *embarazado* means?"

"*Sí!* You mean to say *I* am *embarazado*, not you!" Ana María could hardly breathe now for laughing. Her rounded frame bounced. The worry that had been building up in her slowly released as she pictured her husband in such a ridiculous role.

Peter joined her in laughing, tension rolling off him as his shoulders dipped and hands relaxed. He shook his head. "What an absolute mess I am."

She doubled over until a pang in her midsection reminded her that she had not yet gained full comfort or control over her stomach.

"*Ay*, Pedro. You are *tan chistoso*. Most amusing indeed."

"I am glad that my apparent condition can bring you some amusement," he said, puffing out his flat, muscular stomach and placing his hands around the shape as if he were an expectant mother. This only caused Ana to further lose control of her laugh.

"I don't want you to be distressed, *querida*," he continued. "What can I do to assist you? Shall we move forward with the preparations for the house?"

She held out the list she had been working on, and as he read through it, she dried the tears that had soaked her cheeks.

"I'll pass this along to Miss Thompson and Mrs. Smith. I am sure they will have some excellent ideas about the nursery and any other necessary items for the baby's arrival."

"*Gracias*," Ana managed, tears wetting her cheeks again.

"I thought we had quite our fill of those tears. *Qué, querida*? What is wrong?"

"*No quiero que te vayas*," Ana replied. "Do not leave me, *por favor*."

"You know as well as I do that the only place I desire to be is here with you. But I fear that in failing to respond to these summons, I will only put our future at greater risk. I cannot allow them to think I have abandoned my position, particularly when we know the truth of all that occurred at San Sebastián."

"*Lo sé.*" *I know.*

"Then you understand why I have to leave?"

"I suppose so."

"More importantly, do you understand how desperately I will miss your companionship?"

Ana looked up, expecting to see a teasing, crooked smile on Peter's lips, but instead his eyes were trained on the floor, his cheeks slightly flushed as he gnawed on his bottom lip. He seemed somewhat embarrassed at the admission! She stood and flung herself into his arms, ignoring his sounds of surprise and protestation until at last his arms wrapped firmly around her in return. She savored his warmth, the feeling of his firm body against hers. He was her safety—her lifeboat.

Ana would be all right without him for a day. She had to be.

"I will miss you too, *Pedro.*"

"I may not be the perfect husband. I certainly have not done all I could have done to understand you." His jaw tightened, and his eyes were bright and clear. "I clearly do not understand what it is to be an expectant mother, and I have never had to experience the many changes you are handling with such grace. This conversation has demonstrated quite remarkably how basic my understanding of Spanish is. And to make it worse, I am a man, and I cannot understand the tender and deep emotions you are gifted with as a woman. But I want to understand you, Ana, in all the ways you need to be understood. And I will strive for that, I promise. Even if it requires that I make many more foolish decisions and Spanish errors. But I do promise I will put forward all my best efforts to be more understanding of you. And I pray God will help me do so."

Ana choked with emotion at Peter's open honesty and could hardly hold his gaze for the intense feeling found therein. Instead, she pressed down that feeling of foreboding that refused to leave her and brushed a lingering kiss against his lips. "Thank you for these words so sweet. *Por favor*, return to me as *pronto* as you can."

Chapter 15

December 28, 1813, London, England

Darling Ana,
Querida Ana,
"Dear Ana . . ."

PETER HAD NOT ANTICIPATED HOW DIFFICULT IT WOULD BE TO WRITE a letter to his wife. He had so much he wanted to express to her, and it seemed that none of the words he required would come to him. Even determining how to address her proved a formidable task. After all, he was still sorting through the myriad of feelings that their shared kisses had stirred up in him. Peter shook his head as a rush of tingles ran down his spine, as pleasing as it was bothersome.

I apologize that I do not write with good news. It is evident that this matter of sorting through the repercussions of San Sebastián is going to be a great deal more complex than I previously imagined. I am grateful to have the assistance and understanding of Sir Huntington while I am here. He has proven most helpful, and I am ever so grateful. Do not be concerned, for I am in good company at his side. It is beyond tiresome to hear lies told about the happenings in Spain when many of the men around me know the truth of it all. And that truth must be brought to light, not only for the justice required by the courts and people of San Sebastián but also for the integrity and spiritual welfare of all our souls. I am determined to see this through, although I am not sure how we will come to any sort of conclusion at this time.

I will have to spend a little while longer here than I anticipated, likely a week at most. Do not be worried on my behalf; I am quite comfortable at Heathridge Hall, and Mother is keeping me quite entertained, although I miss your company more than I can say.

I promise to return to you at the soonest possible moment, and we can resume any of the holiday celebrations that we may have missed together.

I miss you, Ana. Te extraño.

Yours,

Peter

Peter ran a hand through his hair, narrowly avoiding smudging his face with his ink-stained hand. He was impossibly torn between wanting to return to Ana at the soonest possible moment to ensure her well-being and wanting to fight for some semblance of honesty and justice regarding the issue of San Sebastián.

But he could not allow Ana to worry, wondering why he hadn't returned after the singular day he'd expected to spend in London. Peter signed the letter and folded it precisely, methodically. He would send it by messenger to Surrey Hills that very day.

"Is everything all right, dear?" Mother said from across the room, where she was seated at her desk, writing some correspondence of her own.

"Yes, Mother. I'm simply writing Ana to inform her I will need to stay here a few days longer."

"And will that be quite difficult for her?"

"I couldn't say." He desperately hoped not. It was already distressing enough to be away from her while she was still in such a delicate state. Peter sighed heavily and squeezed his eyes shut, trying to calm his rising annoyance at Mother's continued prying.

"And for you? I imagine it is a great challenge to be away from one's new bride. Why, you have only been married a few months."

"Of course it's a challenge, Mother," Peter snapped, his voice thin and slicing. Instantly, Mother's demeanor changed. She seemed to fold into herself, and her eyes held a great deal of pain, much more than a simple retort should have earned.

"I am only trying to help, dear. I thought it might do you some good to talk about how you are feeling."

"I'm sorry, Mother. I did not mean to sound vexed. Forgive me." Peter shook his head, wishing he could take back his rash tone. Years apart had not made communication with Mother easier, particularly when he was in a foul mood. A tiny voice of fear whispered that in that respect, he had become more like his father than he had ever wished, even after being anxious to get away from him.

"Matthew frequently discusses his troubles with me, and he finds it helps him a great deal."

But I am not Matthew.

Again, that insistent frustration returned, rising in heat like a fever. Peter bit his lip to keep an impatient, annoyed response from slipping out again. He should have expected that upon returning home, he would be welcomed with a plethora of comparisons to his older brother. After all, who wouldn't compare them? Matthew was a handsome, kind, accomplished earl who was wholly adored by Mother and every other person he came in contact with, man or woman. He had never made a mistake in his life, as far as Peter was aware. Peter, on the other hand, was a voluntary outcast who had abandoned his family in their time of need. And after so many years of minimal communication, Mother had the right to harbor some hurt. At the very least, she had the right to feel confused and to seek understanding.

Guilt hazed his mind, thick and heavy, like an insistent smoke. In so many ways, his choosing to leave Heathridge Hall had been a matter of survival. One more day spent under the same roof with his father would have led to violence. And Peter was so untrained at the time, he surely would have been severely injured. When he had realized that Matthew and Mother herself would not allow him to enter into any sort of physical altercation with his father in their defense, Peter felt he no longer had a place there, at least not in his present state. He had joined the army in an effort to gain strength and discipline that would assist him in putting Mother's home into order once and for all.

But then Father had died unexpectedly of a deadly fever. And now it appeared that Matthew had a wise and firm hand on the reins as the new Earl of Heathridge Hall. The threat was gone. Mother was protected. And Peter had not been the one to do the protecting she had so desperately needed. And all the great horrors he had lived through, all the strength he had gained, would never justify his decision to leave them.

"Never mind that, dear. If you are not ready to speak of these things, I will not force you. After all, we are just becoming comfortable with one another again." Mother patted the place next to her on the sofa, motioning for Peter to sit. He obeyed, sitting rigidly next to her. "I really am delighted to have you here. It's been so very long since I have had both of my boys here together." Peter wasn't so sure that Matthew was equally delighted. But he hadn't indicated that his feelings toward Peter were as complicated as the feelings Peter harbored about him.

"I do wish it could be under better circumstances," he grumbled. "It seems the army is content to bother me even during the months they insisted I spend recovering from the mess they put me through."

"Are you certain there's nothing that Matthew can do to assist in the issue? He has quite an influence, you know."

"I am quite familiar with Matthew's influence." An influence neither of them had ever been able to use to protect their own mother. An influence that attracted all sorts of women in the Ton but that didn't carry the weight to save their armies from being driven to the slaughter . . . or from causing the slaughter themselves. Peter breathed heavily, splaying his fingers on his lap to avoid creating a tense fist with them. "I am quite certain. It is somewhat of a complex issue. But I thank you."

"It is regarding your time in Spain, yes? Is there anything you would like to share with me? Perhaps it would help you."

Peter remembered the weight that had lifted off his shoulders when he began telling Ana of his troubled thoughts and was almost persuaded to reveal the truth to Mother. But then memories of blood-streaked dresses and ale-stained uniforms flashed through his mind, and he could not speak of it. The pain was still too great. He rolled his shoulders and shook his head, as if that could dispel the visions that plagued him.

"I see that it would not be helpful after all. No matter—we can talk about something else. Tell me more about Ana. How is she faring? Is she enjoying Abbeygate? It is such a peaceful place. I always greatly enjoyed our summers there."

"She is settling in well, thank you. Although she is certainly implementing some traditions of her own in the household," Peter said with a chuckle.

"And I would expect her to do as much."

Mother's word snapped in half a cord of tension that Peter had not even realized he had been holding on to. All this time, he had been so concerned that they were not conducting their household in a way that would be expected of the family of an earl. But clearly Mother was more concerned about Ana's happiness, as was Peter. He slumped in his chair, relieved.

"It is quite amusing, after being so caught up in the army for all these years, to suddenly find myself completely consumed with Ana's well-being. And now that I'm away, I am constantly thinking of her, wondering how she is sleeping, hoping that she is eating sufficiently, praying that she remembers enough English to communicate well . . ."

"You care a great deal for her."

"And why shouldn't I? It is my duty to ensure that she is comfortable, well cared for. She has endured so much . . ." *Too much.*

"I was referring to a more sentimental sort of caring," Mother said with a slight smile. She reached across Peter's rigidly folded arms and squeezed his hand.

"Of course," Peter managed. He had spilled enough secrets for one day. He would certainly not admit to harboring any sort of great sentimentality for his wife, beyond what was expected, of course. He felt like he was young again and had been found out during one of his mischievous ventures with Matthew. Mother's brows arched higher on her forehead.

"You mentioned you're concerned about Ana's sleeping and eating. Is something amiss? Is she still feeling ill as she was on your wedding day?" she pressed. Then understanding dawned on her visibly, as her eyes widened and her mouth curved into the shape of an O.

Mother knew. She knew about Ana's condition. And now she knew the timing of it all.

Peter felt his stomach drop violently. It had been years since he had lived with Mother. Did she really know him well enough to believe that he would never harm Ana? That he would never even imagine touching her against her will? Devastating memories, too often shoved from his mind, rose to the surface. Ana, bleeding, limping, crying. Ana, locked in the dark of her boat cabin, insistent that she could not bear the sight of the other soldiers on board. Ana, shaking with sobs when she realized she was increasing. Acute pain and anger fogged his mind and muddled his speech. "She is not . . . it is not what you think . . ." Peter stuttered, placing his head in his hands as misplaced fear and shame overwhelmed him. "I have done nothing wrong."

"I would never presume that you had done so," she replied with a reassuring tone. "I am sure you have always behaved honorably toward your Ana. But are you suggesting that she is with child, and has been for quite some time?"

Chapter 16

December 29, 1813, London, England

Peter had endured another long day of meetings only to see that the army was getting nowhere with the issue of San Sebastián. Nothing could be more frustrating than that. The sun was already setting outside the tall, stone building, and the paned windows no longer provided sufficient light to the room, signaling to Peter that it was high time he left. He shrugged on his knapsack and set out through the door, his legs marching in quick, learned steps. He would have made a fine pace to his conveyance to return to Heathridge Hall if he hadn't collided with a shrouded figure standing just beyond the corner of the building.

"I apologize, my good sir," Peter said.

"Apology accepted, Cap'n, and I don't mind at all being called sir."

London was a crowded place. It was not a difficult thing to run into someone. But that voice. Peter stepped back, blinking rapidly as if it would somehow help him to recognize the man in front of him more quickly.

Price. One of the men of his company. He was a young one, barely eighteen, and had been recruited off the streets of London, like so many other foot soldiers. But what was he doing back here? And why was his presence sending Peter positively reeling? While in his role as Captain Ashmore, Peter was not one to get overly emotional, at least not about anyone other than Ana. And he certainly never showed any level of sentimentality to his men. Loyalty, yes. Consistency, yes. But not emotional softness. And yet for some strange reason, his chest tightened upon seeing Price, and he suddenly found himself breathing much more quickly than he had been a moment previous. He very nearly embraced the man, only to be snapped back into reality by Price's stoic salute. Even in a worn, faded brown shirt and thick work pants, the young man looked a soldier.

"Price! I can't say that I understand how you've come to be here, but I am more relieved to see you than I can say."

"Charley, Cap'n, call me Charley. We ain't riding to battle, so I do prefer to be called Charley."

"Very well, then, Charley."

"And I am mighty pleased meeself to be seeing you, Cap'n."

Peter had more questions than he had words for. It was the first time he had seen any of his men following the sack. "Come, I have a conveyance waiting just down this alley. I wish to speak with you in confidence."

"A conveyance, eh? Cap'n, I never pinned you as one of them high-brow gentlefolk."

"I wouldn't call myself gentle, and I certainly doubt my wife would call me high-browed."

"You went and got yerself a wife now, did you? I'll be. The men won't believe it when I tell 'em."

Peter felt his neck grow hot as he walked up to the conveyance and motioned that Charley join him inside. Price—like most, if not all, of Peter's men—would have been well familiar with Ana, then known as Miss Bailon. Many of them had noted Peter's strange awkwardness around her graceful communication and stunning beauty and had frequently made him the brunt of their jokes. If Charley ever saw Ana, particularly in her current condition, a great many secrets would be revealed, putting them both in danger.

"Indeed," Peter answered. "It was somewhat of a quick betrothal. But I have known her for quite some time."

"Ah, an English lass she be then."

Peter coughed and changed the topic of conversation in desperation . . . and curiosity. "San Sebastián. How did you . . ." *Survive?* "And the others, did they . . ." *How many more had he lost?*

"Once I saw the city start to smoke up, I hid away. I knew there would be a great punishing for burning those many homes to the ground, and I was not about to catch myself in all that business."

Peter nodded his head, tapping on his chin. After the French had retreated and surrendered, a number of soldiers had entered the town to sack and pillage . . . and do much more terrible things than that alone.

"Mighty mad, the men were," Price continued. "Half-starved from months of siege on so little rations. I wager they thought it their right to go find themselves some food and ale."

"And they found—and took—a great deal more than that," Peter said, his voice low and pained. Holy relics from the local chapel. Precious and personal family heirlooms. Not to mention their cruel and merciless taking of the precious innocence of so many women, some of them much too young.

"Aye," Charley agreed, his darting gaze downcast and sorrowful.

"I didn't receive orders to recall you and the other men. How was it that you ended up here in London?"

Charley shifted on his feet, rubbing a hand across his neck as he chuckled. "See, I heard tell *you* would be here, Cap'n, and ain't nobody been able to hear from you since the city fell. I jus' had to see ya to know you survived and all."

"My soul is a little worse for the wear, but I survived all right," Peter said, lifting the corner of his mouth to try to bring humor to his words, which felt all too heavy and all too true.

"An awful lot, that sacking was."

"More horrible than I can say. And it would seem that our leaders are insistent that it didn't occur at all, even though there are many of us who know otherwise."

"Oh, Cap'n, Wellington done had made himself some statements that were mighty clear about that. Published in the *Royal Gazette*, they were."

Peter stared hard at Charley. "Truly? I haven't heard anything official made outside of army tent doors, so to speak."

"'Tis true. There are an awful lot of Spaniards speakin' out about it, seems. I did find me a copy, Cap'n, though it weren't no easy task. Here, now. Take a look for yerself."

Charley handed Peter a wrinkled copy of London's *The Times*, dated October 30, 1813. Just as the soldier had said, the name Wellington jumped out at him from the page. Peter scanned it quickly. The quotation from Wellington implied that the town was not, in fact, sacked; instead, it was merely robbed of wine and other articles. According to him, the destruction of the town had nothing to do with the British troops.

"Makes me sick, it does. And here I was, thinking Wellington was the savior of the country."

"He has been, in many respects," Peter replied. "But in this one, he is doing his troops and the Spanish a great disservice. Particularly when you consider that he was not even in San Sebastián when it all occurred."

"No doubt he heard it all from Graham."

"It's an outrage to see. Even more frustrating is the matter that now our troops are moving into France, while Spanish troops are being sent back to their home country, after we have left it in pieces."

"T'was a devastation. But that is the lot of the soldier, isn't it, Cap'n? Seein' such atrocities and then movin' on to fight the next battle? There ain't nothing we can do to fight it, not when that is our lot. Can't sell me commission like some ranker, pardon me language. This is the only way I can pay for any sort of living at all. An' then I hear about me friends, abandoned after the war, no money or support, an' I know this is me lot." Charley's shoulders were slumped, his face devoid of emotion. He had an air of hopelessness about him, which tugged at Peter's heart in a way it never had before.

Was this how all his men had felt? Trapped in their roles? Destined to kill and pillage and act as if it were their duty, their right? What a sorry existence indeed. And Peter himself had been fighting such a tempest of emotions on the inside each time he received a letter from home, so much so that he had stilled his emotions on the outside. He had become too disciplined, too practiced, too unfeeling—until Ana had changed him entirely, cracking his heart wide open to realize the true horror of San Sebastián and the rest of what they had been living in during the ongoing war with the French.

* * *

Darkness shrouded the library as Peter sat across from Captain Davies, waiting for an explanation. The man sipped deeply from his lemonade, as if he hoped it were something a great deal stronger. Peter didn't blame the man. Theirs was a disastrous plight.

It was difficult to ascertain one solid reasoning as to why the British soldiers had razed San Sebastián—and other towns—so violently, so completely. Perhaps it was the admittance of such actions by the customary laws of war at the time. Perhaps it was the breakdown of trust in command, particularly with months of failed attempts to break through the French's defenses. Perhaps it was the innate wretchedness and greed brought on by delayed payments and poverty that drove them into the homes to loot and search for valuables but turned them to the helpless inhabitants housed there. Perhaps they thought it was their right, having sacrificed a great deal to fight for Spain's freedom, turning their looting into a sort of unholy tithe. Perhaps it was the desperation that so many of the lower soldiers felt, knowing that they were trapped in their positions, that no sort of future awaited them at home, that they would be chained into their uniforms until they died, or deserted, which was even worse than death.

Ultimately, Peter believed that there was some sort of vast transformation that occurred in the sackers, somewhere between the beginning of the war and the moment France's white flag was raised. Their minds were truly altered, overrun with a blur of vengeance, relief, euphoria, and even excitement. So long they had become numb to death—so long they had created terms and codes for their victims instead of names—that they not only lost their humanity, but they lost their ability to see humanity in those around them. Even in those fragile, innocent women and children whose lives they destroyed. It was almost mythic in scale and horror. There was no other way to explain the way disciplined soldiers became demons. And drink made them devilish, even more than war had. In Peter's eyes, they could no longer be considered men, no longer possessed even a shred of humanity to have enacted the atrocities he had witnessed. The atrocities Ana had suffered.

Peter had never felt any such transformation. For so many years, he had found comfort and escape in the discipline of the army. Now the veil had been unceremoniously ripped from his eyes; he saw just the same selfishness here that he had seen in his own home, and he could not allow it to continue. He wanted to remember the lives, the names of their unintended victims. Starting with Ana María. And Major Bailon.

But it was increasingly difficult to come to terms with it all when other leaders, even his friend Captain Davies, saw the actions as unpreventable. And Davies had paid him an unsolicited call at Heathridge Hall to tell him as much.

"Our men were starving, on the brink of death themselves. They would have sooner left the army than continue on for another day without some relief from their lot," Captain Davies protested, shamefaced as he did so. He paced back and forth in the dark wooden library, vacated by Matthew for their privacy.

"Relief?" Peter countered. "Senseless intoxication, rape, and murder. Is that what you truly believe they were in search of for relief? Perhaps it is our greater failing that we do not properly care for our men that they are driven to such measures."

"The laws of war permit the sacking of a fortified city that resists our help. It was our right."

"Then you do admit it was our fault," Peter said, barely resisting shoving his finger in Davies's face. "That the sacking occurred at our hands, not at the hands of the French."

"I . . . that is . . ." Captain Davies stammered before bursting out, "You know as well as I do that higher leadership, even Wellington himself, ordered Graham that our men task themselves with destroying the enemy rather than the town and the people. That was his express wish."

"That certainly worked out in our favor, did it not?" Peter spat, his words rough with sarcasm. "His order that the gates be shut except on strict business hardly lasted an hour."

"You, I, and all other commanding officers were instructed to enforce the strictest discipline. But it is simply impossible to control so many desperate drunkards."

"Yes, well, delegation has never been Wellington's strongest suit, now has it? If the man wanted it done properly, if he truly desired to prevent another Badajoz or Ciudad Rodrigo, he would have needed to be there himself. At the very least for the disciplining."

"And yet disciplining measures were still taken, even though he could not be there. Assistant Provost Marshal Edward Williams reported that he flogged sixty men. Offenders. And there were efforts to recuperate the plundered goods . . ."

"After *three days* of sacking!" Peter thundered. "By all accounts, Wellington wasn't even informed of the burning until more than a day later. You and I witnessed all the destruction and dastardly deeds that were done well before anyone was capable of stopping them. I tried and was threatened and attacked, and very well likely would have stayed fighting my own countrymen until I was shot dead if I had not needed to rescue . . ."—*Ana María*—". . . a person of utmost importance to me."

Davies stepped closer to Peter now, his whisper intense. "Wellington was not pleased with any of it. In fact, he was furious. But as he has said before, it has fallen to our lot to take many cities by storm and siege. We must trust that this will help us make headway against Napoleon."

"But he was furious with good reason," Peter shot back. "San Sebastián contained more atrocities than the sackings of Bajadoz and Ciudad Rodrigo. Not to mention that we left the place a pile of soot."

"You cannot deny that some of the rumors became furious, politicized. Like the unbelievable notion that Graham would have given the order to set the city aflame. That the action was a matter of warfare strategy or policy. And to think that there were reports that the French lit the torches as part of their defense. If anything, the Spanish should be blaming the French, not us. It's preposterous."

"We lost a number of our own officers in that firestorm," Peter said.

"Precisely. Those Spaniards are trying to campaign against us, and after all we have done to defend them from the French."

Smoke overwhelmed Peter's senses, nearly as real as could be. Whether it was emotion or ash forcing him to cough, he could not tell. Piles of soldiers, drunken or dead, were rising on either side of him. A beautiful city burned was hovering before his eyes. Ana's pain-racked sobs rang in his ears, a sound he thought he had long eradicated from his memory.

"Diplomatic tensions have not been so heated in many years," Davies continued. "It has even created quite a sensation in London's drawing rooms. My own mother wrote me, asking . . ."

Peter squeezed his eyes shut, words exploding from him. "*Those Spaniards* saw their country ransacked, their livelihoods destroyed. No house was safe, no convent sacred enough to keep out the fury of their once-protectors. *Those Spaniards* saw their tender daughters and . . . and *wives* selfishly ravaged," Peter's voice shattered, and his hands fisted tight against his legs. "And at our hands, might I add. Those who were not shot down in their own doorways or mercilessly violated found themselves forced to jump from the rooftops to avoid being burned alive." He blinked hard, suddenly unable to speak past the block of emotion in his throat. "It is all a great, unforgivable sin. It ought never to have happened. Not in San Sebastián, not anywhere. And certainly not at the hands of the soldiers who ought to have been defending them. It was not some sort of mistaken skirmish in the wake of the retreating French. It was frenzied but systemic. It was intentional, even if the fire perhaps was not."

Finally, Davies was silenced. And the weighty dip in his shoulders and dark, haunted look in his eyes revealed that he knew the truth of it all, just as Peter did.

"And so, something must be done," Peter concluded. "You must help me. It is of utmost importance."

"Ashmore, you know as well as I do that speaking out against the decisions of our leaders in such open defiance and rebellion would have dire repercussions. Even now, soldiers are being banished for as much."

Peter had heard of one such banishment. But the punishment was not decided for inflammatory comments. Murmured rumors among his men had evidenced that the poor soldier had taken up arms against a drunken lieutenant who was at the verge of forcing himself upon a helpless woman. It had not been a mere act of speaking out. It had been something much braver. A small part of Peter wished he could have done the same. But then he would not have been able to save Ana. And he would never regret that decision for as long as he lived.

He rubbed a hand over his eyes. "It remains unjust that so many have had to suffer for the pride of our superiors."

"My friend, while I regret—and even hate—the unnecessary violence that has happened in the Crown's search for Napoleon, I have served for a few more years than you. I was there at Badajoz. These things cannot always be prevented. In one way or another, they will always be a consequence of war." He ran a hand through his hair, his expression tainted with helplessness.

"But it should not be so. Not when we harm our own. Not when our victims are those we care for."

Captain Davies stepped back from Peter, his light blue gaze scanning across his face. "Why are you acting so entirely strange about this? Do you have a Spanish relation? Perhaps you're half Spanish yourself?"

Peter squirmed, pulling at the starched uniform collar that was rubbing his neck raw. Davies's words were much too close to the truth.

But perhaps that truth was the key. Perhaps if he understood why Peter felt so strongly about this, he would lobby with him, defend the victims. Help him protect Ana.

"I do have a Spanish relation. A wife, in fact."

"You are a married man, and I never had the slightest idea? I would offer my congratulations if not for the look of total distress on your face."

"It is somewhat of a recent development," Peter said. "After the sacking."

Shock and horror laced Davies's features. "Tell me she was not there."

Peter breathed deeply to quell the anger burning in his chest. "She did not live in San Sebastián. But she was . . . impacted in a permanent way by the siege. It has altered her life forever. I suppose this is why I feel so strongly about the matter. I am not only defending the defenseless that remain across the ocean. But I am defending her, or at least making an effort to do so."

"I am sorrier than I can say, Ashmore." Davies placed a hand on Peter's shoulder, staring at him intently. "That any woman had to even witness those horrors is an atrocity I will never forget. Although I daresay your newfound wife is the luckiest of them all, to be sheltered and protected by you. I would that all the victims of sieges and sackings in this war would be equally as cared for."

Peter nodded mutely, anger still heating his neck and mixing his words.

"Although I must give you a word of advice, my good man. After your . . . boldness in San Sebastián, Graham and the other leaders are very clear about where you stand with regards to the sacking. And they are also aware that your brother and mother have no small amount of influence in British society. If you were to campaign against them in some sort of rebellion, you would not just be ruining your future in the army. You would be framing yourself as some sort of threat, both in society and on the battlefield. And you do know what they do to soldiers who undermine and disrespect their superiors."

"I don't care about what happens to me. I just want our men to accept ownership of the grave deeds they have done."

"But do you care for your new wife? The one who you said yourself was greatly affected by the siege? If you are not safe from the repercussions of standing against the army, she will, no doubt, be equally unsafe. I do not merely imply dismissal from the army. You could be labeled as a traitor."

A sick panic twisted in Peter's stomach. After the horrors he had witnessed, he had no illusions about a hopeful, healed future for himself. Not when he refused to sell his commission. But his entire reasoning for bringing Ana to England was to save her from that awful destruction that was enveloping her home country. He could not put her at even greater risk now.

He would not be able to bring San Sebastián to public light, and using Matthew's influence to do so was out of the question. But there still had to be some way to show his great disapproval, even up the ranks of the army.

Chapter 17

December 31, 1813, Abbeygate, Surrey Hills, England

There was something decidedly comforting about being curled up by a warm fire on a snowy night. Ana had spent most of her nights in the parlor doing just that ever since Peter left. Their autumn tradition of dining on the balcony had quickly transformed into taking their nightly tea in the parlor, with the large windows providing a nearly unobstructed view of their frost-topped land. But as Peter was not there to provide Ana with conversation or entertainment, she pulled the large mahogany chair up to the fireplace, along with a few extra pillows, and nestled in for the evening.

Ana dragged her gaze from the depths of the fire to return her concentration to the matter at hand . . . quite literally. She was making her best attempt at a baby bonnet, and it was going miserably. It would not be embroidered—Ana had never had the patience for such activities, but she once had some talent at sewing and needlework. But now, straight, clean stitches seemed to evade her, instead being replaced by crooked, uneven lines that she had been continuously pulling out. Her child would be mortified when she grew old enough to recognize the great sloppiness in her mother's handiwork. Clearly she should have practiced more recently instead of letting the more complicated parts of the art slip while she was traveling *España* with *Papá*.

She squinted her eyes, still smarting from the bright light of the fire, and jabbed the needle through the delicate, floral fabric once again. Clicking her tongue in concentration, she worked the needle back up through the fabric with trembling fingers. There! That stitch had been better, but only just. Perhaps she should abandon the thought entirely. But Mrs. Smith had been so generous to bring over some scraps of fabric for this precise purpose. She could not let the kind woman's action go unappreciated, even if her efforts were an exceedingly poor reflection of her gratitude. Ana held the fabric up to the light to examine her work more closely, then turned to the chair opposite her, eager to poke fun at her failure . . . only to realize, once again, that she was utterly alone. She brought the needle down in a frustrated poke, missing her mark entirely.

Ana had always considered herself to be a fairly independent woman. And while that desire for independence still stoked a constant fire beneath her, she now felt a distinct loneliness without Peter by her side. The sensation of missing him—needing him—terrified her. She had settled into a quiet, comfortable existence at his side these past months, and now, upon being separated from him, all sorts of worrisome questions began to arise in her mind.

Was this aching feeling an indication that she was too dependent upon Peter for her own well-being and happiness? Was she losing herself in depending upon him? And if so, what would happen when he would inevitably be required to report to distant lands again as part of his duties to the army? The pain in her chest almost convinced her that she might fall apart at the notion.

But other women in similar circumstances might decide that their lives would be less complicated and better off in a separated state from their husbands. Her mother had demonstrated as much.

Mamá had left them much too soon. Although anytime would have been too soon. How could a mother ever deem a time as appropriate to abandon her husband and child? But Ana had been at such a tender age, nearly on the cusp of womanhood. It was a time when she had needed the influence and wisdom of her mother so desperately. But *Mamá* would not continue following *Papá* and his *armada* across the country—or world—in the name of peace. It was too great a sacrifice, although following her own selfish designs for her life required a great sacrifice on her part: her daughter.

Ana shook her head in an attempt to rid herself of the painful memory. No good would come from dragging such things into her mind when she was intent upon creating an entirely different relationship with her own child. She had only a few short months left until the time of her confinement would be upon her, and the thought of having her baby in her arms filled her with equal parts terror and longing. She could not allow her relationship with her baby to become like her own relationship with her mother.

Her relationship with her husband and her relationship with her child should be some of the most treasured interactions of her life. Ana already understood that it would require a great deal of effort and vigilance to ensure that those relationships didn't sour, or grow uninteresting, as they perhaps had for *Mamá*. But she was not prepared for what would happen when she lost her heart, completely and entirely, to her husband and her baby. That would be the greatest risk she had ever faced. For how would she survive if she loved them, in her passionate and wholehearted manner, and then lost them, as she had loved and lost *Mamá*?

Peter, of course, knew nothing of this, although Ana was certain he had wondered why she so rarely spoke of her mother. But if they were to be joined in this journey of parenthood together, she would need to help him understand how her own parents had affected her. So Ana took advantage of the unique circumstance of Peter's absence and wrote him a series of letters on the matter. It was infinitely easier to patiently pen the words than say them aloud. It was also easier to express herself in English through writing, given that she had the time to search for correct translations. And she had found that his answering letter had echoed many of the feelings she had herself.

* * *

The last letter Peter had sent to Ana had not been an easy one to pen. He had spent many long minutes staring out the window, a piece of empty parchment in front of him, praying for God to inspire him with the words he felt he needed to say. His time at Heathridge Hall was stirring up many emotions in him, reminding him of the reality that he would soon have a child to claim as his own.

> *I admit that fatherhood frightens me. I have spent most of my life endeavoring to escape the shadow of my own father. He has shaped me in many ways, none of which I want to imitate in shaping my own children. It is because of him that I do not drink. It is because of him that I left my mother, even too young as I was, to escape to the army. It is because of him that I never imagined myself being married or having children.*
>
> *Even with all the structure and rules of the army, men could still let loose on their carnal nature, submitting themselves to their more violent tendencies. San Sebastián taught me this more than anything. Even the best of men can be reduced to savages. I was frozen in the shock of this for quite some time, I fear. It was precisely why I ran away from my own family. I was convinced that the regimen of the army would keep me from becoming the monster that my father was. But ultimately, I saw that same, horrific translation in so many around me.*
>
> *This, I confess, is my greatest fear in becoming a father. I married you because I was convinced that I could better protect you as your husband than I could otherwise. But how will I protect our child from the cruelty of the world? How will I protect her from wicked men when I have gone from this world? It seems I have lost faith in all those around me. All except you, querida Ana.*

Peter paused the motion of his quill, tapping the tip on the parchment. He shook his head, squeezing his eyes shut, but try as he might, he could not fight off the attack of memories that were swarming his head, scrambling over his defenses. He had shut them out for so long, but becoming a father, it seemed, was loosening the formidable stones in the wall he had created in his mind. *Not now.*

Young Peter was crouched in the hallway, outside the door of his mother's chambers. Father had just arrived home from another seemingly rambunctious evening. He'd been able to smell the wine on Father's breath and clothing as he stumbled by from underneath the small side table where he hid. He had prayed, *begged*, that Father would collapse onto his bed and slip into sleep, but instead, he had stormed into Mother's rooms.

"You fool of a woman!" a deep, harsh voice yelled, the slurred tone all too familiar.

Peter bound his fingers together, making a tight fist. He was the worst kind of villain, his father. If Peter were only bigger and older, he would burst through the door himself.

The hard echo of flesh hitting flesh permeated the corridor, followed by a whimper of pain, and suddenly, Peter could not stop himself anymore. He jumped from beneath the table, his fingers only a breath away from the doorknob, when small, but strong hands pulled him backward. Matthew's lanky arms wrapped around him; his tall frame pressed against Peter's back.

"Come, Pete," he whispered, "Mother told us to hide. He's in one of his furies, and it will only be worse if he finds us."

"I can't let him hit her again!" Peter whispered, his voice hoarse and furious, but devastated tears leaked down his cheeks.

"I know." Matthew's own voice cracked. "But you and I both know that he'll treat her even worse if he finds us here. We need to go back to our room and lock the door. We'll wait until Mother comes to us."

Wetness splashed onto Peter's hand, pulling him from the past. He looked down, expecting an offending spot of ink from his wild quill, only to realize that tears had dripped down off his face. It was not an easy thing to recall the pain Mother had endured. The pain they all had endured. He had blocked it out for so long.

Peter had only been a small boy of ten years. And that was when he had vowed that he would run away to the army. He would become strong and seasoned until he could fight off his father and any man who tried to hurt a precious woman in his life. But he had been too late to protect Mother. His father had died over a year ago, and the end of the war with France was nowhere in sight yet.

How distraught that younger version of himself would be if he now knew that any measure of decency, restraint, or ethics was similarly lost among the soldiers he had once called brothers. How long he would carry the painful memory of their grave mistakes, he did not know. But he would strive as much as possible to have a closer relationship with God, with Ana, in the hope that their influence would heal him in time.

Chapter 18

January 3, 1814, Abbeygate, Surrey Hills, England

"A letter for you, Mrs. Ashmore."

Burnsey stood by the library door, the light bleeding into the room in sharp contrast to the rich wood that climbed the walls. Ana waved her hand, motioning for him to approach, as she slowly rose from the overstuffed chair she had claimed as her own. He held out a letter to her, holding her gaze for a moment. His eyes were wide and carefully observant, likely watching for the outburst of emotions that commonly occurred. Ana had always been free with her emotions, but she found that something about pregnancy made those emotions even stronger. She found herself crying, whether they were happy or sad tears, almost every day. And receiving news of her husband's continuous delay in London did nothing to help such outbursts.

"Thank you, Burnsey. I am well."

"Are you certain?" His brow creased, silver, poofy eyebrows raising upward in concern.

"Yes, *gracias*."

Ana breathed deeply and pressed the letter against her chest for a moment. Her eyes scanned the room around her, overcrowded with books, maps, and papers, a bittersweet reminder of her husband's absence. But perhaps he would be returning soon. She unfolded the letter, squinting at the blur of English words that lined the front, addressing the note to her. Writing to Peter in English about complex subjects was exceedingly easier than speaking, but reading in English was still a great matter of frustration for her. It required a laborious effort that often left her with a headache. Still, it was worth any pain or frustration to hear from her husband.

Now, *speaking* English remained the greatest frustration of all. English, Ana had decided, was an exceedingly lazy language. Well, the pronunciation of English, that is. The grammatical rules of English were anything but lazy. Learning Basque and Portuguese had not been too difficult in her time traveling throughout *España* with *Papá*. Their pronunciation was still familiar and crisp, even if certain vowels were slightly altered. But English was a different issue entirely. It was entirely pockmarked with diphthongs and full of flat sounds, halfhearted consonants, and swallowed vowels. When Ana tried to imitate a true English accent, she was sure she sounded as if she were half asleep with a bad toothache. Hence why Ana deemed it to be most lazy indeed. The open, bright vowels of Spanish with trilling *r*'s, song-like inflection, and precise, cutting consonants were much friendlier to her mouth and tongue.

Still, she had spent hours on end carefully listening to the staff at Abbeygate in an effort to more accurately imitate their pronunciation, but it was proving to be a most difficult imitation. She wished for her English to be much improved when Peter arrived home again. Although why she suddenly had the desperate need to impress him, she could not say.

Ana returned again to the letter, anxious to know if Peter would be returning to her soon. Her heart pounded to see her name penned in his hand at the top of the page. Would she ever become accustomed to the thrill of reading words that she knew he had written privately, precisely for her? Even if they were written in English, it was lovely to know she was in his thoughts. In fact, it did all sorts of strange things to her stomach, causing it to twist and flip.

Dearest Ana,

I have found you a maid. Her name is Elena, and she is from Barcelona. She seems quite qualified, and I believe you will find her company to be delightful, seeing that she can speak Spanish and such.

I also need to confess that Mother has guessed at your condition. She is entirely too perceptive. But she is overjoyed for us and anxious to assist you in any way that you require.

And now for the less-than-satisfactory bit. I'm afraid I'm going to be delayed another day or two longer. I am so very sorry. My leaders seem to be completely determined to continue forward without acknowledging the significant errors made in San Sebastián. Even if these men in leadership, particularly Wellington, were not the ones to wreak havoc on the city, I feel they are making a grave error in brushing over the entire event as if it never happened. And then blaming it on the French, when there are innocent women who have testified otherwise!

I truly haven't the faintest idea why they would take the time to deflect these legal allegations when there is an entire war to be fought. Why not make amends while moving forward? It would soothe the anger of those victims involved and strengthen Britain's relationship with Spain.

But I will not worry you with my ramblings. I promise to continue to do my best to resolve this matter . . . if it is indeed possible. And if not, I pray that God will perform some miracle to heal the great hurt done to the people of San Sebastián, as well as you and me.

Know that I pray for you and our babe nightly. You are always in my thoughts.

Yours,

Peter

Ana pressed a hand to her stomach, hoping to still the butterflies that flurried there as a result of seeing her husband's handwriting. Since writing her letters, Peter had stopped referring to the babe as "your child" as he had while he was at home and had instead started asking after "our child." Surely he didn't know the power that such a small word had over her. It locked her throat with emotion and caused her heart to race. And so she returned his correspondence, writing "our child" as if it were the most natural thing in the world, not betraying the increasing hope that it gave her.

Still, despite the girlish excitement that she felt at receiving a letter from Peter, the contents of his letter were definitely a cause for concern.

Lady Ashmore had discerned Ana's condition. But had she done the calculations and guessed that Peter was not, in fact, the father of the child? Thankfully, Peter's lack of distress indicated that it would not matter regardless. Ana's new mother-in-law wanted to help her, and that brought a much-needed sense of relief.

But Ana was pained to read that Peter still carried about the weight of San Sebastián, as if it were his too-heavy army knapsack. And sooner or later, the pain of the weight would build to a breaking point, particularly if he pursued the issue endlessly. Ana also wished for some sort of justice; it was not fair that the English army would brush over the great pain they had caused as if it had never happened. But surely Peter could not force a solution about the issue when he was practically the only one fighting for such things.

"Mrs. Ashmore?"

Ana jolted from her reverie at the warm voice of Mrs. Thompson. The housekeeper approached the desk where she sat, reaching out a hand to help her rise.

"There is a young lass here to see you. Insists she is the new maid, at Mr. Ashmore's request. Calls herself Elain or something of the sort."

Could it be Elena? Had she really arrived already? How had Peter arranged for such a thing?

"*Cielos*, he didn't waste any time, did he, Mrs. Thompson?"

Ana rose, grateful for Mrs. Thompson's assistance. Her figure had not expanded as much as it undoubtedly would, but the additional weight that she carried about her midsection had entirely messed up her equilibrium and sense of balance. She found herself stumbling more often than not these days.

"Let us meet Elena. Peter wrote me about her," Ana said, waving the note in her hand.

Ana moved in careful steps toward the front drawing room, her arm still laced through Mrs. Thompson's. The instant her eyes lit upon Elena, she knew they would get along more than well. The maid could be no more than sixteen, but she had a bright smile, an intellectual gaze, and creamy coffee skin, and she curtsied with the slightest hint of flair that was clearly indicative of her heritage.

"*Hola, Señora Ana. Soy Elena.*"

Ana nearly crumpled at Elena's feet at hearing her native tongue. Had it really been so many months since she had been able to communicate so easily? Once she regained her composure and presented herself, she rushed to Elena's side and pressed enthusiastic *besos* to her cheeks.

"I am so grateful you are here," she murmured in Spanish. "We will be the best of friends, I already know it."

Chapter 19

January 7, 1814, Abbeygate, Surrey Hills, England

Finally, Peter could breathe. He shrugged his knapsack off his shoulders, dropping it to the stone floor with a thud, and took in the warmth of the familiar surroundings that greeted him: Tall, dated windows, framing the winter landscape outside. A steep, wooden staircase, worn with countless running footsteps of two young boys. The inviting scent of plum pudding baking in the kitchens, perfuming the air of the entire house. How he had longed for Abbeygate while he was away.

He was home. *Home.* That was a novel thought, one that he was not accustomed to. Even though he had many fond memories of staying at Abbeygate as a child, he had never thought of it as home, even with the escape from Father's furies that it provided him. But somehow, in only the course of a few months, it had transformed into a haven, the place he felt most comfortable and peaceful in the whole world. What had changed?

"*Pedro!*" His name ended with an enthusiastic trill, a telltale sign of his wife.

That is what had changed. Peter was married. And Ana made this old estate a home.

Peter spun around and opened his arms wide, scooping up the giggling figure that rushed toward him. She smelled sweet and tangy. It was comforting, familiar, and strangely enticing. He tightened his grip on her adorably short frame, a frame that now had a delightful hint of roundness to it. A lump appeared in Peter's throat unexpectedly. He was not yet truly a father. Was he already becoming so soft at the thought? How his comrades would laugh at him. Still, he planted a lingering kiss on Ana's head as he fought to regain his voice and composure.

"How I missed you, Ana. *Muchísimo.*"

"I miss you *también.*"

Without warning, Ana stepped from his embrace. The excitement seeped from her voice, and she froze, desperation squeezing her features. "You not be recalled, no?"

"No, not now. I can remain here with you."

Ana breathed an audible sigh and pressed an enthusiastic kiss to his lips. Peter savored her touch as the reality of his own words seeped into his mind. The thought of returning to battle was the stuff of nightmares. But that was not his lot now, it appeared. And if his time with Ana was to be limited in the future, he needed to enjoy it to its very fullest.

Ana wiggled out of his embrace, only to grab his hand and pull him toward her favorite chairs by the fireplace.

"Come, sit *aquí.* I will call to Mrs. Thompson that she bring us some tea."

Peter watched as she hurried from the room, a hand pressed to her slight roundness. The sight brought a rush of warmth to his chest, and for once, he did not try to ignore it or pound it away.

Soon Ana was at his side again, pouring a cup of tea in an entirely English manner and pressing said cup into his hands.

"*Gracias,*" he whispered, staring into her beautiful eyes. A blush warmed her cheeks, turning her olive skin to more of a copper.

"I am so happy that you be here at home with me again."

That she also referred to their residence as "home" was not lost on him. Peter leaned forward and kissed her temple. It was a wonderful thing, to return to a place that felt so comfortable and so safe. To have a listening ear who he could trust to listen to him and advise him eternally without raging like Father or teasing like his comrades.

"And I am happier than you can imagine," Peter replied. He reached out a hand toward Ana, lacing their fingers together.

* * *

Ana toyed with Peter's fingers, running her fingertips over the calluses worn into his hands. There was a security in the warmth of his skin that she had missed desperately, although she hadn't truly realized it while he was gone. She had not only felt keenly the absence of his companionship; she had missed his touch, his embrace.

"Thank you for allowing me to go to London. It was certainly a complicated endeavor."

"*Y qué pasó*?" *What happened?*

"My superiors, it would seem, are convinced to blame the French entirely for the harm done to the inhabitants of San Sebastián. And yet they know that I disagree entirely with that approach. What is more, they know that I actively fought against the men who were taking such actions."

"*Claro*. You are a *capitán*. Of course they know you were there, and you saw the city burn. Why is this so bad that you know these things?"

"You see, I anticipate repercussions against the army, perhaps even on a large scale. I have recently learned that this was not the first time this type of sacking occurred."

"*De verdad*?"

"Yes. There were other cities that were plundered. It seems that many soldiers realized that their packs would be searched for loot after overtaking a city, which made them careless and resentful. They would get drunk and reckless and take their spoils of the city in an entirely different way. Their actions were inexcusable still, and the instance of San Sebastián seems to be the most violent of them. The poor victims of these crimes, along with all of Spain and Basque Country I would imagine, will continue to fight against such greedy and barbaric behavior."

"*Qué terrible*."

"Indeed. And yet I can't imagine that my superiors will admit to any wrongdoing on their part, particularly when the army is pressed to progress in this war. I feel certain that they will continue to fight against any allegations, as they won't do much to help their momentum against Napoleon. And as a result, I cannot understand what my future with the army will be. They won't hear anyone breathe a word against them. But I cannot allow myself to return to such grave indiscipline."

"Because you know the English and Portuguese hurt and killed the people there?"

"Indeed. And that the French were not at fault, despite being at fault for a great many other issues."

He was right. And his leaders and countrymen should be held responsible for their great errors. It was only proper and just. Particularly when this war played such a large role on the world stage. A battle such as the Siege of San Sebastián would not be forgotten.

"I support you, *te lo prometo*. Tell me how I can help you in this." Ana gripped his hand tighter, although her eyes were clouded over with painful memories.

"But that is just the issue. I don't know of any other way to speak out about this issue. I want justice for those my countrymen ravaged so carelessly. But in speaking out, it is not my reputation I am concerned for. I simply cannot see how I can stand against them, not without risking you and our future. That much was made clear when I was in London. Quite simply, my superiors determined that they could remove me from my position, simultaneously removing my ability to financially support both myself and you. And if they even knew of your existence, I feel certain they would go to great lengths to ensure that your witness of the events there and of your own suffering never came to light. You heard how infuriated they were by the so-called libelous publication *El Duende de los Cafés* months ago."

The fury Ana felt on behalf of the Basque women morphed into fear as she realized that she too was a victim of this particularly grave event of wartime misconduct. And if anyone was trying to collect those wronged to testify against the guilty, she could be called to testify. And in testifying against an army so great as Britain's, she would be dangling an immense sword over her head. The future they had worked to build in England would be destroyed. Peter's life, her life, and the life of her baby would all be at risk. Her hands clutched at her stomach, unbidden. Words escaped her.

"But I will not ask such things of you, Ana," Peter whispered as he gently gathered her hands from their desperate position against her waist. "You are my greatest responsibility now. I must protect you. And even if I did speak out, one voice against hundreds would get stifled so quickly. It seems an impossible, unattainable goal."

Ana was soaking in Peter's distress like a water-starved flower, the words flooding through her, transporting her to another country, another time. Memories pounded in her head, much like the pounding of incessant explosions that had brought down the barricades at San Sebastián. Memories that she had fought to dispel from her mind over the past months. She pressed a hand to her temple while the other clutched at her stomach, as if she could somehow protect the growing child within from the trauma. Even the once-comforting fireplace in front of her transformed, engulfing that desperate city in flames.

Deafening blasts.

Heartrending screams.

Never-ending destruction.

Cruel words, furious fingers, ripping fabric, and aching pain.

"No!" she cried out, rising from her seat and shaking her head against the agony. "I will not feel this again. *No lo quiero!*"

Ana pressed her eyes shut, desperate honesty streaming from her. "You leave me for so much time, and I do not know if you be in danger with the truth you know. And then you come home to *casa*, and you tell me all these things that I be so worried, and I do not even know if you remember that our life is *muy diferente* now. We are not in *España*. We are not in *San Sebastián*. Now we have a *bebé* that we need to protect. We cannot put our lives or *futuro* at risk now, *Pedro*."

Peter was on his feet now too, trying to lower her to her seat again. Ana whimpered and moved away from his grasp, away from the fireplace.

"Believe me when I say that I understand perfectly the risks that we face. I have done so much to ensure that you and your . . . *our* child would be safe." He massaged his temples with one hand, breathing deeply. "But for my own sanity, for the slightest hint of hope that I might be able to someday live without the crushing guilt of what occurred in San Sebastián, I had to go to London. I needed to find out if there was anything to be done to remove the weight of these sins. I would have told you if I thought either of us was at risk. That is precisely why I was writing to you as often as I did. And why I sought out Elena and sent her to be a comfort at your side."

"Yes, I love Elena. She is *perfecta para mí*. But she is not you, Pedro. I needed *you*."

Peter tilted his head back, his eyes shut tightly in a pain so apparent it must have been physical.

"I promise that in the future, I will be more completely honest with you, more forthcoming. Please know that it pains me to see you distressed."

Ana's throat hurt, her voice high and strained. Did he not see how he was hurting her? "It was no easy that you be gone from me. And what will I do when you leave again with the *armada*?"

Tears soaked Ana's cheeks now, running down her jaw. She had already lived through too many farewells, too many abandonments, too many *despedidas*. She could not survive him leaving again, not when she had just started feeling safe in his presence, in his home.

Peter stepped toward her, cupping her cheeks with his hands, his touch warm. "It will be better in the future, Ana. I promise. I will be completely honest with you. You'll never know a more faithful correspondent than I. But now I want to focus on today. On tomorrow. I want to see you happy. Do allow me to try again. Please, Ana. *Por favor*."

"*Bueno*." Ana folded her arms across her chest, dividing her from his touch, as if the action would protect her from further distress or disappointment. Peter dropped his hands to her shoulders, seemingly insistent upon still touching her, despite her clear indication that she did not desire his touch at the moment. He was quiet for a moment, his eyes visibly looking over her hair, her brow, her tear-soaked front.

"Come, let us not forget what we've missed together. It is not lost on me that I've been absent during some traditional holiday celebrations, including one called Twelfth Night."

"*Sí*, Mrs. Thompson told me a little about this."

"I promise it will be most diverting . . . particularly after the great dampening spirit I've brought back home with me from London. Allow me to make it up to you with a belated celebration tomorrow."

"Very well."

"Thank you, my dear." A surge of hope warmed Ana's chest as Peter wrapped her in his arms, holding her firmly, insistently, until she had no choice but to relax and return the embrace. Surely he had not intended to hurt her or cause any strain on her mind. He had simply been trying out that bond of trust that they had been building, believing that she would help him in his moment of need. She sighed deeply, burying her face into his chest. She needed to be a more trusting wife. After all, he had rescued her in more ways than she could count.

Chapter 20

January 8, 1814, Abbeygate, Surrey Hills, England

Peter had returned from his morning preparations for the day's activities expecting to find Ana in her bedchambers, but he was surprised by its vacancy. Instead, she was taking her breakfast at the well-worn table in the kitchen with Elena and Mrs. Thompson. Perhaps it was not seemly or traditional, but it brought her happiness. Peter would never correct her after hearing her laughter light the place as she visited with her friends.

"Mrs. Thompson, Elena, may I be permitted to steal my wife away from you?"

"I suppose," Elena whispered, her pronunciation crisp and rounded and her eyes twinkling with amusement. She rose and helped Mrs. Thompson clear away the dishes as Peter led Ana from the room. Their hands joined as they climbed the stairs together, approaching his bedchamber.

Her new, fruity scent still perfumed the air around her, much as it had yesterday. He breathed deeply. Had she always smelled so enticing?

"Ana? What is that smell?"

She cocked her head and placed a hand on her cheek. "What smell you speak of? The breakfast?"

"No . . . your smell."

"Oh!" Ana blushed, her fingers brushing along her wrist as if feeling the remnants of the perfume. "It is a perfume of Elena's. She had some from *España* that her *abuela* made *especial* for her. You like it?"

Peter chuckled and nodded vehemently. "It smells quite welcoming indeed. What is it made of? I've never encountered such a perfume before."

"*La granada de España.* It is a fruit *como* this size." She cupped her palms together in a shape that was considerably larger than an apple.

Peter shook his head and shrugged as he helped her take a seat on the chaise across from his bed.

"It is red and has the delicious, juicy seeds inside." Her lips were quirked to one side, and her nose was scrunched in concentration. Peter nearly kissed that nose. His wife was entirely adorable. Even if she was hard to understand.

"Let me think back to the fruit I ate in Spain. It was all quite delectable, of course." Peter tapped a finger to his chin. What fruit had large, juicy seeds? It could not be mango or papaya . . . "Ah! Pomegranate!"

"*Sí, eso!* Pom-e-gran-ate," Ana sounded out, her face beaming. "*Me gusta mucho.* It is so nice and reminds me of my country. I am so happy Elena was so kind to give it to me."

"I happen to have a few more things that may remind you of your beloved Spain," Peter said, unable to school the grin that spread across his face.

"*De verdad?*"

"Sí. Just wait one moment and I'll go fetch them."

He stepped into his dressing room and grabbed his knapsack, pulling from it a large fabric package. "The one victory that I did manage in London was recovering a few things left in Spain. I thought I recognized a few of your belongings . . . and your father's."

Tears instantly filled Ana's eyes, causing their near-black depths to sparkle in the light.

"Darling, don't cry. You haven't even seen what I brought you yet. For all you know, it could be a broken shoelace."

"I do not care what you bring me. I only care that you feel it was so important to remind me of my country *precioso.*."

Peter held out the knapsack, expecting her to grasp at it with eager hands, but she pushed it aside, instead reaching for him. Her short arms wrapped around him as she touched her chin to his chest, tilting her face up to him as tears trickled down her cheeks.

"*Gracias, Pedro. Muchísimas gracias.*"

She then rose on her tiptoes, puckering her lips, their rosy bow and curve enticing him. Peter more than happily obliged, lowering his lips to hers in a quick, innocent kiss . . . which turned into a number of quick, innocent kisses. And although they were brief, they still sent sparks coursing down Peter's spine. The flush that rose on Ana's cheeks and neck indicated that she had enjoyed them as well. His wife was beautiful. But she was downright irresistible when she was freshly kissed.

He helped Ana to settle onto the sofa once again and joined her as they sorted through the knapsack. Her clothing hadn't been recovered, and neither had her father's, but he'd managed to gather a number of items that he thought would be valuable: A collection of maps and journals in various languages, tied with a strip of thin leather, a quill still pressed between some of the pages. A well-worn Bible, its Spanish wording long-faded from the front. A length of black Spanish lace pinned with a single pearl earring, carefully preserved from the dusty, day-to-day life of a siege. Perhaps they had been her mother's? Her father's pistol, dented and empty but still preserved with intricate carvings of Spanish flair. His war medals that had been attached to his formal uniform. It seemed the jacket itself had been confiscated, but the medals had been sent along in hopes of finding his remaining family with the rest of the items. Lastly, he had recovered a miniature of Ana and her mother—a rather outdated one. Ana had still been a child. He wondered why she would insist upon carrying such an old painting with her.

When he'd been questioned regarding his claim to the items, he insisted that he had connections to their family members and would ensure that the treasured items reached them. It had seemed believable enough, apparently. And Ana was certainly mighty pleased. She had pressed each of them to her heart, if not her lips. She touched the Bible reverently, tears welling in her eyes. The lingering, wordless looks that she sent Peter throughout the process would be seared in his memory forever. It was not just gratitude that shone in her eyes but peace. Healing.

Peter reached for the Bible that still lay on her lap.

"I was particularly eager to recover this one. I know it may not have been your father's, but I thought that we might take up our studies of the holy word together. It would help bring us some peace, I hope. And perhaps it would even prove an aid to my sorry Spanish."

"I love this idea so much," Ana said, "What a privilege it be to study with you."

"Well then, it is settled. I have made a habit of reading in the mornings. Unless another time would please you?"

"*Está bien*, if I still take my *siesta* later," Ana said with a smile, humor shining in her eyes.

"Of course, I wouldn't deny you of your precious *siesta*. You are doing a hard work, carrying and growing this little child." Peter nodded at her growing form. "Now, I hoped that today we might celebrate some of the traditions that we missed while I was gone in London."

At his words, Ana leapt to her feet and hurried to the door that adjoined their rooms.

"Do wait, before it starts—I as well have something for you. A gift of *la Navidad* even if it may be *un poco tarde*."

"Ana, you needn't gift me anything, really."

"But you have given me so much." Her voice cracked, and her still-wet eyes filled with tears again. "You have given me *todo*. I don't know how to thank you for how you save me. But I can give you *sorpresas* . . . surprises and presents." She giggled and sniffed hard at her tears. Her roundness bumped into the door's edge and she laughed harder now, the sound echoing in her rooms. Clearly she was not used to her growing shape.

Peter felt a rush of pride filling him like a deep breath after a long training exercise. It took his breath away. *She* took his breath away—even if he had to remind himself time after time that he was not properly the father of the babe growing inside her. Just when he thought Ana could not look any more stunning, she started to show lovely signs of becoming a mother. He would have to be careful, as her rounded, growing figure was one that he found to be most alluring. Perhaps they would be having many more children than he had intended. Peter chuckled wryly. It was shocking how comfortable he felt with the notion of becoming a father, even repeatedly, when he had discounted the possibility from his future for so many years. He would simply have to avoid pondering what he and Ana would have to do to ensure that more children were born into their family. He pulled at his waistcoat, all the layers he was wearing suddenly feeling quite restrictive and much too warm.

A moment later, Ana returned, her eyes bright, and her hands hidden behind her back, revealing her rounded middle in a most advantageous manner.

"This *regalo* is not only for you."

"Ah, did you buy a present for us both?" Peter smiled more widely, his imagination already expanding as wide as the sky.

"*Para mí*, no. It is for you and for our child also."

"Children," Peter added, feeling strangely bold as he settled his hands on her waist.

"*Sí*, children. *Hijos*." A reddish blush raced up her neck and cheeks, begging him to kiss the flushed surfaces. She squeezed his hands and then raised them up in front of him, palms upward.

"I am even more excited to receive it than before."

"*Cierra tus ojos*."

Peter obliged, shutting his eyes. Pressed into his hands were a number of oddly shaped objects that felt strangely familiar. "Are these . . ." He couldn't keep his eyes closed any longer.

Knuckle bones and dice. One of his favorite childhood games.

"How . . . how did you know?"

"Mrs. Thompson. She tell me how you and Matthew love so much to play this game *como niños*." Ana's eyes shone with pure contentment.

"I truly don't remember the last time I played. It's been ages."

"I also have some wooden toy *solderos*, and a ball-and-cup. *Se dice así?*"

"Yes, that is precisely what it's called." Peter shook his head, boyish excitement coursing through him. "I haven't the slightest idea how Mrs. Thompson remembered."

"She remembers this because she loves you, *Pedro*."

Peter suddenly found himself with a most annoying lump in his throat, blocking his even breathing and causing tears to rise to his eyes. He blinked hard before they could fall down his cheeks. He knew Mrs. Thompson cared for him, as did the rest of the staff. But this was physical proof of the fact, reminding him, once again, that he could find happiness here. That he *did* belong in Abbeygate. He rubbed a finger over the smoothed wood of the knuckle bones and imagined playing and laughing with his own children much as he had with Matthew so many years ago.

"This is the first Christmas present I have received in more years than I can remember. And I couldn't have asked for a more meaningful one. Thank you, Ana. I so look forward to introducing these games to our little ones."

"*De nada, querido.*"

Peter rested a hand on Ana's cheek, his thumb stroking against her lovely, defined cheekbones. Her eyelids fluttered in response as her gaze lowered to his lips. He closed the distance between them in an instant, covering her lips with his. The sweetness of her lips was a taste Peter would never tire of. Each time, he found it increasingly difficult to pull away and slow the desire that was being stoked to a raging fire within him. But for now, he kissed her slowly, patiently, hoping that he could thoroughly convey his thanks. The curl of her smile beneath his indicated that he did. He trailed kisses down her cheek, in search of that sensitive spot behind her ear that he had recently discovered made her giggle.

But then she pulled away, quirking her mouth to one side and blinking rapidly as she often did when she was thinking hard on a matter.

"What is it?"

"You never celebrate *la Navidad* in *la armada*? You never receive any *regalos*?"

Peter huffed out a laugh. "If you consider the festivities common among the soldiers to be appropriately celebratory. Mother always sent money, expecting me to outfit myself with new clothing and necessities."

"Then why celebrate now?"

"Perhaps because I have something—and someone—worth celebrating."

Ana's face was painted with the most becoming blush at his words. Clearly she understood what he referred to. He ran a hand over the flushed curve of her cheek, having half made up his mind to forgo his plans for the evening and spend the rest of the winter here in his room kissing his wife. But he knew how she had looked forward to this day while he was away. No, he would go forward with their plans and enjoy it immensely. He may not spend the evening kissing Ana, but he would drink in her laugh and smile, which was a very close second.

"It also helps a great deal to have a wife that won't allow you to forget the important days of the year . . . including your *Día de los Inocentes*. You seem to have transformed me into a much more tradition-honoring person than I ever was before. I am a changed man."

"The being *un esposo*—a husband—it suits you, *querido*. That is what change, not you."

Chapter 21

January 8, 1814, Abbeygate, Surrey Hills, England

Ana stepped into the dining room, but her quick, excited pace was stopped entirely by the delightful *vista* that met her.

In the time they had been upstairs, the room had been transformed into the most magical of holiday scenes. The few decorative greenery boughs that the household had put up for earlier celebrations had already been taken down and burned, as was tradition. (Ana had heard murmured words from Mrs. Thompson about bad luck and a goblin, and she had no wish to tempt fate in that regard.) But these new decorations were something entirely unique.

An impressive collection of candles brightened the center of the table. There were thin, spindly candles and short, stout candles, and even a few decorative ones in elegant, glass holders. But even though the candles were mismatched in their great variety, they didn't look haphazard in the least. Their nearness helped the table to look like it held a great collection of stars. The light and the warmth from the display warmed Ana, inside and out.

Above the table, delightfully bright ribbons were secured to the bottom of the chandelier and twisted downward in a cascade of ruby red, emerald green, deep plum, and rich ocher. Hot spiced wine glittered in glasses, giving a jewel-like appearance to the table spread. The estate's finest dishes and silver were set with great care in an arrangement just for the two of them. Between their plates sat a golden cake, topped with intricate, white icing, appearing for all the world to be a real length of French lace.

Ana sat heavily at the table, completely awed. How had Peter arranged for all of this when he had only just arrived home? She had made some arrangements of her own to commemorate *el Día de los Inocentes*, but nothing on this scale.

Again, his surprising thoughtfulness struck her. Peter did not often exude any sort of emotional softness, at least not when she was first coming to know him. His logical mind seemed to rule his decisions, and his life was planned with precise intention. The role of soldier had seemed to fit him perfectly then. He knew his responsibilities. His rules and limitations were drawn so very clearly. And none of this allowed for overly caring acts of tenderness, not to mention the mind-numbing kisses that he had bestowed on her as of late. He was changing. Or perhaps he was just revealing to her more of who he truly was. And tonight was another excellent example of that.

"I see you've already found part of our celebrations," Peter whispered, soft and low in her ear. He buried a kiss at the back of her neck. Tingles ran down Ana's spine, and her heart pounded wildly. It seemed his words now had just as much power over her as his touch. What a weakness she had for him already.

"It is so *hermoso*, *Pedro. Gracias.*"

She rose and turned to greet him, clasping her hands together so as to hide their trembling. Was it nervousness? Excitement? She would never know because within an instant, her hands were captured by his.

"I don't know how you accomplish *todo eso.*" Ana tilted her head, gesturing at the stunning display.

"Oh, I hardly lifted a finger, truly. Mrs. Thompson was delighted to use her creativity to decorate without the holiday evergreens. It is bad luck, you know. And Elena helped by gathering the candles. Said it would give a nice religious touch. Or perhaps she said romantic." He winked, chuckling as he brushed a kiss on her forehead. "Best of all, Cook has prepared a special Twelfth Night cake for you."

"Ah, *qué delicioso*! She knows how I love cake so much!"

"Yes, but this cake is particularly special. It is a fruit cake, as is tradition for the holiday season, but it has a dried bean baked into it. Whoever happens to find the slice of cake with the dried bean inside will be proclaimed the king or queen of the Twelfth Night celebrations and will be able to dictate how we celebrate for the evening, be it in the form of games or dance or song or whatever pleases them."

"*Qué buenísimo!* I love this tradition!"

"So, shall we start our evening of celebrations by enjoying a slice of this cake?"

"*Por supuesto!* But of course!"

Peter helped Ana into her chair and then pushed it, moving her closer to the table. The warmth of vanilla and sugar mingled in the air as she leaned in close to the cake.

"It is so beautiful, this cake. Can we really cut it?"

"We must. How else will we discover who will be the king or queen for the evening?"

"*Es verdad.* I would very much like to be *la reina.*"

Peter cut a thin piece for Ana, who quickly spooned through the soft bake in search of the bean, but it was not there. "Nothing here."

He then proceeded to cut up the entire cake until, with a knowing grin, he handed her the last, large piece. Sure enough, the bean was embedded in the side of the slice, right near the bottom.

"I found it! I win!" Ana laughed, the freeing sound rippling through her.

"And so do I. It will be delightful to watch you rule," he said with a wink.

"*Ay qué* power to be queen. Does this mean I rule you too, *Pedro*?"

"You already do, Your Highness. You are the queen of my heart." Peter slapped a hand against his heart and saluted in an exaggerated, humorous motion, but something about the brightness of his eyes told Ana that he wasn't entirely joking. And that caused her breath to catch in her throat, caused tears to spring to her eyes, caused her legs to tremble.

Why was it so terrifying to imagine being loved?

Ana needed something to distract herself, and fast. She sprang from her chair, sticking a finger in the air and tipping her chin up in a self-important pose.

"As *la reina*, I declare that we begin the *noche* with a game."

"And what game would you wish to play, Your Highness?"

Ana tapped her chin. She hadn't thought that far. "What you think, my king?"

"Well, Your Majesty, what say you of a rousing game of hide and seek to begin our evening of festivities?"

"Hide and seek?"

"Indeed, where the designated individual hides themselves and then the rest 'seek' out the individual who is hiding. If one is lucky enough to find the hider, they can join them in their hiding position."

"I think *está bien*."

"Splendid. And who would you like to be the first hider?"

"*Yo*."

"Are you certain? I know all the best hiding spots this old house has to offer."

"*Sí*, I believe I can find a spot that will be not so easy for you to find. And a spot to fit us both, for when you find me, no?" Peter stepped up to her, close enough that their noses brushed.

"If you wish me to join you, then yes." Peter smiled, winking at her. Ana's chest heated, her ribcage suddenly refusing to expand in a deep, regular breath, a lack of motion that had nothing to do with the growing child within her.

Minutes later, Ana was hurrying down the hall as quietly as she could, a perfect destination already set in her mind: the library. She did not know the house as expertly as Peter, but she had spent enough time pacing in the library while he was gone to know which floorboards creaked. She could hide herself in there quietly enough, and she was also certain that her hiding location would provide room enough for two.

Ana crawled underneath the grand wooden desk that sat in the far corner of the room and pulled the stuffed chair closer to her in an effort to disguise her hiding spot. Then she pushed a hand against her heart, willing it to slow as she strained to listen for any sign of Peter finding her. She only waited for four minutes, perhaps five, before she heard the slow creak of the library door. She strained further and could barely distinguish the slow shifting of footsteps before a shadow touched the hem of her gown.

"Your Majesty," Peter whispered, "I believe I have discovered your hiding place. Would you care if I joined you?"

"Not at all," Ana whispered, moving to one side underneath the desk.

Now that Peter had found her, Ana realized the silliness of the game. With only the two of them, it was already finished. There was nobody else who would seek them. Why had Peter suggested such a game that would be completed so suddenly, especially with how familiar he was with the estate?

Then the way his knee, his hip, his shoulder pressed against hers as he crawled under the desk revealed what she hoped to be the truth. He had wanted to be close to her. She had wanted the same, had desired a moment of solace, of privacy, and of lightness, after the heaviness he had brought home with him from London.

"This was an excellent hiding spot, Ana."

"Not very excellent if you find me so quickly."

"That is because I know you quite well. You love your books and maps. It reminds you of your father, I gather. I thought you might feel safe hiding here in the library."

Ana touched a hand to her chest, pressing against the sharp pain that jolted there at the mention of *Papá*. She blinked away tears at the reminder of darker days laced with loss. Why was it that the feeling of safety was always accompanied by a reminder of the painful devastation of feeling unsafe? No matter how brief the reminder, Ana felt a dip in her spirits. She shook her head against memories that were flashing through her mind, unbidden. Today was to be a happy day, not one for remembering all she had lost.

True, this library reminded her of *Papá*. But this library in particular had an entirely different feeling. Ana had spent many hours here during the days that Peter was away in London. Somehow, being in a space that felt like him, almost smelled like him, managed to quell some of her worries.

"I love this library because it reminds me of you, *Pedro*."

A long pause lit the air with silence, flammable with unspoken emotion. Ana held her breath, waiting for some kind of indication that her words were not uncalled for.

"Then I would hope that you would feel safe here for the same reason."

"I do."

Ana hiccupped, and whether it was a result of her holding her breath or fighting back tears, she could not say. Why must she cry so often since becoming a married woman? Or was it since becoming an expectant mother? Either way, it was quite frustrating indeed.

Peter bent his already doubled-over frame to kiss Ana's cheek. Just as soon as she started to lean into his touch, he started to move away from under the desk. Ana felt cool air rush in at the absence of his warm body and missed him instantly.

"*Qué?*"

"I confess I am quite constrained in so small a space," he said with a laugh. "Would you care to join me out here? We can still sit on the floor, beside the desk, if you wish."

"*Bueno.*"

Ana joined Peter, pushing her back up against the wall as she moved herself even closer to him than before. She rested her cheek on his shoulder and laced her fingers through his, telling herself that she desired it only to be comfortable and not because of the surge of butterflies that the closeness gave her. Breathing deeply, her unexpected emotions began to calm.

Ana had quieted significantly since they had snuggled close together. They relaxed that way in cozy silence, neither one eager to move, but she had not continued her usual stream of commentary. Few things stilled her tongue so.

Peter's tone lilted in a teasing tone. "Your Majesty, I propose that you are hiding more than just your location secreted away here in this library. Now what is the secret you are keeping from me?"

"*Qué?*" Ana's stomach dropped in an instant. She squeezed her hands in her skirts as her heart sped up in a wild, anxious pattern.

Her forehead creased in genuine concern. "I promise, *Pedro*, I have no secrets from you." Her bottom lip trembled.

What secret could he possibly be thinking of?

Of course, the origin of her condition was a secret they alone would share till their graves. But Peter had never jested about such things. He would never say anything to make her feel guilty or uncomfortable in the slightest, having witnessed the terrible circumstances she had endured. Surely he could not be referencing that. At present, it seemed that Ana's very existence was a secret. He had implied that if some of his leaders knew of her condition, they might try to call her in to testify about San Sebastián, or worse, they might try to hide her further. But it was very well understood between the two of them that Peter wanted her to feel as if she had a normal life here. He would not be teasing her about such things.

Secret-keeping had always been a pain-filled point in Ana's life. She had been entirely too young and tender when the burden of a large, life-altering secret had been placed upon her. The evening before *Papá* was scheduled to return from his responsibilities, Ana caught a glimpse of *Mamá* packing a valise. Although Ana had understood that she would be leaving, it had not crossed her mind that she would be leaving permanently, especially when *Mamá* had kissed her the following morning, telling her she was going to visit a cousin in the south for a time. Why else would she leave her closets full of dresses and her home full of possessions if she did not mean to return?

And why else would she leave Ana?

It was an excruciating secret. One that continuously ripped open her heart as the months—and then years—passed and *Mamá* never wrote and never returned. But Ana had never breathed a word to *Papá* about what she had seen, what she had heard. This secret was largely why Ana had sworn to be as open and honest with her husband and children as she possibly could. She would not put them through the turmoil that she had endured.

Perhaps that was just it: *Mamá*. True, Ana had not told Peter very much about *Mamá's* absence in her life, but he had also never asked about the issue, and she had never found an appropriate moment to divulge such a heavy topic.

Ana had tried her very best to be open and honest with Peter. It had not been a simple task, all things considered, particularly when she was dealing with the unexpectedly wild emotions that her condition had brought her. And after all her efforts, she felt that somehow,

Peter was the one who had not been completely honest with her. After all, he had spent much longer in London than expected and had returned with a burdened spirit indeed.

A few traitorous tears escaped now, though she tried to put the heaviness behind her in favor of the lightness of the evening's celebrations.

"Ana darling, I was merely jesting." Peter wiped her tears and pulled her into an embrace. "It is only a game and an ill-timed jest on my part. Don't cry. Not on our special night. Please, forgive me."

"*Bueno*, I forgive you." Ana tried to believe her words, much as she was trying to calm her aching heart.

"Are you certain that you are all right?"

"*Sí.*"

"And you wish to continue?"

Ana nodded, brushing the wetness from her cheeks and moving her hair back from her face.

Peter stood, reaching for her hand. "So, Your Highness, have we spent sufficient time hiding away here? Shall we continue with our celebrations?"

"We shall, *mi rey.*"

"Do tell me, what do you have planned for us now?"

For a moment, her mind was foggy, still caught up in painful memories, but soon happier memories replaced them: Glimpses of *Papá* wearing a fuzzy hat, fake nose, and silly costume as he chased the town children around the square. Echoes of the laughter they shared that filled the quiet emptiness of their home. *El Día de los Inocentes* was very good for that, for bringing laughter and lightness to one's home, even on a dark day. After all, it commemorated a dark day indeed, the day when King Herod of old commanded that so many innocent children be killed in his search for the babe *Jesús*. And still, they could celebrate the clever and inspired trick that Joseph and Mary had played on him in escaping with the Lord *Jesús*. Even so, Ana could put dark memories behind her and enjoy this evening with her husband.

"A simple game for *el Día de los Inocentes.*"

"Somehow I do not trust that it will be truly as simple as you say."

"*Sí*, it will be. You will wear a silly costume while the whole *casa* will say how *ridículo* you appear and make . . . how you say? Jests."

Peter shook his head, chuckling. "It sounds simply delightful."

Chapter 22

January 8, 1814, Abbeygate, Surrey Hills, England

Ana was having a simply awful night. Comfortably settled in bed as she was, she could not seem to fall asleep. Perhaps it had been the *Roscón de Reyes* cake that Peter had surprised her with late in the evening. Eating sugar near her regular time of retiring had never done her any good. Or perhaps it was her silly reaction to Peter's earlier jest about secrets. He had been trying to flirt with her, hadn't he? And she had made a grand old mess of it all.

Regardless of the reason, sleep was evading her continuously, much as Peter had attempted to evade her silly costumes and jests. But this situation was much less humorous. The later the hour, the weaker her resolve grew to block fearsome memories from her mind.

Out of doors, a rainstorm progressed ever fiercer. Thunder caused the house to tremble and the glass panes to rattle. Ana's body tensed as she held yet another pillow over her head in an attempt to drown out the sound. Why must the storm sound so much like the gunfire and bomb explosions of the battlefield? Another crash was accompanied by splitting lightning that cast her room in foreboding shadows. Ana jumped at it, whimpering, and in her wild movements, she slammed her elbow into the thick wood of the headboard. She moaned. Would she ever be blessed with sleep tonight? A few more minutes passed, and when thunder pounded in her ears again, tears slipped down her cheeks. In her exhaustion, she could not separate the storm outside from the violent dreams that tortured her.

She could smell the ash, hear the screams, feel the ripping of her dress . . .

Then a knock cut through the noise of the battlefield. That certainly seemed out of place. Sure enough, it sounded again, soft but insistent, at the door adjoining her rooms to Peter's. Ana latched onto the sound, begging it to pull her from the horrors that were running through her mind.

"Ana? Are you all right?"

Tears streamed down her cheeks even harder. She opened her mouth but couldn't form words; instead, a cry emitted from her throat. It had been months since she'd been plagued by night terrors.

An instant later, the door swung open, and Peter strode to the side of her bed. His nightshirt hung open, exposing the shadows of a muscled chest, even in the dim light. Clearly he had not had time to pull on the additional cover of a nightgown or banyan. He rubbed a hand over his eyes, breathing heavily. "I have been hearing you all night. I cannot stand the sound of your cries anymore."

Ana heated with embarrassment, which worsened at the intimacy of Peter's lack of dress. Humiliation lit upon her skin, burning over its surface until it roared like a great fire in her belly.

"*Lo siento* for disturbing you. I am so sorry . . ."

"I am not bothered in the slightest by your noises, or by being awoken. But I cannot abide the thought of you suffering alone while I am right next to you." He shook his head, running a hand through his hair. "Please allow me to help you."

"Hold me please." Ana sniffed and held out her arms.

"Here?" Peter sat at her side, but it was clear by the way that his eyes kept darting back to his room that he was not comfortable in Ana's space. Curious. But her head was pounding. She desperately needed sleep and didn't want to deliberate any longer.

"I go with you. I need to feel safe."

Peter scooped her up. He seemed to hesitate for a moment, looking around, before he carried her to his room. She sighed heavily, letting her eyes, so heavy with exhaustion, fall closed at last. His warmth, his closeness, was the only thing that could stop the pounding of her heart.

* * *

Ana woke up in the most stunning bed she had ever seen. Rich mahogany wood shone with hues of red and copper, swirling into four intricate posts that nearly touched the ceiling. The mattress was supportive but deliciously soft, the yielding beneath her indicating modern and luxurious rope supports below. Numerous blankets swirled around her in soft textures and delicate patterns.

But the most comforting feature of all was the presence of Peter beside her. She was tucked into his side, her cheek resting upon his chest as his arm circled her back and waist, pulling her to him. Ana felt entirely safe, more than she ever had before.

"*Buen día*," he whispered above her.

Ana rose on one elbow, turning her head to meet Peter's eyes. His cheek was lined with the mark of her hair, and his eyes were squinted from sleep. And he had never looked so handsome.

"Welcome to my room." Peter's cheeks reddened adorably as he cast her a sheepish smile.

Ana gazed about the space. It was all so beautiful. And so decidedly feminine. More graceful details greeted her in the form of dried floral bouquets, gilded candelabras, various leather-bound books, and a large painting of a young mother and two rosy-cheeked boys. Then it dawned on her.

"This was your mother's room, *verdad*?"

"Yes. It is foolish of me that I didn't have you stay in here from our first night."

"With you?" Ana's cheeks heated, and her breath caught in her throat. Had he really desired her closeness all this time? She would admit that the feeling of waking alongside his warm, comforting body was one she had relished. Perhaps they had made a mistake in taking to their separate rooms for so long. But when she looked upward, Peter's cheeks were brighter than her own.

"I didn't mean to imply . . . that is, I would never insist upon your company . . . unless you were willing. Although I certainly have no complaints about your being in my bed this morning." His cheeks were flaming now, and Ana found he would not meet her eyes. "I meant to say that from the beginning, I should have offered you this room instead of my father's. This one is certainly more feminine and perhaps more suited to your tastes, although it is quite English, is it not?

"My room does not bother me, *Pedro*. But is there a reason why you feel more comfortable here? In the room of your *mamá*?"

Peter began to tap his hands nervously on the bedclothes. Ana was certain that if he weren't comfortably tucked in next to her, he would be pacing the room. It seemed he was always moving when something was troubling him.

"*Qué?*" she pressed. "What is it?"

"Your rooms used to be my father's. And although he rarely came here, I still had no desire to be connected to a space that used to belong to him, not when I am also trying to determine how to be the sort of husband and father that I want to be."

"Did your *Papá* spend much time here?"

Peter tilted his head in thought. "In all honesty, I don't remember him ever coming here. But Mother always wanted to keep his rooms prepared if he did decide to appear. At the beginning, the three of us lived in constant fear that he would descend upon us. Although I don't believe he was bothered in the least by our absence. He had Heathridge Hall to himself for all sorts of diversions."

It all made sense now. His reluctance to spend time in her rooms. His enthusiasm at her desire to redecorate her dressing room. His private nature when it came to the time he spent in his own rooms each morning. Clearly it was somewhat of a haven for him, a safe space. But if he felt so about a mere room that his mother had once occupied, why didn't he want to spend more time with Lady Ashmore? Of course, they had been hiding Ana's condition for a few months, but now that Lady Ashmore knew, perhaps they could travel to see her more often. If it would bring peace to Peter's heart, Ana desired that it be done.

"*Pedro*," Ana spoke, her voice quavering slightly. "You are not your father, just as I am not my mother."

"I know." His arm tightened around Ana's waist, pulling her in closer to him. "And your being with me in this room helps me to feel even more sure of that." He traced circles on the delicate skin of her upper arm, sending delicious tingles racing up her neck. Ana had to stifle a sigh of contentment. She never wanted the affection that was flourishing between them to wilt. But Peter's continued touch made Ana foolishly bold.

"*Entonces, quizás* I should sleep here with you, *no*? If you would be happier."

Peter's fingers froze. Ana's heart dropped.

"I'm so sorry. I speak my mind too fast, no?"

Had she jumped to a conclusion that he was not yet ready to make? To share a room with her husband was no small feat . . . it was something Ana had once feared she might never do. But their shared kisses and soft words had transformed the trust between them into something more delicate, more valuable. They were a great distance from the formalities of their original marriage those months ago. The closeness between them was new but increasingly precious. And Ana found that she wanted more. She knew she could trust him to care for her so completely.

She propped her elbow beneath her so she could look into his face. His brow was not scrunched in frustration, his jaw not set in distress. Instead, his eyes were wide and clear, a new, shimmering emotion visible there that made Ana want to cry or kiss him senseless. Or both.

"Please do," he said, his voice low and vulnerable. "I would like nothing more than that."

A rush of satisfaction accompanied by a warm anticipation spread through Ana's chest.

"*Bueno*. I will." Ana shifted upward and kissed his cheek, lingering in his warmth and closeness. When she drew away, it was only just. Being so close to him, she could see every fleck of scruff on his cheeks, could trace the perfect sharpness of his jawline, could memorize the many shades of blue in his eyes—eyes which were flicking back and forth between her gaze and her lips.

"I thought this was already a calming space, but now, with you here, it is incomparably peaceful. Perhaps we could make a nice morning routine together. We could study the Bible together when we wake. It would help my Spanish and your English."

"And we can take breakfast in bed together?"

"Of course. So long as I am allowed to remain here, close at your side, we can do whatever you wish. Although I may find it much harder to leave my rooms each morning and go about my responsibilities." Peter chuckled and shifted, rolling onto his side so their faces were aligned, but his hands did not leave her waist. Ana was suddenly, delightfully aware of the firmness of his embrace, the heat of his gaze and his touch.

"*Yo también.* Me too," she whispered without moving a single inch. Her eyes were trained on his mouth, her lips parting involuntarily. The few kisses they had shared had been delicious, incandescent. How she wished he would kiss her every day. She leaned in closer, her lips barely floating above his.

He was breathing fast now, each breath warming her face, and his hand was searing as it cupped her jaw and threaded through her hair, pulling her face to his. His lips enveloped hers in a gentle but insistent motion, each kiss further convincing her that she would never sleep without him again. Ana sighed in delight. If she had known her husband could kiss her with such passion, she would have married him much sooner. Ana began to return his kisses now, her lips slow but firm as they explored. She laced her arms around his neck, pulling herself as close to him as the rounding of her middle would allow.

But instead of melting into her embrace, Peter froze, a shadow in his eyes. Fear? Hesitation? Desire?

Then without warning, he leapt backward out of bed, tangling himself in the bedclothes and falling in a great heap onto the floor. The jug of water on his bedside table bumped against his Bible, teetered at the disturbance, and wobbled ever more uncontrollably.

"*Pedro!*" Ana dove for the jug but to no avail. It was already careening over the edge, landing upside down in Peter's grasping hands, entirely dousing him with water. He sputtered and gasped, surprise written across his face.

Ana squealed with laughter as she fumbled with the covers in an effort to escape the large bed and assist her husband. She took the jug from his hands, replacing it on the bedside table.

A knock came at the door, "Mr. Ashmore, are you all right in there?" called Elena.

Ana and Peter froze simultaneously. Peter raised a finger to his lips, indicating that they remain quiet. The staff hadn't the faintest idea that she had spent the night in his rooms.

"Hush now, he's with his lady, you know. Leave them be," said Mrs. Thompson in her nasally whisper.

Or apparently they did. What sort of grand teasing would they be in for today?

Ana's side ached, her eyes still blurred from her tear-inducing laughter, as she rose to her feet. Peter stood, his night shirt plastered to his muscular form as he shook drops of water from his hair. The wetness of his shirt revealed not only the strength of his chest and arms but also a series of scars laced across his shoulder and neck. At the sight, Ana felt it incredibly difficult to breathe.

"*Estás bien*?" she asked, her voice abnormally, annoyingly high, and she bit her lip in some effort to calm herself.

Peter stepped forward to where Ana was bent over the side of the bed, his eyes simmering with amusement and some other emotion that made Ana feel as if she would melt completely under his gaze. Then he leaned his head toward her, barely hovering over her mouth.

"I am better than I have ever been before."

Ana could feel his whisper against her mouth. She licked her lips and held her breath, waiting for him to fall into the bed again and warm her mouth with his. But his mouth moved away. It flipped into a teasing smile and glanced against her cheek instead. Ana groaned, collapsing backward against her pillow as Peter started for his outer clothes.

"And with that, my dear wife, I will take my leave of you."

Chapter 23

January 22, 1814, Abbeygate, Surrey Hills, England

"Ana, dear, I've fetched your warmest cloak. Do come wear it. I will not have my wife catching a cold."

There had been a blessed break in the heavy snowfall that had kept Ana cooped up for the past week, so Peter had been insistent that they take a walk about the gardens. The snow had melted and seeped away almost completely on the gravel paths, although the same could not be said for the grass fields that could take them to newer destinations. They would have to stick to the gardens for today.

Soon Ana was at his side, adorably wrapped in a ridiculous number of layers and prepared to embark as they stepped through the back door. She felt the cold much more acutely than he did, having lived in a warm coastal town for much of her life. So long as she was comfortable, Peter himself was content.

Leaving for London had been a risk. But since Peter had begun to open up about some of his concerns regarding the army and some of his difficult past, there had been a renewal of trust and openness between them. Ana in turn had hinted at a unique understanding of some of the difficult feelings he had regarding his father and his own lack of a typical upbringing. Somehow the pain of their pasts was beginning to mold them into better friends and spouses. And he hoped that the same would be true when they would become parents.

"Peter!"

He froze, impossibly stuck between feelings of bliss and terror at hearing his wife use his Christian name in English for the first time. Gone was the teasing, overdramatic *Pedro.* She was calling him because she needed him.

"What is it? Are you all right?"

Ana's hand clutched at his arm, the other pressed against her roundness.

Peter drew her in, his bliss quickly turning wholly to concern. He gently touched a hand to her torso as well, as if he could feel what had her so taken aback. "What is the matter?"

"The *bebé*! I feel her move!" Ana looked up at him, her cheeks rosy and rounded in an impossibly wide smile, while tears sparkled in her eyes.

"Truly?" Peter found it even harder to breathe than it had been a moment previous.

"*Sí.* I am certain."

Peter dropped to his knees, not caring in the slightest about the wet gravel soiling his pants. He cupped the roundness of Ana's midsection with his hands. What a miracle it would be to feel their child moving within her. The thought brought an entirely new and heady rush of excitement to Peter's mind.

"*Querido,* it is so early still. I feel her inside me. I don't know if you can feel her too."

Ana's hand stroked Peter's cheek as her smile softened into one that he hoped was affectionate of some sort.

"But I want to."

"*Lo sé.* Soon, I am certain."

Peter huffed out a heavy sigh, one that was visible in front of him in the crisp winter air. He pressed a hand to his knee, raising to his feet again, and resumed their walk. Beside him, Ana was quiet but glowing as she wrapped an arm around her round torso, basking in the tender surprise.

Once the initial excitement of the moment had resolved, Peter had to broach the topic of her using his English name. He could not resist it.

"You do realize you called me Peter, do you not?"

Ana pursed her lips in a pout and sighed heavily, a look of pretended disappointment written all over her lovely face. "I so sorry. *Lo siento mucho.* In this my moment of excitement, I forget and call you in this lazy language. But *Pedro* is much better, you know—so very much romantic *es Pedro.*" She shrugged her shoulders, the same shoulders that were trembling with the laughter contained inside her. Peter couldn't resist chuckling as well.

"I do believe Peter can be just every bit as romantic as this Pedro, as you say. I also believe that you have insisted on calling me that in Spanish all these months just to tease me."

"*Bueno,* you find me out, *Pedro.*" Ana laughed fully now, but the softening of her gaze seemed to indicate that perhaps there was an additional reason to her insisting upon calling him *Pedro.* Perhaps it had been a protection or hesitation of sorts. Because there was definitely a certain intimacy upon using one's Christian name in one's own language. It implied an emotional nearness that they had not yet experienced. Peter could not deny the thrill that had coursed through him at hearing his name upon her lips, even as it had trilled dramatically upon delivery. It tightened his chest with breathlessness and caused the undeniable attraction that he felt for her for so many months to become cemented more deeply within him.

"And seeing as I have found you out, as you say, could you be persuaded to continue to call me Peter?"

"*Quizás . . .*" Ana said, tapping her chin with a finger, "but I would like to see how you do this persuasion, no?"

Peter did not need any more encouragement. Her lips were entirely too flushed and becoming as it was. "Well, if you insist." Peter pulled Ana into his arms, dipping her dramatically, and kissed her soundly. At least, that is, until she wriggled in protest and sent them both tumbling slowly into the snow, tangled up in each other's embrace.

Chapter 24

February 10, 1814, London, England

London felt much more familiar this time, Ana decided.

Or perhaps it was being in Peter's company that felt more familiar, more comfortable. She snuggled into Peter's side, wrapping her arm through his.

Estás bien? Peter squeezed.

Estoy bien. Ana squeezed in response, and Peter leaned more heavily into her.

Ana sighed at the comfort that came from the warmth of his touch. Months, even weeks ago, the prospect of traveling to London again would have brought her great distress. Abbeygate had become a safe haven for her, and the looming, bustling landscape of London was overwhelming. But somehow, being with Peter quieted the noise, both inside her mind and outside the carriage. Ana pressed her cheek into his shoulder, squeezing her eyes shut. So much had changed in so little time. And now she felt as if she could never endure life without his touch, his companionship, his smile, his wry jokes.

She loved him. She could no longer deny the reality of her feelings. The comfort of waking up at his side each morning had stripped her heart bare, revealing that truth. And loving him somehow flooded her with elation and terror at the same time. Elation that she could discover so pure a love in the darkest moment of her life. Terror that she would lose him—that more important responsibilities would come along, and he would leave her, just as *Mamá* had. Just as *Papá* had.

Peter had planned this trip for Ana's benefit. Her swelling form had started to grow past the constraints of her current clothing, all except the loose night shifts and dressing gowns he had purchased for her a few months past. And although she protested that Elena could help her to make some adjustments to some of Lady Ashmore's old gowns so they would be more serviceable, Peter insisted that they would take a trip to London in search of some garments that would be comfortable for the coming months. Lady Ashmore had been kind enough to arrange for a seamstress to come to her home so Ana could have her measurements taken in a more comfortable setting, given the privacy it provided.

Ana admired Peter as they stepped out of the carriage in front of Heathridge Hall. His double-breasted greatcoat was a vibrant Prussian blue, its length long and flowing, as was the apparent style, but the cut of the garment indicated that Peter had worked directly with the seamstress to ensure it fit the demands of his daily activities. The fabric had a durable flexibility that suggested it could be worn for years without revealing signs of distress. The definition of the shoulders and collar also had a specific military-esque appearance, as well as the numerous pockets that he had apparently requested to be sewn into the interior. Ana had already seen him slip half a dozen items into his person, and he surely couldn't be storing them in his cravat.

She was sorry to see Peter's relaxed, country manner of dressing disappear for the day, but she had to admit that his slightly more formal outfit had its own type of allure. It was, in a way, reminiscent of their days in Spain. And although those memories were hazy with pain and trauma, they also had the faint, shimmering remnants of attraction. Perhaps Ana had nursed hidden feelings for her husband longer than she realized. She hoped that this trip to Heathridge Hall would have dual benefits. He needed to experience the healing of being close to his mother again after so many years, a healing that Ana desperately wished for herself, although she knew it was impossible. It would be good for them both to have this short stay.

"Mr. Ashmore, what a delight to see you."

The Ashmores' butler ushered them inside and led them up to Lady Ashmore's private sitting room, where the dowager was waiting for them, an eager smile on her face.

"Ana, my dear, you look simply beautiful. Do tell me, how are you feeling?"

As if on some cue unheard by the room, the babe placed a firm kick to Ana's ribs. Ana pressed a hand to the spot, as if patting could ease the child's motions. "Thank you. I feel well as I am able. I am much tired but happy to feel the child move in me."

A peaceful smile crossed Lady Ashmore's face, and she placed a hand on her own midsection, as if she could still feel the same movements. "That is one of the most precious experiences a woman can have."

"*Es verdad* . . . um, yes, it is true." Ana stumbled over the Spanish words that seemed to naturally make their way out of her mouth. She and Peter had been practicing using more English in the past days, knowing that Lady Ashmore didn't have the partial understanding of Spanish that Peter did. But some of the most instinctual responses always seemed to come out in her native tongue.

"I have inquired with a number of the ladies in my society about the most modern preparations to assist a mother in her lying-in and confinement, and I hope you don't mind that I've made arrangements to provide some of those comforts for you."

Ana licked her lips and darted a glance at Peter. She had always known Lady Ashmore to be exceedingly kind, but she didn't want her or the child to be a burden on her, particularly when her marriage to Peter was so unexpected. "We don't need anything so *grande*. I know Peter will care for me very well."

"I don't doubt Peter's abilities in the slightest. But I do want you to be comfortable. The process of bringing a child into this world can grow quite complicated, and it is wise to have the necessary preparations so you and your child can endure the process safely."

"Thank you, Mother," Peter interjected, "I would be most grateful for your arrangements, and I know Ana would too."

"That is what I hoped to hear. Dear Ana, I hope you know that I am so grateful to you for joining our family and for caring for my Peter, perhaps in a way I have never been able to care for him myself. I hope you will allow me to help you in any way that you might need. Do think of me as another mother. I truly desire to be that for you."

Ana's throat tightened, and her eyes blurred with tears. This genuine, natural declaration of affection from this kind woman was also the confirmation that Ana had longed for. She knew that she was wanted in this family, and not only by Peter. She also knew that she had a mother who would care for her during the difficulty of the coming months. A small piece of her heart that had been shattered so many years ago seemed to mend itself.

"Thank you," she cried as she launched herself into the woman's arms, unable to restrain her tears anymore.

"We love you," the dowager whispered as she rubbed Ana's back.

"I love you too," Ana whispered, her voice breaking. Had it truly been so many months since she had heard that she was loved? Or since she had expressed the same sentiment herself?

"Now, shall we discuss some of the arrangements we can make? Lady Gray told me of a special bed that has been invented for the lying-in process. And we must find an accoucheur to assist you. That is a modern type of male physician, dear, a discreet, gentlemanly type. An accoucheur will be precisely perfect—that is, if it is what you wish."

"I wish for anything to help that it be easier," Ana said with a laugh as she patted her belly nervously.

"One thing that will do a great deal to make things easier for now is to obtain some special stays for your condition and some dresses that will adjust with your growing form. Don't blush, Peter dear, it's not as if you've never seen your wife's stays!" Lady Ashmore chuckled.

The color of Ana's face now matched Peter's, and her gaze, like his, suddenly found great interest in the carpet. She would not be the one to reveal that although they had grown a great deal closer as of late, there was one aspect of their marriage they had yet to approach. Ana knew that Peter would never initiate that final step in their relationship. It would go against every vow he had made to protect her and honor her. And despite her savoring every kiss they shared and every moment she slept at his side, Ana likewise was not convinced she was ready for things to change further between them. Besides, the arrival of their baby was fast approaching now, which would bring a great deal of physical and emotional change as well. Perhaps it was for the best that they remain safe in the familiarity they enjoyed at present.

Chapter 25

March 10, 1814, Abbeygate, Surrey Hills, England

Peter thumbed through a stack of correspondence, wishing desperately that it would disappear. The large majority of it contained reports about Wellington's further invasions into France. He'd won significant battles at the Nive and Orthez in recent months, gaining a very real foothold against the French. Peter's regiment had been stationed in Spain for so long that he was not surprised that he hadn't been called to journey to France, but he *was* surprised that he had yet to be recalled at all. Part of him feared that he was being punished for speaking out so boldly against his superiors—that they would resist calling on him as a result. But surely they needed loyal captains who would not sell their commissions after only months of service, as so many officers of the Ton were deigned to do. They were in the middle of a war, after all. The sickening fear lay shrouded in his mind, but at moments such as these, it was difficult to ignore that possibility. Peter now had a family to support, a future to plan. He was not running away to the army to ignore life in England as he once had.

"*Hola*," Ana murmured as she entered the room, relieving him from his less-than-savory reading. He smiled, glad to banish his fears to that corner of his mind again.

"Hello, dear. Allow me to make you more comfortable," Peter said, rising from his chair to reposition the room's furniture.

Ah, he would never grow tired of the sight of his expectant wife.

Ana's new form was somehow even more beautiful than her previous one. Her gowns flowed over her round abdomen most becomingly, and her cheeks were rounded and rosy. She was prone to increased emotion—including daily bouts of tears, as she admitted herself—but she was also prone to prolonged embraces and long, lovely kisses. Although Peter knew very well that Ana's condition weighed upon her more than she would admit, he continuously admired her hopeful optimism.

Already, he found himself anticipating seeing her in this lovely condition again. That is, until he remembered what achieving such a condition would require of them both. And then he found he needed to stop staring at his wife's becoming figure and cool off out of doors.

Ana navigated Abbeygate in a new way, squeezing through doorways and bumping into furniture, unfamiliar with her newfound size. Peter found himself moving the obtrusive objects multiple times a day until the house was in a more satisfactory layout. And today was no exception. They were currently situated with the task of making the library more maneuverable so they could go over an overly large stack of unpleasant papers. Peter shoved the desk up against the wall and positioned the chairs next to it, leaving ample space around them.

"Is that all right, *querida*?"

"*Sí, gracias*," Ana murmured as she rose on her toes. Peter angled down his chin, prepared and anxious for the kiss that surely awaited him.

And it was just as delicious as every other kiss.

Peter reached out, grasping Ana's hand, and lowered her into the chair.

"Now that we are comfortable, shall we endeavor to attack the enemy at hand?"

"The enemy being *todos los papeles*?" Ana said, laughing and nodding her head at the stack.

"Precisely."

"*Bueno*, I suppose. You will have to help me so much with the *entendimiento*. You know the English is *muy complicado* in these things."

"Of course, I will help make matters clear as much as I possibly can."

Peter grabbed the papers and thumbed through them. It had been quite some time since he had looked over any sort of legal instructions. But the years he spent at university and the Inns of Court started seeping back, and the jargon began to make a bit more sense. He needed to explain the process of determining and preparing a will to Ana before the proper witness arrived for the arranging and signing of the papers.

Mother had been invaluable in helping them prepare for Ana's eventual lying-in. But this step of the preparations was somewhat less-than-savory. They needed to make sure their accounts were all settled before that time arrived in case . . . Well, in case something terrible happened to Ana or the child. But Peter could not allow his mind to spend even a moment reflecting on such a possibility. Because he did not want to endure a life without Ana.

"Right, well, shall we get started then?"

While it was a rather dampening activity to help Ana put her affairs in order to be prepared for the unlikely circumstance that her lying-in didn't proceed as they hoped, Ana was strangely calm and orderly about it all. She was very clear that she wanted everything to be arranged to give their child the greatest opportunities possible, despite the flaws of the country's laws where daughters were concerned. It was rather quick business, especially since Ana had very little to her name, all except a small family cottage in Valencia, given that it had not been claimed by some other family member, which likely already occurred.

Every time Ana mentioned her potential passing, Peter felt his chest seize and his breathing begin to quicken. The only reason he stayed somewhat calm through this process at all was because of the quick and orderly way that Ana was proceeding through it. He hoped she was acting in such a way because she felt confident that she would indeed survive.

Peter knew there was always a possibility of death when bringing a child into this world. And he was certainly acquainted with death after years in the army. It had never been a casual thing for him to see. Peter had mourned the deaths of each of his men and comrades, perhaps more than he should have. But death now had a certain terrifying finality when it was threatening someone whose life was inseparably connected to his.

"Peter, there is one thing *muy importante*," Ana said, squeezing his hand hard, her voice trembling. His eyes rose to her face in an instant, surprised to see tears brimming in her eyes. After an entire conversation of pure, reserved rationality, this emotion was concerning.

"What is it, dear?"

"The matter of inheritance." Her words were stilted, whether from emotion or difficulty of pronunciation, Peter could not tell. Ana clutched her abdomen as tears leaked down her cheeks now. "This child is not yours, Peter. Not *de verdad*."

Peter froze as his heart dropped at an alarmingly quick pace. But the child *was* his. He wanted it to be so. Whatever could she mean?

"And I no want that this be *complicado* for you in the process of inheritance. Mrs. Thompson tells me that when some *familias* receive a daughter, it is not so happy a thing for the matter of inheritance. That *quizás* some *familias* prefer a son."

Why would Mrs. Thompson say such things to Ana, even if this was an unfortunate reality in some circumstances? Peter rubbed a hand across his forehead.

"And *quizás* you want another child, one that is yours, truly yours—that child can be the one for the inheritance . . . I do not know how to say."

He stood, splaying his fingers out in front of him as he shook his head.

"Ana, we are making arrangements for your accounts, not mine."

"But we are *esposos*. We will have a child. Our accounts, they are together, no?"

Peter sighed. They were indeed married and shared nearly every aspect of their lives. But from a legal perspective, it was not so simple. But Ana needed to know that if the worst circumstances occurred, their child would be taken care of. Some part of him even hoped that the child *would* be a boy so he could show her, in a very literal sense, that this child would be his heir. But how else could he show her his loyalty to them both? He knelt in front of her chair, wrapping her hands in his.

"Ana, I promise that our child will never lack, not in a temporal sense. The child will be well provided for and have all the resources I can possibly provide." He pressed a gentle hand to the firm roundness of her belly. "I will claim the babe as my own, even if there is not some legal way to do so. This child will be mine just as much as he or she will be yours. This child, *our* child will be *loved*, Ana. By you and by me. Whether the child is a daughter or son. And I truly look forward to this addition with great anticipation, but even more than that, I look forward to creating a new family at your side, with your great passion and wisdom and love."

Ana hiccupped as a smile spread across her face.

"I will not lose you, Ana. I promise."

Chapter 26

March 29, 1814, Surrey Hills, England

Peter tried to still the trembling of his hands as he helped Ana from the carriage onto the wild grasses below. Ana would comment on it, surely, and realize how he was blastedly, annoyingly anxious about the very outing he had planned himself. Mrs. Thompson, clever as she always was, suggested that he tie a length of fabric about his wife's eyes to prolong the surprise of their special destination. He had done so, resulting in Ana's needing to lean on him more than she usually did, and he could feel the way that her walk had shifted with the additional weight of her growing child. She now took wider, slower steps, and her body rocked slightly as she moved.

It was no small feat, carrying a child. Peter knew that now more than ever. He truly believed that his wife was as strong as a soldier. Every day, her condition tried her in every sense. Even on the days when she was not sick or aching or incredibly exhausted, he knew that her condition caused great changes in her mind and sent her emotions spinning out of control. He would never assume such things, particularly since Ana was already a passionate woman who would never hesitate to speak her mind. But she had confessed as much to him. Thus, he knew she was performing a great sacrifice in carrying this child.

But he admired her greatly for it. A woman with less mental strength could be bogged down by the literal, physical reminder that she was assaulted. That reminder was growing in her each day. And his wife had suffered the effects of her attack for months, and likely still even did to a small degree. But now, Ana had chosen to allow this coming child to be an inspiration and a hope for them both. Already, the prospect of parenthood had healed them in ways he had not anticipated possible.

"*Casi llegamos?*" Ana questioned, squeezing his arm.

"Yes, dear, we're almost there."

Peter wrapped an arm around her waist, giving her extra support and balance as they rose over the lip of the gradual hill they had been climbing. Finally, they reached the view that he had hoped she would enjoy as immensely as he did. They were not near an ocean view here, as that would remind her of her hometown in Valencia. So Peter had chosen the next best destination: a vineyard. Spain was dotted with vineyards, even in the region where he had met Ana. This particular vineyard was not yet overflowing with fruit, it being March, but the snow had thawed nearly a month ago, and now green growth was beginning to curl about the wooden supports. At the edge of the vineyard, trees with sweeping limbs were sporting the first hint of white, fluffy blossoms. It was truly a stunning sight.

"We're ready," Peter whispered in Ana's ear as he worked at the knot in the fabric at the back of her head.

"*Por fin!* At long last," she huffed teasingly. Peter chuckled. How grateful he was for her ability to find levity and humor in the best and worst of situations. Even a year ago, he never would have imagined himself married, much less to someone who could make him truly laugh.

Finally, he pulled the fabric clear of her face and shoved it into his pocket. "Ana, open your eyes."

Her body was motionless, her voice silent, nothing at all like the squealing and jumping that Peter had imagined her reaction would be. "Is something the matter?" He stepped around her side, taking her by the shoulders so he could see her face. Her eyes were glittering with unshed tears, her mouth partly open in an awed expression. When she finally tore her gaze away from the scene and locked eyes with Peter, the tears spilled over her cheeks.

"I feel I am in *España*," she whispered. "I feel I am home."

An ache tore through Peter's heart at the words. She was experiencing every sentimental emotion he had hoped she would, but it was not filling him with the happiness he had imagined. Instead, he had to resist the urge to rub at his chest, so physical was the pain he felt. But why?

Because to Ana, Spain was still home.

Suddenly questioning all of his carefully made preparations, Peter moved to the side, no longer obstructing the view, and slipped an arm around Ana's waist.

After many minutes standing in silence as Ana wiped at her tears, Peter was finally brave enough to speak. "How are you faring? I did not intend to make you cry, you know."

"I cry because I am happy, silly," Ana said, blinking her dark eyes at him and smiling despite her emotion. "*Gracias*, Peter. This beautiful place make me feel so close to my country. It is perfect."

"Oh, this is only the beginning of what I have planned."

"*Qué?*"

Peter led Ana up to a table that he had specially positioned in view of the vineyard. The tabletop was swirled in vibrant floral patterns of white, blue, and red, all shining with their ceramic glaze. He swept his arm across, gesturing at the spread of delicious food he had arranged for.

"Peter! This look so delicious! And this table is so beautiful, it almost look like something . . ."

"Spanish?"

"*Sí.*"

"You once mentioned to me that Valencia was famous for its ceramic tiles. Elena assisted me in finding a merchant and collector who often visits that region, and he brought back the most beautiful table I've ever seen. I knew I had to get it for you. I thought we might take our evening lemonade at this table all summer long."

"I would love that so much!"

Peter helped Ana lower herself into her chair before reaching across the table to arrange a plate for her. Elena and Cook had been most helpful in arranging this picnic for them. In addition to a few English dishes, Elena had suggested they prepare a paella, a rice dish topped with an assortment of vegetables and chicken. Peter had something similar during his time in Spain and heartily agreed. She had also helped to prepare a sweet milky drink spiced with cinnamon called horchata. Peter never had the opportunity to try such a drink before, but he could tell from the closed-eyed bliss on his wife's face that it was more than satisfactory.

After they finished eating, Peter suggested they go sit beneath the shade of one of the blossoming trees while enjoying a slice of lemon cake.

"Shall I bring you another glass of your 'or-cha-ta'?"

"*Sí, por favor,*" Ana responded. Soon they were settled on a blanket beneath the large, flowering branches. Ana leaned forward to reach for her glass, her forehead nearly touching his. The afternoon sun cast her in spotted patterns. He was tempted to reach out and finger the spots on her cheek, as they appeared in velvet hues. Then she met his gaze with hers. In the light, Peter glimpsed facets of deep chocolate and bronze in the depths of her eyes. He stared, frozen, until she exhaled, her breath felt upon his lips, so close they were. Then she settled back, leaning against the trunk of the tree, the shade shrouding her eyes into blackness again.

He could not simply go about kissing his wife at every moment she came close to him. So he would have to distract himself. A slice of lemon cake would have to do.

"Cook certainly has outdone herself with this cake," Peter murmured as he guided another bite into his mouth.

"With *todo* she has outdone herself!" Ana exclaimed, "It is *perfecto, todo.* I do not know how she manages. But I suspect that you help her a great deal, *no*?"

"Perhaps a tad, in the planning and such." Ana's black eyebrow arched as the corner of her mouth quirked to one side. Clearly she did not believe him. "I simply wanted it to be a special day for you."

"And it has been a *día* most *especial.* I am so much grateful to you."

"I would do anything to help you, Ana. I hope you know as much."

"I do."

A gust of wind rolled through the vineyard, causing leaves to twirl on their stems and warming Peter's skin. It was hauntingly reminiscent of the region surrounding San Sebastián. How Peter wished that memory did not have to be accompanied by such horrors. But as he turned to his wife, her face was smooth and serene, her lips upturned and peaceful. Here she did not seem to be troubled by reminders of her homeland as he was. Perhaps that was something to be grateful for.

"Ana?"

"Yes?"

"Do you miss Spain very badly?"

"*Sí,*" she whispered, her voice breaking. "I miss the food, all the things so familiar to me. I miss hearing the most beautiful language all around me, like music. I miss my *familia* most of all. Every day I remember their faces, their voices." She paused, her voice thick and low with emotion. "I miss them *tanto*."

With a flush of shame, Peter realized that he hardly knew of her family. The dire conditions they had faced had forced them together out of necessity, and the physical closeness they had found had blossomed out of such circumstances. But there was still a great deal that he didn't know about her past, and that she didn't know about his.

"Do you still have family in Spain?"

"*Sí, mis abuelos*."

"Your grandparents?"

"Yes, and some aunts, uncles, and cousins as well. But many of them left Valencia long ago and move far away. Even fewer maintained contact with *mi Papá*. And so when I live with him in the army, I lose contact with them as well."

"Perhaps you could write to your grandparents. Surely they would like to hear of your whereabouts and your condition—that is, if you wanted to share such things."

"When I leave with my father, they consider me dead. *Me desheredaron*."

"They disinherited you? For following your father to war?" Peter ran a hand through his hair. It was completely confusing, all of it. "But why?"

"Because *Papá*, he choose the war instead of *Mamá*."

Peter's chest tightened, and he clenched his hands into fists. It was heartbreaking to learn how Ana's family had fallen apart, but it was even more devastating to realize that his own act of joining the army could have left his family similarly estranged. It had certainly strained his relationship with Matthew, to say the least. Had he made just as difficult, as injurious a choice as Major Bailon? But the man brought Ana with him. She had not been left at home to wonder after his well-being and whereabouts, as Matthew and Mother had in Peter's case.

"But he chose to remain with you, did he not?"

"Yes, because *Mamá* choose to leave me with him."

"Ah." Peter's heart broke anew for his wife. But as he reached out a hand to her, pulling her into his arms, her face was strangely cold and dispassionate. It seemed she did not harbor the same great mourning for her mother as she did for her father. "I apologize. I do not mean to dampen our lovely Spanish picnic with difficult memories."

"*Está bien.* It is good that you know. Perhaps I should have told you much time ago. My relationship with *Mamá* was *muy complicada,* and I not like to think on it very much." Her forehead creased and her lips pressed together in frustration or distress, Peter did not know which.

"You are already familiar with my feelings toward my father. Our relationship was just as complicated as yours, it would seem. He did not leave our family in a physical sense, but he abandoned us in every other possible way." Peter rolled his shoulders, a familiar tightening of anger already winding them upward. "In a twisted sort of way, he has become a sort of inspiration for me as I anticipate becoming a father. I must become everything that he was not. I will be faithful, attentive, understanding, and compassionate. I want to enjoy my children rather than treat them as if they are a great inconvenience, always caught underfoot. Most of all, I want them to know they are loved."

Peter's voice tightened now, his throat aching with emotion.

Ana reached for him, their fingers interlacing as she brought his hand back to rest on her rounded stomach. He paused for a moment, moving his palm about her shape until he could feel the slight movements of the babe therein.

"I understand. I know it is *difícil* to have these feelings so complicated. A parent should be a place of refuge for a child. And I know you will be that for our *bebé.* You will be a *Papá maravilloso*, Peter."

Peter moved closer until he was sitting next to her, their shoulders and knees touching. He laced his arm about her shoulders and brought her forehead to his lips.

"Thank you. And you will be a splendid mother, Ana, just as you already are."

Chapter 27

April 2, 1814, Abbeygate, Surrey Hills, England

ANA BRACED HERSELF ON ONE ELBOW, PUSHING HERSELF TO A SITting position in her bed, a task that now took a great deal more effort than it used to, now that her body swelled with child. Ever since her Spanish picnic with Peter in the vineyard, Ana's thoughts had been running through faded memories of cousins whose names she could hardly remember. Aunts who once loved to sing and dance with *Mamá*. And *Abuelita*, *Papá's* mother, who had spent endless hours playing with Ana and teaching her words in Portuguese and English. *Papá* and *Mamá* had created distance between themselves and their families that had caused Ana to feel as if they lived on the other side of the world rather than the other side of the country.

But perhaps there was something that Ana could do to remedy that, at least in some small way. And it would have to start with *Abuelita*. How had she not thought of it before?

"Elena?"

"*Sí, Señora*?"

Ana smiled at the beauty of their native tongue, continuing their conversation in Spanish. "Would you know where Peter keeps his stationery? It seems I have used the last of mine."

"I will ask Burnsey and return with some in a moment."

True to her words, Elena returned in a short moment, her arms full of a large stack of parchment and a few newly sharpened quills clutched in her hand. Ana moved over to her desk, eager to start writing. She had so much to tell her grandmother—that is, if she actually received the letter. She needed to know that she would have a great-grandchild. With an ache in her chest, Ana realized that she would also need to inform *Abuelita* of her son's passing. How she missed *Papá*.

"Elena, do you have any family left in Spain?"

Her tongue rolled, twisting delightfully around the Spanish words. Even just speaking the language of her heart brought a sense of contentment that was difficult to express to Peter.

"No, we have all come here to England, or to Portugal. The war has been so terrible for our country, you know."

"It has been heartbreaking, to lose one's country,"

"It is more than my homeland—it is who I am," Elena whispered, her voice soft and her face still with melancholy.

Ana nodded as her throat tightened with emotion. "What do you miss the very most about Spain?"

"I miss the delicious food, of course. Even just to smell it walking down the street, it was a thing of comfort. I miss the music and how people felt the music in their souls, always dancing in their words and with their feet. But most of all, I miss the feeling of being understood. That bone-deep comprehension of each other's experiences, each other's challenges, just by sharing the same language and same country."

"It is a miracle to experience, truly," Ana murmured.

"It is impossible for the English to understand," Elena continued, her dark eyes shining with emotion as she twisted her apron. "To them, everything foreign is bad. They see how I look different, hear the accent in my voice, and they fear me. They assume I am dangerous, or at the very least, entirely uncivilized and minimally educated. All the things that make me belong to my heritage, my culture, seem to be all wrong here."

Ana had seen that same shock and alarm on too many faces as she and Peter traveled across the ocean, and then again as they made their way up to London—although she much preferred those sorts of reactions, as uncomfortable as they were, to the disgusting leers she had endured too often at camp in San Sebastián. Peter had protected her in so many ways by bringing her here, to Abbeygate.

"Your *Pedro* was the first to recognize that my heritage could mean something good—not just for you but for your family. He is special."

"I know. I am most fortunate to have found him. I would not have survived without him." Ana's hand went to her rounded stomach, feeling for the movements of her baby as her throat choked with emotion.

Peter did so much to ensure her comfort in every way imaginable. And on the whole, Ana truly was feeling safer and happier than she had in quite a long time. Every day, she spent time with the man she cared most for in the world. Every night, her babe tapped out rhythms on her stomach, which were normally delightful though occasionally exhausting. The ache of the absence of *Papá* was beginning to lessen somewhat, just as it had for *Mamá* years ago.

But still, there was a portion of her soul that would always yearn for Spain. And that was something Peter would never truly understand. But perhaps reestablishing this relationship with *Abuelita* would satisfy that yearning in some small way.

Chapter 28

May 5, 1814, Surrey Hills, England

Peter sat back in his saddle, surrounded by the quiet morning of the Surrey Hills. The only noise that interrupted his heightened breathing and pounding pulse was the warbling of a few insistent birds. It would have to do. Normally, such surroundings brought him a steadying peace. But not this morning.

Isolation. That had been his aim. He did not want Ana overhearing his cursing or outburst when he read the missive that had arrived late last night for him. His name and address were scrawled in an unfamiliar hand, although the army's official crest indicated the letter's origin. Fear squeezed Peter's heart. This was no letter from David or Matthew, or even Captain Davies. This would be a summons, likely back to battle.

A cruel fate it would be indeed to be recalled weeks before the birth of their baby, when Ana would need him most. She had already lost her father. And, somehow, her mother. How would she fare if she lost Peter, and in such a needful and delicate time? Peter knew that on his part, life in the army would never be the same again. Not after San Sebastián—not after Ana. Instead of being an escape, a place of relief, being at camp and on the road in foreign lands would fill him with loneliness and longing. He felt it already, just at the thought of leaving Ana and Abbeygate. Would he really be called back, forced to end the lives of so many when the tiniest, most precious life was just beginning back at home? Would his child even know his face, his voice? The grip that fear had on his heart clenched ever tighter.

Peter offered up a desperate prayer and allowed his mind to spin through the comforting verses he had studied in the Bible that very morning. If there were ever a moment to need God's strength, it was now. For this letter could decide his entire future—not only with the army but with his family. Finally, he tore through the wax seal. The letter within was not signed, nor addressed specifically to him. It must have been a mass communication sent out to officers.

> *Paris is secured. Napoleon has been deposed, abdicated by the French Senate. Wellington was hailed a hero and was made the Duke of Wellington on 3 May 1814. An armistice was signed on 23 April 1814, and a treaty is currently being constructed between France and the Sixth Coalition, including Great Britain, Prussia, Portugal, Russia, Austria, Spain, Sweden, Sardinia, and a number of German States. This will ensure that stolen and conquered territories are returned to their respective countries, reducing the expanded borders of France.*

Peter's heart thudded irregularly in his chest. His shoulders had been wound so tightly, his chest tight, braced for pain . . . but instead, relief flooded him. He hardly knew whether to whoop with joy or to set back immediately to tell Ana. Instead, he slid off Warrior and planted his knees into the dewy morning earth. Tears trickled down his face, catching in his rough whiskers.

"Thank you, God, for saving many people from continued war. Thank you for this second chance at life, at forming some sort of home and family. Thank you for Ana and our child. Thank you for peace."

Peter rubbed trembling hands over his face, breathing deeply. No longer would he have to prepare to face home with devastating, heartbreaking news of a recall. Instead, he would return to Ana, renewed and reinvigorated with a passion to make everything right before her lying-in time—before the babe would arrive. He would get to treasure the precious moment of holding his wife *and* his infant child.

Inevitably, an official assignment would come again, but Peter would surely be spared at least a few months in the peaceful wake of the end of such a long and disastrous war. Finally, he longed for a respite from his duties. He longed to be home. And it seemed God would grant him an answer to that prayer.

He hopped to his feet and mounted Warrior in a smooth, learned motion. After snapping the reins and shifting forward in his saddle, they set off at a gallop toward Abbeygate. The ride was not a short one, but after what seemed to be only a few moments, he was arriving at the stables, handing the reins to the stablehand, and bounding through the back entrance of Abbeygate.

"Ana!" he yelled. "Ana, where are you?"

"Peter?" Ana's voice trembled as she descended the stairs as quickly as her cumbersome form would allow. Her brow was wrinkled in concern as she hurried toward him. He had frightened her.

"All is well, my dear. Forgive me for startling you."

"*Qué?*" Ana whispered after folding herself into his arms.

"Only the most wonderful of things. Napoleon's army has been defeated, and he is to be exiled. The Allied forces are returning home. The war is over."

"So you not leave me?"

"I will not leave you, Ana. I will be here for you and our babe."

Ana let out a sob, a sound that was part relief and part joy, and pressed her lips against his. She tossed herself into his arms anew, and Peter's knees buckled at her weight and his emotion. They knelt on the floor, there in the hallway, making a great heap of their embracing arms and mingling tears as they thanked God profusely for hearing their prayers.

Chapter 29

May 18, 1814, Abbeygate, Surrey Hills, England

"Peter, do be a dear and fetch Ana's favorite chair from the drawing room and bring it up here."

"To our bed . . . *my* bedroom?" Peter's neck heated at the implication of his question.

"Yes, dear," Mother said, unable to hide the laughter in her voice. "Ana will require a comfortable place to sit as she is tending to the babe throughout the night."

"Yes, Mother."

"Oh, and Peter?"

Peter turned, cocking his head as if to ask whatever else Mother could require. "I am not surprised in the least that Ana is sharing your bedroom," she said, "so you needn't continue to pretend that it is yours alone."

"Very well," Peter choked, then nearly ran from the room. Apparently Mother had guessed at the true progression of his relationship with Ana.

Preparations for Ana's confinement had officially begun. The birth of their child would be, at the physician's best estimate, only a few weeks away, and it was Peter's priority to ensure that she be given the greatest accommodations to ensure her health and safety. Mother had been a great help in arranging these things. She had even found a highly acclaimed accoucheur to assist in the lying-in time and a monthly nurse to help Ana with her recovery afterward. Ana's bedroom had started to be transformed into the lying-in chamber. Her bed was moved to the far wall, and an innovative bed now stood in its place. A new table had been brought in to house the supplies needed for the lying-in and recovery, as well as a few additional chairs. It unnerved Peter somewhat after spending too much time in battlefield medical tents visiting his wounded men.

Peter reached the drawing room downstairs, squatting to brace his legs with strength as he hefted the armchair into his grasp.

Fortunately, Ana was staying in his room now and had been for a number of months now. Peter didn't know if he would ever be able to sleep again without her warm form pressed up against his side. The velvet softness of her skin was intoxicating, and her slow, insistent kisses drove him nearly to madness. The thin boundary that remained between them, held there by the insistence of his honor, seemed to waver every time she pulled him to her lips. In such moments, he frantically reminded himself how incredibly uncomfortable she already was in her current condition, in addition to the shadows of her past. She did not need any sort of pressure from him. And he certainly found enough satisfaction in her kisses and companionship alone.

How would he ever survive without her when he was recalled to the army?

Even more than her presence in his arms, his bed, Peter found he could no longer live without her company and her character. Her quick wit brought him out of any dark memory, and her compassionate speaking had already made him more of a caring neighbor and friend. And the tender way she spoke of their child made him dream of the future—and future children—in a way he had never allowed himself to do. The fear of the reality of death on the battlefield had limited his vision and imagination to merely surviving the next day. He had never allowed himself the privilege of thinking of the next month, let alone years in the future. But now, with Ana, he envisioned them taking their nightly lemonade on the terrace, surrounded by a great gaggle of toddling children, blissfully, incandescently happy. Happiness. That was something he had certainly never guessed he would achieve in life, but it was a treasure he had already found in the presence of his darling wife.

That said, they would likely both be a great deal more comfortable once their child was no longer performing a jig in Ana's stomach each night. Her moaning, tossing, and turning kept both of them up each night. Peter only wished there was something more he could do to ease her comfort. And so he was following Ana's every bidding and Mother's every command in rearranging their rooms for the imminent birth of their child.

Peter carefully squeezed the stuffed armchair through their bedroom door, finally bringing it to rest at their bedside with a great heave and a satisfied sigh.

"Peter, *es perfecto*!" Ana exclaimed from the doorway adjoining their rooms. "Thank you." She crossed the room, rose on her tiptoes, and brushed a kiss against his cheek. Peter noted that Mother was conveniently occupying herself with the bedclothes, her lips curved knowingly with a smile. So Peter took advantage of the moment. He pressed his lips quickly but firmly to Ana's, breathing in her contact as if it were just as necessary to his survival as air.

"I do wish the two of you could have visited us for the ball at Heathridge Hall," Mother said. "I would have loved to present you to my friends. And our home looked more beautiful than I ever remember it being." A peaceful, serene smile crossed her lips as she folded yet another incredibly small piece of clothing for the baby.

It had been the first large event Mother had hosted since she was out of mourning, and she had been talking—and writing—about it ever since it occurred two weeks past. To see hope in his mother's eyes again buoyed Peter up in a way that was hard to express. For so many years, he had longed to wipe the grief-worn lines from her brow. And even now, he had not been able to do so. But Matthew had.

"I am truly sorry we couldn't be there, Mother. But as you know, Ana's condition would not allow us to travel and stay at such a late event. She requires much rest, particularly now."

However, the true reason for declining the invitation was because Peter had been fearful of who might be there. Would they encounter a fellow soldier who knew Ana? Would someone guess at their plight? He could not risk it. The privacy and seclusion afforded by Abbeygate was a blessing, one that would not last forever.

"Of course, dear, I don't hold it against you in the slightest. I understand completely why you were unable to attend. But it was a most wonderful night, particularly for Matthew."

"Matthew—he become betrothed, no?"

"Yes, and to the most wonderful woman," Mother gushed, placing a hand to her heart.

Peter gripped the back of the stuffed armchair, adjusting it slightly yet again. Of course Matthew would have an ideal betrothal, one that Mother would be proud of. It seemed yet another example proving why Peter was a disappointment.

"She is kind and humble and compassionate, much like yourself, Ana," Mother continued. "In fact, I believe that the two of you will become dear friends and sisters. That is, once your condition permits that you can meet her."

Peter's fumbling with the furniture paused as he slowly raised his eyes to his wife. Theirs had not been a typical betrothal or marriage. Indeed, nothing about their lives would ever be typical or normal. But Mother was clearly able to recognize the unique ability that Ana had to spread love through her eager expressions of affection and fond embraces. A rush of warmth clouded Peter's chest. Perhaps finding some measure of comfort within his family would not be as impossible as it felt, at least not with Ana at his side.

"And why she not come here with Matthew?" Ana turned to Peter, reaching for his hand. He folded her hand into his eagerly, rubbing his thumb over hers. Her gaze was bright, shining with that same hope that reflected in Mother's eyes.

"Dear, it is a particularly lovely idea. But with your lying-in soon approaching, I am not certain that making plans to receive visitors for an extended period is the wisest idea."

"Oh, not now. After the *bebé* perhaps? After the *boda*? The wedding? *Quizás* that time will be easier for us all."

"They are to be married in June," Mother interjected. "The timing of it all would work rather well."

Peter sighed. He knew that the recovery after the confinement period could be difficult; Mother had told him as much. But if he was completely honest with himself, he was more nervous about the prospect of hosting his brother in his home at such a vulnerable time, particularly when they had not yet had the opportunity to resolve things between them.

"Very well, dear," Peter said to Ana. "If that is what you wish."

Chapter 30

June 8, 1814, Abbeygate, Surrey Hills, England

The very day Ana had been born, *Mamá* had walked all the way to the square from their home just on the outskirts of town to buy food for the day. When she had nearly arrived home, her waters came rushing, and *Papá* carried her the rest of the way, which Ana had always thought was terribly romantic. Within only a few hours, *Mamá* had her new babe in arms. She always attributed the speed of Ana's arrival to her long walk in the fresh air, in addition to her brief stop at the *Catedral* to pray to the *Virgen María.*

Ana's current experience could not be more different. Instead of having the luxury of moving about outside to combat the pains heating her back and midsection, she was confined to her room and, most often, her bed. Even the windows were locked shut and the curtains drawn. The accoucheur protested that opening a window could increase the risk of Ana falling ill, but she ironically felt even worse stuffed up in the warm room. It was entirely uncomfortable, particularly the bed that Ana was confined to. It was lightweight and would make it quite easy to change the linens, but it certainly was not as comfortable as Peter's bed.

In their preparations, they had arranged her adjoining dressing room into somewhat of a gathering room for Peter. There was also a makeshift bed arranged for the monthly nurse. It had all resulted in quite a crowded affair, but Lady Ashmore had insisted these preparations would make her lying-in and recovery much easier.

Lady Ashmore had requested a wet nurse, but Ana had finally strongly insisted that this additional arrangement was entirely unnecessary. She may not experience the lying-in period that had been typical for her own mother, but she would nurse her own child, much like her mother had done and her grandmother before her.

Ana lay flat on her back, breathing slowly and heavily, in an effort to stave off the growing sharpness of the pain surrounding the lower half of her body. Elena pressed a cool cloth against her forehead.

"I need to move. *Por favor*," she moaned. "It cannot hurt the *bebé*. It will help me, no?"

"Married to the son of an earl and she hasn't bothered to properly learn English. A great shame it is," the monthly nurse, Nurse Williams, grumbled in the corner, clearly believing that Ana could not understand her. "You simply cannot allow her to leave the bed. Her temper, her passions, could run wild. Your reputation as a physician could very well be put at risk."

Ana clutched the sheets to keep herself from springing from the bed and running from the room, pains and all. Women like Nurse Williams were not understanding in the least and certainly not forgiving. If Ana lost her temper, she would jump to even more judgmental conclusions and would quickly start blaming Ana's intelligence or nationality for any issues between them. In this very moment, when Ana's life—and more importantly, the life of her child—could very well be at risk if even the slightest complications arose, tension and arguments would not help either of them. Ana would simply have to do what she had always done when her wisdom or her character had been questioned by soldiers, foreigners, or even *Mamá*. She would clench her jaw and bite her tongue to ensure that a word would never escape her lips.

But then another, stronger wave of pain struck Ana. She could not help but moan aloud. Dr. Lee, the short, stocky accoucheur, had beady eyes that were darting between Ana and Nurse Williams while his nervous hand brushed a few spindly hairs over his balding head.

"Mrs. Ashmore, with my assistance, I will allow you to move about the bedroom." Hope filled Ana's chest like a full breath of air, such as the type of breath that had evaded her for months now, thanks to the growing body inside her. Now she just needed her husband beside her, to support her physically just as much as emotionally.

"Peter can help me?"

"I am afraid it cannot be permitted. It could be unsafe to allow him inside while you are in such a delicate state."

That puff of air deflated as quickly as it had come. Dr. Lee held out a hand to Ana, and Nurse Williams reluctantly moved to her side, helping her to rise to a sitting position once the wave of cramping passed.

* * *

"Mrs. Ashmore . . ."

"It's Ana!" she nearly yelled as the pain-filled pressure heaved downward yet again. The baby had to be nearing birth now. She had been exerting all her strength in pushing for what felt like hours. And her patience for hearing her formal name had at last worn thin.

"Very well, Ana," the physician finally surrendered, his voice urgent. "The baby is in position. You're very nearly there. Push again, please."

Ana moaned through a wave of agony and then began to move her trembling limbs when relief finally came. But nearly as soon as it passed, another wave attacked her.

"Yes, that is precisely it. Now, please bring your knees forward a bit more."

She complied and groaned as force and pain mounted. Then pressure flooded Ana's body. She found she could not contain her vocalizing; her yelling was innate and visceral. Elena gripped her hands. Somehow Ana's body knew what to do, and she pushed with all her might.

"That's it, Ana. Wonderful, wonderful!"

One last strong push, and there was a splash and a thump and a great, blissful relief. A small, wet, wriggling form was plopped into

Ana's arms, and the most heavenly, helpless cry mingled in the air in perfect harmony with Ana's own sobs of joy. Tears blurred her vision, and she blinked hard as she looked into the small, delicate face of her baby . . . her *daughter.*

"*She is a girl, Elena*!" Ana exclaimed in Spanish. "*I have a daughter!*"

"*Hermosa!*" Elena responded, her voice filled with awe.

Small, perfect lips. Dark, wide eyes that were now blinking against the harsh light of a new world. And wet, messy hair that was already curling insistently, so similar to Ana's own hair. A ferocious feeling of protective, all-encompassing love slammed into Ana as she pressed the babe to her skin. This child was her flesh and blood. Part of her very soul. Ana very nearly laughed as pure elation and relief coursed through her. This was heaven. It had all been well worth it.

Still, distant painful memories pushed at the safe bliss that surrounded them, reminding her that *Mamá* had borne her in a similar manner, *Papá* had treasured her tiny body in this same way, and it had not been enough to keep them.

"I will protect you from the bad things of this world," she whispered. "I will not abandon you. *Te lo prometo.*"

* * *

Finally, Peter was to be allowed into the lying-in chamber.

Before Dr. Lee could even fully and properly open the door, Peter pushed past him and very nearly ran to his wife's side. She was now comfortably resting in her bed, the temporary birthing bed discarded to the side of the room. And while exhaustion was written all over the lines in her brow, the circles beneath her eyes, and the trembling of her hands, pure, unrestrained happiness shone from her gaze, unlike he had ever seen before. It brought tears to his eyes and made his knees buckle, bringing him to his knees at her bedside.

"How are you?" he whispered, his voice hoarse.

"*Perfecto,*" she murmured. "I am mother to *un ángel.*"

"It was . . . beyond frustrating that they would not allow me to be here at your side."

"Dr. Lee says it was for my health."

"But I needed to witness your health, your well-being, for myself," Peter said, his voice breaking. "I needed to protect you." The helplessness that had him pacing all throughout the house like an injured beast was akin to the desperation that he had felt upon finding her after the siege. Never had he felt such panic, such distress. His need to ensure Ana's safety had very nearly become his purpose for living, and being separated from her, even for the space of a day, had almost made him a madman.

"Peter, *amor*, I am safe," Ana said. "I did not need protection. I am well."

"You are so strong. So brave. You are simply marvelous," Peter breathed into Ana's neck as he embraced her with gentle, careful hands.

"And so is she." Ana tilted her arms, exposing the tiny, caramel-toned face that had been previously lost in a bundle of swaddling.

"She?" Peter choked, emotion clogging his throat.

"Meet my . . . our daughter, Esperanza."

Hot tears doused Peter's cheeks and he blinked rapidly, not wanting to miss even the smallest detail of the tiny being his wife had brought into the world. Dark, wavy hair capped the top of her perfectly round head, and bow-like lips wiggled in an echo of sucking. She was already learning to love her mother's sustenance, it seemed. Peter's gaze darted to Ana's form again, just now seeing the loose gown she wore. It had quite a low neckline and two buttons at the front, likely making it easy to feed the needy babe. Her body was clearly swollen and exhausted from the immense transformation she had just endured, but to him, Ana had never appeared more beautiful. Pure, abiding love wrapped around Peter like an embrace, and he found himself weeping again. He rose to press a gentle kiss to Ana's lips.

"Say her name again for me, please, that I might pronounce it correctly."

"Esperanza."

"Esperanza," he repeated slowly, feeling out the inflection of the syllables. "A beautiful name. What does it mean?"

"Hope. Because she is my little hope."

"She is *our* little hope." He pressed a kiss to the top of her head, and Ana María turned, tipping up her chin to welcome his lips and his embrace.

"Esperanza seems a fine name for such an adorable babe, but also a mighty long one. And it never sounds as beautiful off my tongue as it does yours, although I do practice, I swear. I think I shall call her Essie for short."

"Essie," Ana repeated, as if tasting the name for its authenticity. "Yes, *está bien*."

"Well then, may I hold her?" Peter's palms were sweating, reflecting both his eagerness and his nervousness to hold his daughter. But at his inquiry, a new emotion rippled across Ana's face, her lips tight, jaw clenched.

"Yes."

"Are you certain you're all right?"

"*Por supuesto*," she said, shaking her head slightly. She met his eyes again, and her expression was clear of whatever tension had clouded it a moment earlier. Her smile warmed him as she held out the small, squirming bundle.

"*Hola*," he whispered. A sniffle sounded at his side as Ana's head came to rest on his shoulder. "*Hola, mi ángel*."

* * *

After Peter held Esperanza and arranged Ana more comfortably for a nap, he slipped from the bedroom into the dressing room, intent on speaking with Nurse Williams. He had not been so overcome by the blissful moment with his daughter that he had been blind to a certain appalling behavior interrupting Ana's peace and care. And he would always listen to his wife's needs, whether they were expressed in English or Spanish.

"*Pedro, te necesito*," she had moaned.

That, Peter had understood perfectly. His wife required his help. He hurried to her side but didn't miss Nurse Williams's grumbling about Ana's audacity to speak another language in her presence, despite Elena being there to help translate. Peter had balled his fists as he lowered himself to sit on Ana's bedside.

"Yes, dear? How can I assist you?"

"The nurse. I know your *mamá* says she is so *buena*. But I no can continue with her. She is so *terrible* to me." Tears simmered in her eyes. Elena pressed a cool cloth to her forehead, whispering in a calming manner. Anger clenched in Peter's stomach, hot and insistent. He would not allow this fool of a nurse to threaten his wife's safety and recovery. He would protect her.

"*No hay problema, amor.* I will take care of it, I promise."

And now he was fulfilling that promise. He approached Nurse Williams in two quick steps, his voice thundering.

"Nurse Williams, you are dismissed."

The woman lifted her sharp chin, her nose wrinkling with indignation. "Mr. Ashmore, do you have the faintest idea of what your mother has paid for my services? She would not agree with my dismissal."

"I believe she would. Because Mother cares about Ana's happiness, recovery, and well-being, and you, it would seem, do not."

"It is awfully presumptuous of you to dismiss me over a mere disagreement."

"It was not a mere disagreement. You purposefully insulted my wife's home country and intelligence and even brought into question her being worthy of your attention. You need to know that Mrs. Ashmore has seen more difficulty in her life than you could ever imagine. And not only is she strong and resilient, but she has also made this home a welcoming place for her culture and fiercely loyal heart. You would have been fortunate to spend the month here learning from her. And perhaps if you would learn from her compassion, you could have a more promising future."

"Oh, I can promise you, I would not learn anything from that woman."

"And thanks to that woman, her husband, and her mother-in-law of great influence, you will have great difficulty finding any ladies who would be interested in your services ever again. Unless, that is, you resolve to treat your patients based on their needs and not on their country of origin."

The thin, wiry woman was speechless, her mouth opening and closing several times before she sneered at him, grabbed her things, and stomped from the room.

Now, there was one final matter of business. Peter opened the door and found Mrs. Thompson waiting eagerly at the end of the hallway. "Mrs. Thompson?"

"Yes?"

"My wife was delivered of the child quite prematurely. The physician estimates about six weeks or so. Even still, the babe, a lass, is quite healthy and faring well."

"And we are quite glad for it, Mr. Ashmore. A blessed babe she will be."

"Any reports that are to be made should mention the earliness of her arrival and her good health. Am I understood?"

"Of course." Her brows raised in questioning, but Peter saw a fierce loyalty shine in her eyes. Ana had grown quite close to this faithful woman. They could all trust her to convey this important message.

"We simply wish nobody to be concerned."

"Certainly." Mrs. Thompson bobbed a curtsey and continued on her way.

Peter's stiff posture slackened in relief . . . but also due to a familiar sensation of helplessness. He was amazed at the great feat his wife had just accomplished in bringing their babe to the world. But in holding that impossibly tiny child, fear had doused him. He had spent so much time trying to become a good husband that he had completely neglected any sort of preparation to aid him in becoming a father. What was worse still, the time he had spent with Ana earlier today showed him that he had very little to offer them both at present. He could not feed the hungry, needy babe. He could not help Ana heal as a physician or monthly nurse would. Yes, Peter could offer them love, support, and company but little else. Most of all, he did not wish to alarm or overwhelm Ana when she had just undergone something so entirely life-changing.

Peter ached to hold his wife. But perhaps it would be better for all of them if he allowed Ana the peace and privacy he needed during this time of healing and learning.

Chapter 31

June 14, 1814, Abbeygate, Surrey Hills, England

Ana reached for the small buttons at the front of her soft, cream-colored dress, unfastening them to prepare to feed Esperanza. Tiny, bowed pink lips wrapped around her breast, latching and sucking with a pinch of pain. It had taken some time to learn to feed her small babe. Nursing was not as intuitive as the monthly nurse had protested it would be. And she had scoffed when Ana had worried about discomfort. What a great relief it was that Peter had dismissed her. But he had not done so before the woman's cruel words had planted seeds of doubts in Ana's already exhausted mind.

Perhaps she was not capable of being the mother that Esperanza needed. A better mother would not have complained about the pain of feeding her child. A better mother would think nothing of the aching that stabbed through her each time she rose from her chair or took steps to the water closet. A better mother would welcome others into her home to meet her new babe, no matter how it wreaked havoc on her unbalanced emotions and tender anxieties. But Ana would not leave her child to be tended to by others. She would, at the very least, be a better mother than her own *mamá* had been in that regard. But the pressure of it all, increased by Ana's helplessness in caring for her own recovery, made her feel like she was drowning.

That feeling was only worsened by Peter. It seemed he was retreating from her. He was incredibly attentive to Esperanza, always eager to change her *pañales* or rock her to sleep at night. He often asked if there was more he could do to help the babe. But did he not see how desperately Ana needed help herself?

He had always been dependable. Steady. Safe. Consistent. And yet it seemed that he could be that for Ana no longer. The blissful feeling of being cared for—understood, protected—that she had enjoyed for months was crumbling. Of course, Peter would never hurt her intentionally. He was too honorable. But now it was clear that his priority was to fulfill his honor-bound responsibility to protect her and provide her a safe place to deliver her child. Nothing more. They would not truly be a family, not as she had dreamed. She was nothing more than a task to be completed in his life. How inconvenient she must be.

First *Papá*. Then *Mamá*. Now Peter too. But she could not bear to see him distance himself from her. She would not survive him leaving her. Would she have to leave him first if it came to that?

Esperanza was no longer sucking, her hungry fists now relaxed as her breaths came slow and sleepily. The only moments of peace and clarity came when her daughter was in her arms, against her skin. Ana brushed kisses down the babe's velvety cheek and set her down in her cradle. She was suddenly incredibly thirsty, and the glass on her bedside table was empty. Bracing herself on the arms of the chair, Ana gingerly stood. The throbbing pain transported her somewhere else entirely. Smoke and sweat stifled her breathing, and tears dripped off her chin as she stumbled over rocky, uneven ground in search of *Papá*. Such a similar pain laced down her hips and legs, so familiar that Ana grasped her dress, feeling for the rips and the burn marks.

And then Peter had been there. He had protected her. Rescued her. Bound her wounds and nursed her to health, emotionally just as much as he had physically. But would he abandon her now? After all he had done to ensure her safety?

* * *

"Ah, the budding new father himself."

"Sir Huntington," Peter replied. "Thank you for coming."

"Do call me David, please," the man said, his smile deep. "It may seem boyish, but it is what your brother has called me since our school days together. I find the familiarity to be fitting with any Ashmore."

David had sent a missive informing Peter that he would be in town and asking him to meet at the local café so his visit would not disturb Ana. Peter was grateful for an excuse to leave the house. The tightness that constantly bound his chest seemed to loosen upon seeing another soul outside his household.

"How fares Mrs. Ashmore?"

"I believe she is well."

"You *believe* so?"

Peter's thoughts blurred with anxieties, desperate for an outlet. So much had changed in so little time. But Matthew and Mother trusted David deeply, treated him as family even. Perhaps Peter should do so as well.

"Well, since Esperanza was born, she has seemed entirely independent. Before, she valued my help, or at the very least, my thoughts. Now it seems that she desires to do everything by herself. And it leaves me feeling more helpless than I can express."

Even more distressing was the feeling that the tender affection they had shared was seeping away. The time when they had enjoyed kisses and embraces and shared the same bed now felt like an entire lifetime ago.

"Well, perhaps I have a reason for you to renew your efforts to help her—to break down whatever barriers she might be hiding behind."

"Oh? And what would that reason be?"

Regret and pain shone on David's face. "I have heard tell that your regiment is being called back to Spain. And so your time with your wife and new little daughter may be more limited than you expected."

While panic seized Peter's chest, he was not entirely surprised at the news. His regiment was made of foot guards. They were rigorously trained and held to the highest standards of discipline. In short, they were a valuable asset and likely should have been recalled earlier. Then again, he had been quite vocal about his opinions regarding leadership's approach to San Sebastián, so perhaps that extended leave had been intentional.

"Who told you as much?

"Captain Davies."

Peter dropped his head into his hands. Once, Captain Davies had been a trusted friend. Their men had worked closely together, and Davies had trained him in his duties as a new captain years ago. But it seemed that his fear of crossing his superiors had drawn a line between them since the sacking. Peter hadn't heard from him in months. Still, the remnants of friendship had instilled in him enough loyalty to warn Peter that they would be leaving. And the man hadn't the faintest idea that Peter was a father now. He would be shocked.

"I cannot understand how it must feel to leave your daughter. But I do recall how I mourned leaving my sisters the first time I was recalled. I thought my heart would burst at the sound of their weeping and begging me to stay. It still brings tears to my eyes to think about it now." David wiped a hand over his face. "Tell me how I can help your family, and I will be at your service in an instant."

"Thank you for being a loyal friend to me just as much as you have been to Matthew over the years. I hardly find myself deserving of such kindness."

"I have seen how much your mother *and* Matthew have missed you. And now I have seen the hope restored to their home upon your return. It has healed a wound Matthew has nursed for too many years."

Peter wondered at that. Matthew had given no indication that the tension that had existed between them had loosened. True, he had never treated Peter with contempt or bitterness for leaving. But Peter had always imagined he had harbored such feelings. What if he had merely longed to have a brother close again?

"Even more than that, you accomplished what I most desire in this world: to have a family. I envy you, brother. I would be a married man and the father of a fine gaggle of children if I had found the right lady by now."

Peter chuckled too at that. "I admit I had not imagined such a future for myself. And while it is a complicated one, it is also incredibly fulfilling. I have not felt such peace in . . . well, in my entire life, as I have these past months being married to Ana."

"And your mother has noted that change in you and told me as much. Since I do not have my own family to care for, I will care for yours. I will not easily allow such a sweet family to be broken up over a badly timed recall, and I intend to assist your mother and Matthew in any way that I can in supporting your Mrs. Ashmore."

Peter's throat tightened with emotion at the thought of leaving his little family, and so soon. But didn't he know this was inevitable? Could he truly have expected otherwise? He had spent years in the army and had always known he would be recalled at any time. But perhaps that was one reason why he had never gone home for a long period before. Because if he had done so, he might have never returned.

He might not even return now. There was always the option of selling his commission. It was his property, his right to sell, although the practice of gentlemen achieving a certain rank for money or prestige and then selling their commission unexpectedly was one of his great frustrations of the army. It made it difficult to maintain effectiveness and consistency when their leaders were constantly wavering and leaving. He had always looked down his nose at such men. Thought them foolish for betraying their responsibility to God, the Crown, and their men. But he had never stopped to consider that many of those men might be returning to wives and children who needed them desperately. It certainly changed his perspective now.

* * *

Ana ventured downstairs for a rare breath of fresh air on the terrace. Lowering herself into a chair while she clutched Esperanza in the other was no easy feat. Her body was slow to recover. But feeling the warmth of the evening air helped to clear the fog that made it so difficult for her to concentrate as of late. And hearing the song of the nightingale reminded her that there was a calm world outside her tumultuous mind.

She wasn't certain when the anticipation of Peter's presence had started to make her so nervous. But whenever he offered to help her with Esperanza, it made her feel as though she was not capable of caring for the babe herself. Perhaps he recognized her faults as a mother and was trying to cover them with his own efforts.

But deep inside her heart, Ana knew that his presence pained her because it reminded her that their arrangement was entirely too temporary. It would not remain like this forever. He would be called back to his responsibilities as a captain in the *armada* and would be leaving her, much as *Papá* and *Mamá* had done. And why would she prolong the inevitable pain of his leaving by allowing him a greater place in her heart, in Esperanza's heart? No, she needed to do it all on her own. His absence would require such independence from her.

Army life did not lend itself to attentive fatherhood, in her experience. Perhaps that was why Peter always mentioned he had never planned to be married or have children. In all likelihood, they were a great inconvenience to him now, and he would be more than glad to return to the army. It had always seemed that *Papá* was at his happiest when he was away. Why would it be any different for Peter? She would not allow herself or Esperanza to be dealt the same heartbreak that she received from *Papá's* recurrent absence. She knew better than anyone how it broke *Mamá*—broke her so completely that she couldn't even be bothered to take young Ana with her when she abandoned *Papá*.

None of it was rational. Ana wanted to believe that Peter was not like *Papá*. He was not blinded by his responsibilities to his country—not so blinded that his family would crumble and he wouldn't even notice. He was not leaving her, at least not now. But that rationality couldn't discount the very real panic that descended upon her when she saw Peter. It made her pulse quicken to a sickening rate, and not in the delightful way it had before when she was anticipating an embrace or a kiss. How had everything gone so terribly wrong in only a matter of weeks?

"Might I join you?"

Peter. Ana's entire body tensed, her arms tightening instantly around Esperanza. Her moment of solace had been cut short again.

"*Por supuesto.*" *Of course.*

"Can I interest you in some horchata?"

Cook had been making the drink after Elena taught her to do so for their vineyard outing. And Ana would utter no complaint about it. She nodded and darted a glance at Peter's face as he poured her a generous cupful. His normally open expression was clouded with tension. A muscle jumped in his jaw, and he bit on the inside of his cheek, as he often did when he was nervous. The anxiety that Ana harbored began to lessen out of concern for the man that she loved much more than she dared to admit. Horchata forgotten.

For the first time in weeks, she crossed the invisible threshold between them, reached for his hand, and squeezed twice. But instead of squeezing in response, Peter's jaw only tightened. Ana's heart pounded dangerously fast.

"What is the matter?" she managed, her voice high with fear.

"I have received quite a bad bit of news."

Ana's stomach squeezed with pain. She wrapped one hand around her middle, as if that would keep her from falling apart. "You are leaving."

"Sir Huntington paid me a visit. It seems that the regiment is going to be called back within a month or so . . ." The roaring of blood in Ana's ears quickly drowned out Peter's explanation as she bounced Esperanza in her arms at an increasing speed.

He was leaving them both. Her daughter would grow up without a father, at least an available one. And she, without a husband. How had she ever allowed herself to enter into such a marriage? To create such a mess for herself? Now the agonies of her own childhood were to repeat themselves, and Ana simply could not bear it.

"You need not share your plans with me," she burst out, squeezing her eyes shut against his reaction, but shocked silence was heavy in the air.

"I thought you would be grateful for my honesty. I did not wish to repeat my mistake of keeping these things from you. I only wish to give us more time to prepare for my absence. There are plans to be made to ensure that you and Esperanza will be—"

"I have been preparing already," Ana interrupted, schooling her features to reflect a calm demeanor instead of the panicked hurt that was tearing apart her heart on the inside. "Simply tell me when you leave."

And, it seemed, that silenced him. Surprise lifted his brows and clamped his lips shut. "Ah. I see," he managed before awkward silence enveloped the space between them. "I have not yet received official notice of the recall, but Sir David has led me to believe it will be in about a month's time."

"Very well." Ana rose on trembling legs, no longer able to endure Peter's presence. One look into his crystal eyes and she would be falling apart, sobbing, begging him to stay. But such things had not worked for *Papá*. Or *Mamá*, for that matter.

"Ana?" She froze at the door, the raw emotion in Peter's voice already causing silent tears to wind their way down her cheeks.

"I will miss you terribly. You and Essie."

Papá had said as much. But it had not brought him back in time. Ana pushed the door open without giving him a reply and ran to her rooms, where she could cry out the aching in her heart.

Chapter 32

June 20, 1814, Abbeygate, Surrey Hills, England

Ana was running, a small, whimpering bundle in her arms. Shards of glimmering ash dimly lit the sky in front of her. The dark forest seemed too far away. Would she ever reach it? She risked a glance backward, only to see a city collapsing in flames and dark, roaring figures running after her. Her feet pounded the ground even harder, slipping over ash-wet stones as Esperanza slipped from her arms, and she fell down, down, down . . .

Then she was alone in an achingly cold ocean, quickly losing every bit of her strength as waves crashed down, overwhelming her with exhaustion. Salty water shoved itself down her throat, choking her. Esperanza's wails carried over the wind toward her from the small lifeboat that drifted ever away from her. Some small portion of her mind knew she was dreaming, but with each memory of her current reality, the waves around her only seemed to grow taller and more ferocious. Esperanza needed her desperately. And Ana was aching and overwhelmed and so, so tired. And the hope of the lifeboat, the hope of Peter rescuing her, was being carried away by the waves that separated them. He was leaving her, and not only in her dream. That reality threatened to drag her so far into the depths below that she would never see daylight again.

Finally, she clawed herself through the dreams that were pulling her deeper downward into the waves. Her chest heaved as she gasped for calming air, and she rubbed at her eyes and the exhaustion that blinded her.

Then ice-cold panic doused her as she found her arms to be much too light and entirely too empty. Esperanza had been feeding only a moment ago. She clutched at the blankets bunched in her arms, tore all the bedclothes off her bed, and tossed the pillows to the floor. Where was she?

"*Mija?!*"

Her feet hit the floor as a panicked sob ripped through her.

"Ana?" Peter grumbled from the rocking chair in the corner, his voice lowered and rumbling from sleep.

He stood, stepping forward into the moonlight that was printed in the shape of windowpanes upon the floor. In his arms was a small, blanketed bundle with a fuzzy head of black hair peeking out from the top.

Relief rushed through Ana, nearly causing her knees to buckle. Before she could as much as take another breath, she rushed to him, her arms encircling the babe and cradling her close to her body again.

"You were quite asleep, and Essie was beginning to fuss. I only wanted to help rock her before I laid her down." Peter's voice blurred with exhaustion and confusion.

The relief that had warmed Ana only a moment before was quickly sapped away by a cold, crashing wave. Jealousy, panic, helplessness, and frustration swirled in her mind so powerfully that it was difficult to put her thoughts in words. She squeezed her eyes shut and shook her head against it all. She felt all out of sorts, a stranger in her own mind.

"You should wake me."

"But you need to rest."

"Why are you so *obsesionado* with my sleep?"

"Because your health requires it," Peter replied, looking a bit taken aback. "Your body still has much recovering to do. Sleep is what you need more than anything else."

"I *need* my daughter. My body *needs* my daughter."

His eyes held hers for a long moment as he wiped his forehead with the cravat that lay undone around his neck. He was still dressed in his day clothes, rumpled and disorderly as they were. Had he truly been waiting in here so long?

"Look at you. *Vaya a tu cama.* Go sleep. It is late."

"Only if I can rest assured that you'll be sleeping as well."

Again his obsession with her sleep! A high wave splashed her, slapping her in the face with a possessive jealousy. He only wanted to see her return to sleep so he could take Esperanza for himself again. How could he not understand that every part of her soul and being required being near her child at this time?

"I can assure you that I will rest. As will Esperanza. And as will you. Now, *por favor*, I ask you to go to your rooms."

Peter's cravat was practically wound into a rope in his hands, so tense his grip appeared to be. But at her words, the tension, the visible fight in him melted.

"Very well," he murmured. He approached Ana, who instinctively held Esperanza higher and tighter to her chest. "Good night, *Preciosa*." He pressed a quick kiss to the top of Esperanza's head, then turned to Ana. His eyes were on her lips, but the thought of kissing him when her mind was in such a state of turmoil only brought Ana greater distress. She turned her head, and he brushed her cheek with a quick kiss that she wasn't entirely sure she had felt at all.

"*Buenas noches*, Ana."

Ana lowered herself back into the pillows with great care, wincing at the lingering pain that ached when she moved. How had everything become so *complicado* so quickly? All it had taken was the birth of her daughter and too many sleepless nights for her relationship with Peter to dissolve almost completely. She felt that she was more of a burden than a wife or friend. And that was even more evident now that he was leaving. Arrangements were to be made.

Surely he wished for another marriage, one that he wasn't obligated to enter into. Or another child, one that was truly his own. There was one last narrow path that she could follow if she became certain that she was truly burdensome. If she could convince Peter to do so, he could go to court, testify that Esperanza isn't truly his child, divorce

Ana, and disinherit Esperanza. After all, she had borne a daughter, not a son, and that meant that she wouldn't be required by law to stay with Peter, since Esperanza was not his heir. Ana would be ruined, at least in the eyes of English customs and society, but such things would hardly matter upon returning to Spain. More importantly, divorce was a grave sin according to her religion. She could possibly be putting her own salvation in jeopardy. But how could she live out her entire life as a burden to the man she loved, and while being separated from the country she loved? Living beside Peter without being able to love him was a torture she would not survive. Surely God would understand her need to find relief from the agony she felt, even if it meant seeking out a divorce.

Perhaps Peter would be happier returning to the army. Or starting a completely different life anew—one that didn't tie him down with responsibilities that were not truly his own.

Chapter 33

June 30, 1814, Abbeygate, Surrey Hills, England

Ana María was lost.

The waves that had lapped at her skirts in moments of worry during pregnancy had now grown to an insurmountable height. She was on the verge of drowning. Despite Ana's being besotted with her round-cheeked babe, she was exhausted with her never-ending cries to be fed. She felt she had lost herself and her closeness with Peter in so short a time. It left her impossibly disoriented.

Strangely enough, the only semblance of contentment that she could find was in the middle of the night—those moments when the entire world was silent and asleep, unable to bother her, and she was entirely at peace, alone with her daughter.

Every day that passed, she felt her desperation growing. A small part of her mind knew that she was in no sort of shape to be caring for her daughter every hour of the day or night. She should be relying upon help, particularly when her body was so weak and tender still, her bleeding still flowing. But she could not do it. The sight of her baby in someone else's arms filled her with panic and anger. She would find herself in the ocean again, being dragged downward in the waves, water clogging her throat. Only once she had her baby back would her head break above the waves.

She was exhausted. Her head throbbed constantly. She could hardly walk. Peter had kindly donated his dressing room, creating a sort of private parlor where she could receive visitors. They hadn't had much company yet, only the Smiths. But still, every part of Ana was craving isolation, screaming out for someone to protect her. Having visitors in her home would be an excruciating reminder of the life that Ana would never have now that Peter was leaving her too.

And yet she needed to tell Peter of the waves in her mind. But how could he understand the vast, brutal ocean of some threat she was unable to understand?

"Peter?" Her voice trembled with tension and trepidation.

He froze, halting his preparations in their makeshift parlor.

"Yes?" he said, his confusion physically manifest in the tension bunched in his shoulders.

"I need . . . your help."

"Name it, and it will be done."

But how could she name something that she didn't know how to identify? How could she tell him of the waves constantly throwing themselves over her head? She wet her lips, begging words to come. But instead, she crumbled to her knees, her body arching over the sleeping babe in her arms.

"*Estoy perdida*," she said as tears doused her cheeks in a sheet of emotion. *I am lost.*

Steps sounded loud and fast, and strong arms pulled her up from the waves.

"Oh, but you'll be all right, dear. You simply need a good rest. A *siesta,* no?" he said.

"No."

"Believe me, you'll feel much better after a rest. Here, hand me our daughter and . . ."

"*My* daughter." She gripped Esperanza.

At that, he froze.

"Yes, she is yours," Peter said, his gaze intent. "But I have also agreed to father her. I want to help you, but I do not understand why you will not allow me to do so."

But how could he be Esperanza's father from the great distance of the battlefield? *Papá* had proved it quite difficult indeed.

She sighed, shoulders slumping. "*No entiendo nada.*" *I do not understand anything, not even myself.*

"Please, will you rest? I see your exhaustion, though you try to hide it from me."

"But Esperanza . . ."

"She will sleep here in her cradle at your side. I'll be in my rooms if she cries."

"*Bueno.*"

Light sleep had arrested her quickly, but it did not have hold over her. Every few minutes, she had burst awake, sitting upright in her bed, panic flooding her, an untouchable sea choking her until her gaze found Esperanza at her side. The maddening pattern repeated for nearly half an hour until exhaustion finally overtook her and she sank into sleep in the watery deep.

Chapter 34

July 6, 1814, Abbeygate, Surrey Hills, England

JUST WHEN PETER HAD THOUGHT HE HAD BEGUN TO UNDERSTAND his wife more wholly, she had been delivered of a child. And everything had changed most drastically. He knew the delivery of their child had been incredibly taxing upon Ana's body and mind, more than he would likely ever truly understand. But he only wished he did not feel so helpless. Even if he changed every one of Essie's soiled diapers, it seemed he could never do enough to relieve the burden on Ana's shoulders.

As of late, she was irritated when he spent long hours at her side but seemed equally as bothered when he spent long hours away from her. To see their trust and bond begin to crumble like the walls of San Sebastián sent panic through Peter's heart.

Fortunately for them both, Esperanza was an incredibly sweet babe, even at such a young and needy age. She had the sweetest lips, and her skin was unbelievably soft. Even her wee cry seemed musical. Peter was entirely besotted with her. It was a blessing he had never even hoped to pray for. Could he really leave her?

Peter looked up from his pacing, finding himself outside the nursery door, unanticipated. But all was quiet inside. Esperanza must be asleep. So, he continued down the hall to Ana's rooms. He tapped his fingers on the door.

"*Sí?*"

He cracked open the door and saw Elena arranging the bedclothes on Ana's bed.

"Elena, have you seen Mrs. Ashmore this afternoon?"

"I believe she is taking a *siesta* in the nursery, sir. And the *beba* as well."

"That is a rest that is well-deserved. Will you please come find me when they are both awake? I wish to speak with her."

"*Sí, claro.*"

"Thank you, Elena."

The accoucheur had clearly instructed Peter that a lying-in or confinement period should be continued for about a month following the birth of Esperanza. Ana had gone through quite a trying ordeal and required plenty of rest. He knew that she was growing restless despite her exhaustion, and he wanted to arrange a diversion for her but doubted how such an idea would be received. As it was, Peter would have to present his idea to Ana after her much-needed nap.

Now, was there not somewhere he was meant to be right about now? Peter pulled a small pocket watch from his waistcoat and scratched his head. He was nearly overdue for his visit with Mr. Smith. How was it that such a small baby could throw off a well-planned schedule so entirely? He strode quickly to the back door and chuckled.

His groom already had Warrior brushed and saddled. Peter swung himself up into the saddle in a practiced, easy movement and snapped the reins. His would have to be a quick journey to the chapel today.

Peter's journey was so automatic, so well-traveled by now, that he hardly noticed his surroundings. But a shadowed bundle dragged his gaze down to the dusty dirt path. Was it a cloak, forgotten by one of the chapel's visitors? As he neared, a faint sound pulled painfully at his heart.

"*Ayúdeme, Papá . . .*"

Peter leapt from his horse and ran, his stomach sore with panic. "Ana?" She continued to moan but didn't move. "*Amor!*" His voice cracked painfully in his throat.

He scooped her into his arms, his panicked tears mingling with her desperate ones.

"Why are you here? And all alone? What were you thinking?"

Her cheek, torso, and hands were dusty, and her eyes were nearly swollen shut from crying. The sight froze his heart. Memories of a bloody and bruised Ana lit by firelight mingled with the sight of the exhausted, defeated Ana before him, and Peter could not still the pounding in his chest.

"Answer me, please, *amor.*" He felt her face, arms, and legs for injuries. "I need to hear your voice."

"*Papá?*" Her voice was childlike and pleading.

"No, *querida*, it is Peter, your husband. I'm here."

"No, Peter, no. Leave, *por favor.* You should not see me *así.*"

"I am your husband. I have seen you in all manner of conditions." He brushed a hand over her hair, her curls tangled in disarray. "Tell me how you ended up here alone. Did someone leave you here? I will deal with them myself." He scoured his mind, thinking of who could possibly know of their residence here. Did someone from the army find her and try to silence her? He would hunt them down.

"I wanted to go for a walk."

"You should have been taking a *siesta*. That is what Elena said!"

"But I had to escape the *desastre.*"

"What disaster? Esperanza? Is she all right?"

"No, the *desastre* in my mind." Finally, Ana's dark eyes cracked open as they poured out hot, large tears, tracking stripes down her dust-caked face. Her eyes were distant, unseeing. She looked haunted.

Peter was familiar with the mental distress that a traumatic injury could bring. He had seen many panicked states among his soldiers upon suffering a serious blow. Ana herself had endured a very difficult lying-in, which is why it was so distressing that she would have ended up so far from home.

"You are in no state to be exerting yourself in such a manner."

"But if I stayed inside any longer, I would have drowned. *Me vuelvo loca.*"

"So you do not wish to be trapped inside any longer?" That much, Peter understood. But what could she mean by saying she would have drowned?

"*Sí.*"

"Shall we make arrangements for you to have a place to rest with Esperanza out of doors on the balcony?"

"Perhaps it would help. Perhaps not." Her eyes were frozen in a distant, enraptured fear, reminding him of her state during their escape from San Sebastián. Her silence had echoed through their journey. But she had never looked so defeated.

"Come, we need to get you home. Mr. Smith will have a horse and cart we can use." She was in no condition to ride on Warrior with him.

Peter stood, scooped Ana into his arms, and grabbed Warrior's reins. He felt something warm trickle down his arm. Blood. The hems of Ana's skirts were spattered with it. "Blazes," Peter cursed as he hurried his steps, soon bursting through the chapel doors. "Mr. Smith, please help me!"

Bending down, Peter laid Ana gently on the long, wooden pew.

"Ana, it appears that you are bleeding, and I need to examine . . ." Peter looked up at Ana's face, only to see that she had paled and fallen into unconsciousness. He would not delay any further, despite the momentary hesitation he felt at lifting her skirts. He was her husband and needed to know what care she required.

The large vicar stayed at a distance once he saw Peter lifting Ana's skirts. Her feet or legs were not cut from her long walk. Instead, blood had trickled down her legs after soaking through her stockings and underclothes. Clearly this was an injury related to her recent lying-in and rough recovery.

Fear stabbed through Peter, just as violently as any battle wound. He did not know much of what was required of a woman's body during childbirth, but he could imagine it to be quite extensive, even in the months following. He would not diagnose the seriousness of her condition himself, not when it could put his wife at risk.

"Mr. Smith, I need you to take Warrior and ride for the physician, as quickly as possible."

Chapter 35

July 7, 1814, Abbeygate, Surrey Hills, England

PETER SAT AT ANA'S BEDSIDE, RUNNING HIS FINGERS OVER HER HANDS. It had been hours, but he would not leave her. He needed her to know she wasn't alone when she woke.

But why had she been so desperate that she ran from the house?

Running from trouble was something Peter was familiar with. When life at Heathridge Hall had become too dangerous, too complicated, he had run and enlisted. Even now, a small, scared part of him worried that if being a husband or father proved too distressing for him, he would be forced to run again. He cared so greatly for Ana; he would never abandon her. But if he started to feel that he was creating more discomfort in her life than he was safety, he would have no option but to leave. But it was a difficult thing to feel needed as a husband, father, and protector when Ana appeared so distressed by his presence.

So distressed that she would leave the house unattended and try to run away by herself.

Being witness to her pain was an agony Peter wished to forget. But he would not leave her now, or ever. She needed him. They needed each other to heal from the great challenges they had endured together.

"*Mami?*" Ana whimpered, her voice audibly clogged with emotion and exhaustion.

Peter shook his head to clear his complicated thoughts and leaned in closer, "*Soy yo*, Peter. I'm here."

The fogginess slowly seeped from her eyes as she blinked. Finally, recognition cleared her features. Peter's stomach plunged as her lips drooped in disappointment as she realized that it was her husband and not her mother who had been caring for her.

"*Ay, qué dolor*," Ana said, pressing a hand to her lower abdomen as pain flashed across her features. "What happened?"

"Do you not remember?"

"I remember Esperanza was sleeping. And then I go for a walk *afuera* . . ."

"Yes, quite a walk you had, dear. I found you collapsed near the chapel."

"*Tan lejos?*" Surprise was just as apparent in her widened eyes as it was in her heightened voice.

"Indeed, that far. I found you, and you were bleeding and barely conscious. Mr. Smith assisted me in calling for Dr. Lee, and after he determined that you could be moved, we returned. Blessedly, there is nothing to be greatly concerned about. Your bleeding increased due to your long exertion."

"But if I bleed, that is bad, no?"

"Dr. Lee determined that it is somewhat normal to experience some bleeding in your condition, although such a long walk is not advised for now. It certainly aggravated your bleeding."

Ana dipped her chin, pressing her eyes shut. "And Esperanza?"

"She has been sleeping soundly, although I suspect she will be quite hungry soon."

The wrinkle of tension that laced Ana's forehead smoothed at his words. "I think I wanted to find the chapel to talk with *mi Dios*. I only remember this. But all is well, no?"

"I'm afraid all is not well."

Peter recognized the stubborn set of her jaw all too well and forged ahead before she could stop him. "Dr. Lee inquired after the state of your feelings. He said it is typical for new mothers to experience a wide, confusing range of feelings, particularly in the weeks that follow the birth of a child. While this symptom is normal to an extent, some cases become prolonged or complicated."

Ana's hands clenched the sheets. "*Estoy bien*. I feel *bien*. I have none of these *problemas*. How can Dr. Lee say these things when he not know me well?" Her voice cracked, tears flooding her eyes.

"Dr. Lee only wished to ensure that you are able to fully heal from Essie's birth, both in body and in mind."

"In mind, I am fine," she protested, waving a hand at him. "But yes, I see I need to rest for this bleeding, *no*?"

This was going terribly. Peter heaved a sigh. He ought to have requested that Dr. Leestay to explain the symptoms himself.

"To aid in your recovery, he prescribed a longer-than-typical lying-in period. You are to stay about the house for a month more. I will write Mother to delay our trip to Heathridge Hall. And seeing as you were so desperate to enjoy the fresh air, I do believe we can make some exceptions as far as taking short walks in the gardens, and even attending Sunday services so long as we take a carriage . . ."

"But why I need a longer lying-in when I say that *estoy bien*! Does Dr. Lee not listen to me? Do you not listen to me?"

Peter barely resisted the urge to drop his head into his hands. Dr. Lee had warned that she may grow defensive, indicating that Ana was experiencing great emotional difficulty. Desperation gnawed at him. But how could he help her?

"Perhaps you would like my mother to come back to help for a time? The diversion of her company could help your recovery feel more enjoyable. And she would help with Essie if permitted. Perhaps then when I . . . when the army is recalled, you will be more comfortable with her help."

Ana's eyes darted to the bassinet at her bedside, where a rosy-cheeked Esperanza lay slumbering peacefully. "Yes, *está bien*. Your *mamá* can come."

"Very well, I will write her. But only if you are certain."

Ana shifted closer to Esperanza. "I am."

"Very well." Peter leaned down to kiss her cheek, but she leaned away. He tried to smile and ignore the pain that stabbed through him. He was losing the very fragile connection he had with his wife, without knowing why it was happening at all.

* * *

Mother arrived quite speedily upon receiving his letter. The next morning, she was on their doorstep, bearing Peter's favorite raspberry tarts, fresh linens and gowns for Ana, and adorably knitted blankets for Esperanza. She interrogated him now, eager to help Ana.

"I cannot understand it, Mother," Peter shook his head. "Ana is so entirely changed. She is unceasingly anxious for Essie's welfare and does not trust another to assist her. And while she tries to deny her changed state, she also acknowledges that she is not herself. She has begun to question whether God is punishing her for having a child that is not her husband's by sending these moods and dreams that torment her so."

"Do you suspect she could be suffering from melancholy?" Mother asked.

"Melancholy?"

"A time of deep sadness and listlessness that occurs with some new mothers. I even experienced a short bout of it myself, following the birth of Matthew."

"But how does it come about?"

Mother took a long sip of her tea, a serious, pensive look knitting her brow together.

"From fatigue, I'm sure, and perhaps the pressures of motherhood. From what you have told me, it appears that her lying-in period was most difficult. Surely all these things combine to create quite a blow to a woman's peace."

In truth, it didn't sound so different from the terrifying emptiness that gripped soldiers after too many weeks in the thick of battle. And carrying and being delivered of a child was certainly a battle of sorts. He had seen soldiers who no longer looked at the miniatures tacked into their pockets and no longer wrote home. They were listless creatures. Such sadness could kill a man.

Peter had not carried or borne Esperanza. And his knowledge of the health of the feminine physique was somewhat limited. But being by his wife's side during those first days taught him that she had been through a war of her own, both in body and in mind. It was not so outrageous to conclude that such an event could leave Ana so altered.

Is this what she had meant when she said she was lost? And drowning?

"Please, how do I help her? I cannot allow her to take on this burden alone."

"In many ways, it is her burden to bear," Mother said. "You cannot see into the inner workings of her mind, cannot heal the great pain in her heart, nor erase the memories of the difficulty of Esperanza's birth. But you can aid her in other ways."

"Believe me when I say I would change as many of Esperanza's linens as she would allow me."

"Yes, do care for the child, as she permits you, but if you see that it makes Ana distressed, do not take the babe from her mother more than necessary. In these early days, a new mother needs her child just as desperately as she needs to breathe or to eat."

"But surely she needs to rest just as desperately."

"Yes, dear," Mother replied, gently patting Peter's cheek. "But imagine you just fought a hard battle to protect your foot soldiers. Then, without much preparation, they were taken away from you. After dedicating great portions of your energy and health to the well-being of those soldiers for many months, wouldn't you feel panicked at not knowing how they were faring?"

"Well, of course. But I wouldn't feel like I needed to embrace them constantly, if that's what you mean." He quirked a half-hearted smile at her.

"Silly boy, you know what I refer to. You have always felt a strong urge to protect those around you, me included. It is even stronger for Ana María, as that urge is now innate and buried deep inside her. That, my dear Peter, is motherhood."

The tightness that had captured his chest loosened at long last. Finally, Ana didn't feel lost to him. Instead, he understood her in a way that he never had before. Her instinct to protect their daughter mirrored his own protective instincts. Perhaps they were more similar than he realized.

"Helping her in this way will enable her to feel calm and safe," Mother said. "With time, she will heal, and not just her body but her mind as well."

"I promise that everything I do is to protect her. I don't even take a breath without thinking of her." He ran a hand through his hair. "It is exhausting to worry so much about someone."

Mother's eyes softened as a gentle smile curved her lips. "Oh, my dear. You have come to love her."

"I . . ." Peter stammered. Why had Mother just come to this conclusion now, so many months after their marriage? It seemed rather late for such a statement, although for Peter, it felt rather soon. *Did* he truly love Ana? He cared for her more than anyone, that much was true. He would sacrifice anything for her. But did he love her? And how would it appear to Mother to admit he wasn't sure of his feelings for Ana when they had just welcomed their first child into the world? He rubbed a hand across his forehead.

"Now, Peter, you may have removed yourself from London for a number of years, but you are still my son, and I still pride myself on knowing you better than anyone. I would be ashamed if I couldn't tell when my son was in love. And on the day of your wedding, you were not yourself. You were distant, lost. It was clear to me, even more then, that yours was a wedding of necessity, although I had guessed as much when you wrote me after so long a silence and asked me to seek out a special license. What a surprise that was."

Peter's mouth dropped open. The nervous bouncing of his knee was stilled by Mother's comforting hand.

"I didn't need to know the particulars of your original arrangement, dear. I had seen enough to know that you were—and are—a great protector of your Ana María. It was merely an observation that it appears you have found love at last. And one that I am glad to know. I have always wished you would find a wife to love."

Peter stood, his shoulders back and rigid. His arms snapped to his sides as he began to pace. In a moment such as this one, when his mind was so utterly occupied, his body reverted to years of discipline and muscle memory. "I care a great deal for Ana. She has given me great purpose, has helped me to adjust to a manner of living that I never thought possible. I never could have married another. But I am not quite certain if it is love that I feel for her." He stopped his pacing in front of Mother, shaking his head. "I have not decided to love her, you see."

"If only it were so simple," Mother chuckled, her tone hoarse with amusement and a hint of . . . could it be pain? Peter's gaze darted to her face. Yes, pain was written there, evident in the small crease in her brow and the tight twist of her lips. "Peter, dear, you cannot decide when or whom you love. You may be able to decide whom to court, or even whom to marry, but whom to love? No, that is not something you can decide of your own volition. Love is like a summer rainstorm. It cannot be hindered, cannot be stopped. One can only shelter from the rain or choose to relish it, rejoice in it. For after a summer rainstorm, there is the possibility of growth. But a tiny seedling of attraction can either grow or drown." Mother's voice broke, and she put a hand to her throat. "And that is the choice that you do have, Peter."

Peter laced an arm around his mother's shoulders, pulling her into his side, and pressed a kiss to her cheek. He did not miss the tear that raced down her face at the contact. It had been years since Peter had seen this type of emotion from her. Did she have love in her past that he had never detected? Surely the love she had felt was not for his father. The mere flicker of memory of the man brought a heat of anger to Peter's head. And yet she had remained by his side for all those years, even through numerous scandals. She had borne him two children. Was there more to his parents' story than Peter had ever seen before?

"Now that the truth of your feelings for your wife is free between us," Mother continued, "how can we ensure that she knows she is well loved by you? Because I suspect that knowledge will do a great deal to calm, comfort, and heal her during this fragile time."

* * *

"Lady Ashmore." Ana slowly bent, curtsying on trembling, exhausted legs. "Forgive me for being so slow to attend you."

"Not at all, my dear. I understand that it takes some time to move about after delivering a child. I remember it well,"

"Just so, my lady."

"Please, call me Eleanor. We are family, after all."

"Very well, Eleanor,"

"You have been through quite a challenging ordeal. How can I be of help to you?"

"I assure you I am all right. *De verdad.*"

"And I assure you that cannot be true. Not entirely."

Lady Ashmore's deep blue eyes didn't waver from her own, burying Ana in a wave of overwhelm that was difficult to sort through. This woman *saw* her. Ana blinked quickly in an effort to dispel the tears that quickly gathered in her eyes.

"I know what it is to struggle with a myriad of feelings after the birth of a child," Lady Ashmore shared. "And I also know that familiar weight of guilt that appears alongside them. You have a beautiful daughter. Shouldn't you be grateful? But instead, you feel exhausted, overwhelmed, alone, and unequal to the task at hand."

The anxiety Ana had held in her shoulders, her neck, slowly started to melt.

"I also know what it is to be mistreated, even violently so, when you least expect it." Lady Ashmore's voice broke. "That builds in you a protective nature that only grows upon becoming a mother. And there is no shame in that." Lady Ashmore placed a hand on Ana's shoulder, her touch light and careful. "It is no fault of your own how you have come to carry, and now birth, this child. It is even less your fault that you now feel a great need to defend yourself and your daughter against any hint of discomfort or pain. In fact, I believe it would be expected of anyone who has lived through even a fraction of what you experienced before coming here to England."

Tears soaked Ana's cheeks now. Lady Ashmore knew. And whether Peter had told her, or whether she had divined Esperanza's true heritage herself, Ana found she didn't care. Instead of panic, she was doused in aching relief at the knowledge that someone understood at least part of what she was feeling at present—and didn't criticize her for it.

"I felt—feel—that same protective nature for my boys. I have not lived through wars in my homeland like you, but I have seen battles of a different sort in my home. And it is no easy thing to experience the delicate changes of new motherhood while also trying to maintain some semblance of defense against a threat."

Pulling Esperanza closer to her chest, Ana tilted her chin so her tears would run down her face and neck instead of dripping onto the sleeping babe. Her thoughts strayed to *Mamá.* Had she also suffered from these innate, unpredictable emotions as she tried to hold together a family that would unavoidably fall apart? Did she mourn as she saw her husband report repeatedly to his duties, leaving her the lone witness to her daughter being heartbroken at his absence? What if *Mamá* left because she too was drowning and had nobody there to pull her above the waves? What if it was the only way she could survive?

Although Ana could never understand nor forgive *Mamá* for leaving her, she started to understand the intricacies of emotion that may have caused her to leave *Papá.* The ache that sat heavy in her heart started to soften as she afforded *Mamá* that small portion of forgiveness. A great sigh released from her chest, as if it had been trapped there for months, even years. And yet even with the beginnings of understanding, she had yet to find any words to speak. She wished so desperately for her parents. She wanted to embrace them, forgive them. Most of all, Ana wanted to place their granddaughter into their arms and see their joy. But those were blessing she would never have.

"Regardless of the past difficulties you have faced, this beautiful infant is a miracle. She is a gift from God above, a great blessing for both you and Peter." Emotion washed over Lady Ashmore's face, her eyes shimmering with tears. "I felt that I was blessed with my boys for a reason, that God had entrusted them to me specifically, despite the challenges I faced within the walls of my home. And I know with all my heart that God has given you this darling girl because He loves you and trusts you."

The spiritual peace that Ana had been searching for, even unknowingly, clicked into place, like the latch in a lock, holding her heart secure and whole once again. Love and forgiveness from above enveloped her like an embrace that was difficult to describe. Her tears continued to flow, although for an entirely different reason.

"I know it is difficult to speak of these things, dear. I only wish you to feel more comfortable knowing that I understand, at least to some degree, what you are feeling. And please, know that you are safe with me. And with Peter."

At the mention of her husband, an ache ran through Ana's heart. But it was duller, dimmer than it had been in weeks past, as buoyed with newfound peace as she was. If Lady Ashmore truly understood so much of what she was experiencing, there had to be some truth in her words about Peter, did there not? Their path ahead would be difficult. He would undoubtedly have to leave them again to report to his duties. But how had divorce ever crossed her mind? It must have been brought on by the desperation of sleepless nights when all her will and rationale disappeared.

Ana watched as Lady Ashmore's eyes lingered on the babe in her arms, a dim light of sad longing there. Ana bowed her head, breathing deeply so as to fight off the waves that threatened their way upward. "You wish to hold her?"

"Only if you are not in need of her."

Ana glanced upward, meeting Lady Ashmore's clear gaze. She noted crinkles around her eyes and a clear focus in her gaze. Was it sympathy she saw there? And understanding? The waves slowly lowered, draining from her mind.

"I would be delighted that you hold her." To Ana's great surprise, there was truth in her words. She felt safe with Lady Ashmore. There was an understanding between them, from their roles as women and mothers and from their mutual connection to Peter.

Ana draped a blanket across the sofa to cushion herself and then settled in at Lady Ashmore's side. She handed Esperanza over to her grandmother, the babe's round fingers grasping at the air and squawking in protest. Ana opened her mouth to comment on Esperanza's fine constitution and set of lungs when she was silenced by the sight of her mother-in-law. Tears were dripping down her cheeks, a peaceful smile played across her lips, and her eyes were completely flooded with light. It was a look of awe, much like one Ana would see in a devout worshipper at church in Spain.

"My dear, I have told you before, but she is truly beautiful."

"Yes, she is."

Ana supposed she too would feel that sense of awe to the same degree if she hadn't been fighting to keep her head above water. She adored her daughter with desperation, with every ounce of her energy. She had given up her country, her family, and her future to bring this child into the world safely. But still, there was a distinct weight that seemed to push downward on her, one she could not shake.

"And now that I have talked a great deal of my own experience, I wish to know, truly, how are you faring?"

"Well enough, I suppose," Ana mumbled.

"Are you certain about that?"

Suddenly, Ana found she could not meet Lady Ashmore's eyes. For if she did, this most perceptive woman would surely see the inexplicable torment within. Surely it would break her. Even avoiding her gaze, tears were beginning to fill Ana's eyes for no apparent reason.

"Motherhood brings the greatest joy imaginable, as does it the greatest pain. Being separated from one's own child is like losing part of one's soul."

"Is that what motherhood always is, then?" Ana replied. "Pain?"

"If you didn't know pain as a mother, then you wouldn't know love."

"But why must love, something so good, always have pain?"

Lady Ashmore met Ana's eyes for a long moment and then rubbed a hand along her cheek. "Perhaps this will help me better explain myself. Do you enjoy walking in the golden, late afternoon sunlight?"

"Yes, the sun is warm and gives comfort," Ana said with a slight smile. "The light is always so beautiful as well."

"Precisely. It is one of my favorite times to walk outside as well. But have you ever noticed that during that particular time of day, the shadows cast by your silhouettes are much longer than earlier in the day?"

Ana was completely confused now. "I suppose so." She bit her lip and scrunched her nose.

"To some, it may be easy to focus on the length and depth of the shadows that seem to cut through the light and drown out the brilliance of those golden moments. But the shadows should not discount the existence of the most beautiful sunlight of the day at precisely the same hour."

Ana imagined the long shadows of the trees, the house, her form moving throughout the garden. She could practically feel the aching of her shadowed body, the weight in her arms so heavy but so light at precisely the same moment. Exhaustion came in waves, lapping nearly at her waist, each shadow around her driving the tide higher. But then she looked down into the wide and watchful eyes of her daughter, and golden sunlight streamed in. And then she felt arms around her, embracing her and strengthening her as she carried Esperanza.

It was Peter. And the sunlight was even brighter now.

"Motherhood comes with many days—and long nights—of shadows, my dear. But that also means that it is overflowing with sunlight. Because shadows only exist in the presence of strong, warming sun."

"I believe I am beginning to understand," Ana choked as tears started to run down her cheeks.

"Being a mother can be exhausting and even painful at times. But it is also more joyful than you can even comprehend. I have been reminded of that reality twice over this year upon seeing my sons married. I would give anything to return to the days of my two young, toddling boys, so close in age that they almost appeared to be twins. And now they are husbands, both."

A greater sense of guilt splashed down over Ana. How could she have taken this woman's son from her? Particularly when Peter hadn't ever planned to be married at all?

"I am sorry. Peter didn't mean to . . ."

"Oh, my dear, the pair of you are very well suited. I expressed myself badly. I only meant to say that it is difficult to be separated from one's child, no matter how old or young they may be. As a young mother, I found myself near desperation when I was separated too long from my own little babies."

The guilt and panic that Ana had felt moments earlier started to fade. "I admit I have felt something like this myself."

"And that, my dear, is my cue." Lady Ashmore smoothed the curling black locks on the top of Esperanza's head and handed her carefully back to Ana.

"What can I do to help?"

"I don't know. Esperanza is so young, and I feel I fail her already."

"You are not failing her, dear, you are just learning a great deal about her and about yourself all at the same time. It is quite normal to feel overwhelmed. Any woman would. It can help some to share the burden with your husband. He may be gruff at times, but I promise he is a good man. He endeavors to assist you. And he is accustomed to quite a lot of work, you know."

"I know. I try to allow that he help me, but sometimes I do not know how to let him. I feel so tired, but I still feel I must do *todo*. I have not even spoken of the difficulty of feeding *mi hijita*, you know. She has hunger all the day and night." Ana chuckled at that despite the heaviness of her feelings.

"That is simply the role of being a mother, my dear—bearing all those responsibilities as if it were the most natural thing in the world. But it is not a simple thing, nor an easy one. We are called to carry some of the weightiest matters in our minds, hearts, and hands," she said, inclining her chin in the direction of Ana's arms, cradling her babe. "But that is because God knows we have the strength to do so."

"And if I do not know if I have this strength?"

"Then you must let Him give His strength to you. Through those around you who love you most dearly. Through Peter."

Finally, Ana realized that God was the one who would heal her and protect her, not Peter. She needed to trust that He would mend the broken parts of her that felt they would never be pieced together again. He would carry the burden of loneliness and self-doubt that she could not seem to rid herself of. He would mold her into the mother—and wife—she could not be on her own. God would save her. And He already had, long ago when He felt her pain and gave His life for hers.

God would make her whole—in body, spirit, and mind.

Chapter 36

July 9, 1814, Abbeygate, Surrey Hills, England

Ana was seated outside on her favorite stone bench in the garden, surrounded by vibrant red roses. Breathing in their fragrance, touching the soft silkiness, seemed to ground her in the reality of her surroundings. It also brought a feeling of comfort, of home. *Mamá* always loved roses. Red roses, much like these, had encircled their house throughout her childhood. Until *Mamá* had left. And without her care, the roses had died.

But Peter had seen how she loved these roses. He had cared for them personally, ensuring that they would blossom to their full potential this summer. That had to be an indication of how he cared for *her*, did it not?

"Might I join you, Ana?"

Ana started at the sound, surprised to see Peter slowly, hesitantly walking up the garden path toward her, a rose in hand. They had not spoken in such a private setting since the incident of her leaving the house. Was she truly ready to be alone with him? Would she know how to make words of the great, confusing mess inside her mind?

She wanted to try.

So she smiled and answered, "*Por supuesto.*"

"Where is Essie?" he asked as he stepped closer and saw Ana's empty arms.

"With your mother."

A look of surprise flitted across Peter's face, lifting his eyebrows and causing his mouth to gape slightly. "How fortunate for her. I am glad you felt at ease leaving Essie with her for a time. It is so very needed for you to spend time in the outdoors."

Ana nodded in agreement and scooted to the side, indicating that Peter sit beside her. The tension or stress that had him locked into his military stance started to release at her invitation. His shoulders loosened and he sat. He was at the other end of the bench, but still, he was seated.

Ana motioned to the rose in his hand. "It is *hermosa*. Beautiful."

Peter fumbled with the flower, his voice halting. "I thought it might look particularly nice in your hair. If you would agree . . . and allow me . . . but only with your approval."

"*Por favor*," she said, inclining her head. She wanted to close the distance that had driven them apart as of late. But she was not prepared for the sparks that raced down her spine as Peter's hand brushed her cheek as he slipped the rose behind her ear.

"*Gracias*," Ana whispered with a smile.

Before her eyes, a more familiar Peter began to emerge. His eyes softened and his shoulders dipped, relaxed. He sat beside her, a tentative smile on his lips, and even held out a hand toward her.

Ana hovered her hand above his for a moment. Becoming close to him again meant endangering her heart—and Esperanza's—in the case that he would leave them. But she had given a great deal of thought to what Lady Ashmore had said. She needed to trust that God had sent Peter to help her, and not only during San Sebastián. So she laced their fingers together, leaning into the warmth of his arm. A sigh shuddered through Peter's frame, and Ana bit her lip to keep from crying at the great comfort that ebbed into her, merely from his closeness. How she had longed for—and feared—this touch.

"Ana, I have something to confess," Peter sighed, squeezing her hand.

"As do I," she responded, trying to keep her voice steady.

"Please, allow me to begin. I have much I wish to say. And I do hope I won't make a blasted mess of it all." He ran a hand through his hair. "I need to ask your forgiveness—no, beg your forgiveness. I have talked to Mother, and it appears that I have left you without the precise type of support you have needed in a very delicate and trying circumstance." His voice broke, pulling at Ana's heart. "I have always sworn to protect the women in my life. I failed to protect Mother, and now I see that I have, at least in recent days, failed to protect you. And for that, I am most deeply sorry. So sorry that I doubt I can forgive myself for it."

"I know." Ana swallowed thickly, testing her voice. "I feel so alone these weeks. I am so entirely exhausted, and I do not know how to care for Esperanza in a perfect way. I feel my body and mind are so changed. Will I ever recover?"

"It is true that your body and mind bear scars of the great love you've shown our Essie in bringing her to this world. Mother has taught me it is a badge of motherhood, one of great honor."

Ana smiled through her emotion, "Your *Mamá* is wise,"

"I know you will recover, Ana. It will not always feel so difficult as it does now."

"I want to believe this," Ana said. "But also I feel so sad. Because I love Esperanza so very much. And I do not know how *Mamá* could love me like this and abandon me still."

And she could not survive being abandoned by Peter as well. Even a hint of that over these past weeks had been excruciating. She crossed and uncrossed her arms, unsure what to do without the comforting weight of Esperanza in them.

A sob caught in Ana's throat now, but Peter laced an arm around her and whispered, "Please, tell me whatever is on your mind."

"You know *mi Papi*. He was *un gran hombre*. Always bound to the honor and duty of the *armada*. But sometimes to be so focused on his *responsabilidades en la armada,* he lose his *responsabilidades* at home. To *Mamá*. To me. To himself, as a *Papá*. And our family fall apart like the leaves of a tree in fall—so dry, so weak, so tired. First, *Papá* spent more and more time away from us. He was given great honors and his choice of assignments, so he returned home even less often than before. And *Mamá no pudo aguantar más*. She could not live her life alone. She needed people, she needed love. But I thought she needed me as well."

Before Ana realized it, she was tearing at the delicate edges of the rose in her hands and spotting the front of her dress with tears. Peter gently eased the flower from her hands and tucked it behind her ear before threading her nervous fingers through his own. "It will serve you better here, *querida*. Go on. I am here."

"One day I come in from playing with my friends and I see that *Mamá* was packing *una bolsa* with dresses and shoes and *todo*. She said that *Papá* would be home *pronto,* that she was going to visit her mother. *Papá* returned later that week and cried for a day and a night. Then he wiped his tears, locked *Mamá's* armoire, and said for me to travel to the army with him, that *Mamá* was not going to return. But I did not believe him."

She rubbed a hand down her neck, as if that could ease the throbbing ache that grew there whenever she cried. "Years ago, when I wrote *mi abuela*, she said she heard nothing from *Mamá*, that she never visited. She disappeared to start a new life. One without *Papá*, without me."

Ana found her throat was so tight, her voice so thick, that it was difficult to continue, despite the racing words in her mind. The warmth of Peter's hand pressed against hers was the only thing that seemed to calm her at the moment. She brushed her palm against her cheeks, drying them, and continued.

"And so I left with the *armada*. *Papá* would not have me fall to the life of a camp follower, even in name alone, so he taught me languages. I became a translator, even as a young woman. It was not the life I ever imagine for myself."

Peter was silent for a long moment, as if he was trying to map out the history Ana had laid bare for him. Finally, he whispered as he squeezed her hand, "I am so sorry. I am sure they loved you very much, despite their difficult circumstances."

"I love *mis padres,* even now that they both are gone. But how could they hurt me so?"

"It seems to me that your parents were trying to survive in a life that had proved quite difficult together. I admire your father's drive to give you a future, to train you as a translator. And in a sad sort of way, I admire your mother's courage for recognizing her own need to be loved."

That Peter would justify their actions, even in some small way, only caused Ana's chest to throb harder. "But was my love not enough?" she said, the words ripping from her deep inside heart, leaving a wake of tears behind them.

"I do not know. But I know it would have been enough for me."

Ana's heart very nearly stopped beating at the admission. Had he meant to imply that he valued her affection? And if he had, would it truly be enough to fill the great gaping hole *Mamá* and *Papá* had left behind? Nervousness fluttered in her stomach and journeyed up her body to freeze her tongue. Peter, it seemed, had been grasped by the same nervousness at his apparent admission, but it instead propelled him to speak freely and in a great rush of words.

"There were many times when I wished that my mother would have the courage necessary to leave my father's tyranny, if not for our sake, then at least for her own. It was not merely uncomfortable for her to remain his wife—it was dangerous. Her safety was continuously put at risk as she was subjected to the blows of his temper, and I was too young to defend her." His jaw was tightened with anger, and one lone tear leaked down his cheek, his jaw. "But such things are not so simple in London's society. We would have had no future, least of all her. And so, although her life with my father was torturous to endure, she remained to ensure that Matthew and I would have the opportunity to choose the sort of lives we would like to have. I will always be indebted to her for that."

Ana pictured the two little brothers running around Abbeygate joyously free, only to return to the terror of their home in London. Her heart ached for them, ached for Peter, who never knew what it was to feel love from a father.

His grip on Ana's hand tightened. "I do not wish to justify the behavior of either of your parents. It was entirely wrong of both of them to abandon you in their own ways. But perhaps there is some light that can be found in the knowledge that their decisions have led you to me. To our family and life here."

"I only wish I could have them *and* you. Some part of me still belongs there in *España*."

"Do you have any family that lives there still with whom you might wish to correspond?"

"*Mi abuela*, the same one I wrote about *Mamá*. I have not seen her in many years, not since I left with *Papá*."

"Perhaps we could visit her. When you have healed and when Esperanza is stronger."

"*Me gustaría mucho.* I would love that indeed. Actually, I wrote her again."

But Ana would not admit that it was not merely a letter to renew a relationship. It was a letter of pain, of desperation. After painfully relaying her heartbreak at Papa's passing, she had asked for *Abuelita's* help once again. Ana begged her for advice, asking her if there was a life for her here with Peter or if she should take Esperanza and leave. But she had yet to receive any kind of answer, and deep in her heart, she knew that she should not wait for one. She did not even know if *Abuelita* was still alive.

"Truly?" Peter's eyebrows rose to his hairline. "And did she respond?"

"Not yet, although I know that communication must be *complicada* with the war."

"Of course. Well, if there is anything I can do to assist you in contacting her, please allow me to do so."

A slow, seeping peace began to spread through Ana's core. It was a feeling that had left her since Esperanza had been born. But Peter was showing his willingness to help her, even offering to take her back to visit her homeland. Surely he cared for her in some way and saw something of a future for their lives that were impossibly intertwined. For the first time in weeks, Ana was well above the waves. With every word, Peter pulled her from the water, welcomed her into his boat, and kept her warm and dry.

"*Gracias, Pedro, por todo,*" she whispered.

"It is my pleasure," he said. "And Ana?"

"*Sí?*"

Peter shifted next to her until their noses were nearly touching. He cupped her cheeks with his hands, his touch as gentle despite his rough skin.

"I will always be with you, as will our God. And I am learning that God will heal your wounds which time—and I—cannot. We must trust Him."

Chapter 37

July 15, 1814, Abbeygate, Surrey Hill, England

Over the past week, Peter had seen a slow shift in Ana's behavior. She had appeared calmer, more peaceful, and even more energized. They had taken to walking daily in the rose garden, as he had promised. Mother's being there greatly helped as well, as she assisted Ana in understanding the many changes she was undergoing. In turn, Ana felt more comfortable leaving Esperanza in Mother's care and even in Peter's. It was surely an indication of the safety that Ana felt in her presence. There was a unique understanding between the two women that seemed to exude the quietude of soul that could only be found after crossing through a great deal of similar difficulties.

Peter was more grateful for his mother's wisdom than he had ever been before. And more regretful that he had ever imagined himself better off enlisting without her continued counsel and communication. But that would change now. It had to. He would become a most devoted correspondent, with both Mother and Ana. They would need his support, it seemed, nearly as much as he would need theirs. Ana needed to feel that familial closeness that had been so absent for much of her life, and Mother would do him a great service in visiting

Abbeygate as often as possible to ensure their relationship flourished. Perhaps Ana could even visit London with her when she had to return.

Peter's mind turned to his surroundings. Feminine flourishes jumped out at him, from the paintings on the walls to the drapes at the window. Even the mahogany chair on which he sat was carved with great intricacies. He only wished that this room could become a haven for Ana, much as it had been for Mother. Ana had not shared his bed, or even spent more than a brief, required moment in his rooms, since Esperanza had been born. While having distance in that precious aspect of their relationship tore at him, he found solace in the trust that was beginning to build between them again. Ana's smile was beginning to widen again, and her gaze did not look so guarded, so numb. Soon he felt that his wife, his love, would return to him—that is, if he treaded carefully and cared for her as he ought to. That was the more difficult part. For how could he care for her when she wasn't entirely certain how she needed to be cared for? Still, Mother had told him that the love that burned in his heart would inspire his mind and propel forth his actions. Soon he would be returning from abroad and all would be well between them, as it once had been.

A hesitant knock sounded at the adjoining door. "*Pedro,* you call for me?"

"Yes, *querida,* please do come in."

The door opened, and Ana stepped across the threshold, a hesitant smile on her lips, even as her nervous eyes scoured the room. The tie of her deep ruby dressing gown cut across her figure, emphasizing the curves of motherhood that were so perfectly becoming on her form. And her arms were empty.

"Essie?"

"*Ya duerme.* Your *mamá* and *Elena* soothe her to sleep with their songs."

"They have quite a talented touch, although she much prefers yours." He smiled up at Ana, holding out a hand for her to join him.

"It is true," she chuckled, "but with their help, I can rest."

"Indeed. And as you rest, you can better care for Essie and yourself."

Ana nodded as she lowered herself into the matching mahogany chair next to his. She did not move as gingerly as she had in past weeks, one of many signs that she was healing, in body and in soul. Peter was more than glad for it. He reached across the distance for her hand, convincing himself the movement was just as natural as it had once felt. To his great surprise, Ana enclosed his hand in hers.

"*Qué necesitas?*"

Peter very nearly chuckled. That was his Ana, sparing the niceties to get to the point..

"I needed to tell you how beautiful you look tonight."

Her brows lifted, her lips tilting to one side. "If you want to flatter me, you can do it in the morning when it is not time for me to rest."

She did not believe that this was what he really needed. But Peter did not miss the rosy blush that bled through her cheeks. Progress. A small victory that he would tuck away in his heart for safekeeping.

"You are entirely correct, of course. Just a bit of nerves, *querida*."

He rolled his shoulders and, with his free hand, reached for the letter tucked in his waistcoat pocket, the official wax seal tugging against the fabric. "You remember how I told you some weeks ago that I was anticipating my being recalled to my duties?"

"*Sí*," Ana whispered, her voice a ghost of pain and panic. Her grip went limp and clammy. Peter gently pressed her hands, not wanting her to pull away.

"Well, I am to report to a meeting in London. The letter doesn't say as much, but I suspect the London meeting will confirm where my official orders will lead me next, and for how long. There is still quite a bit of unrest throughout the surrounding nations in the wake of the war."

The words pained Peter, particularly as he thought of the sweet, round-cheeked babe dozing down the hall from them just now. But the agony that lined Ana's face slashed straight to his heart. Had he not prepared her sufficiently for this moment?

"I promise that all will be well while I am away." He forged ahead, desperate to ease her panicked features. "We can move Essie's things over to this room if you feel you would be more comfortable here. Mother has agreed to make arrangements to stay here for two weeks each month. In her absence, perhaps you might visit her in London so you won't be alone."

"But I won't be with *you*!" Her voice was high and tight now, her hands having abandoned his completely to clutch the arms of her chair.

"You cannot be. We both understand quite well why it would be a mistake for you to return to the battlefield." Peter clenched his fists. He would not allow her to return to the nightmare that was their beginning.

"But you tell me you will always be with me!" She was on her feet now, hands pressed against her cheeks, her eyes shining with desperate tears.

"And I will!" Peter had sworn he would protect her, and he would do all that he needed to see that she was cared for.

"How, Peter? How you be with me when you are across the ocean so far away?"

"I will be in your heart, and you will be in mine. We have Esperanza, connecting us permanently, inseparably . . ."

"But I will not be left behind, *abandonada*!" Her voice raked against the ceiling just as she crumbled to a heap on the floor. "Not again!"

Finally, Ana's words in the rose garden made complete and entire sense. She had not only been speaking of her mother's and father's abandonment. She had been begging Peter to not do the same. That was the real source of her grief and pain over these past weeks. He rubbed at his chest, as if it could quell the ache that was growing ever present there.

But couldn't she see that he would never abandon her? That instead, he was providing a life of safety and peace for her? It seemed the reality of a recall was shattering her.

"I will write you daily. Mother and Elena will help you care for Essie here. And when I return, we will be a great, happy family, as you and I both have always wanted."

"But when you return, you will only leave again," she whimpered from her place on the floor as sobs shook her curved form.

Peter sighed heavily. There was some truth to that, a truth he could not prevent nor deny. But then Ana had crawled to where he sat and grasped his hands.

"*Por favor*, let us go with you," she begged. Even as her eyes were wide with hope, awaiting his words, a familiar haunted look cut across her features. Ana would never truly desire to return to a war camp again, not after what it did to her family and now her. She must be truly desperate. But the mere thought of Ana and Essie traveling across the ocean with him to a war-torn Spain or France sent shivers of horror down Peter's spine. A nightmarish vision of Ana limping across the battlefield, her arms baby-laden, flashed before his eyes. And he could never ensure that he would be there to rescue them both, as he had before. Fear wrenched painfully at his stomach.

"I will not have you lower yourself to the life of a camp follower. Even as a translator, I cannot permit it," he said, squeezing her hands. "I will not have you or Esperanza be put at risk in any way."

"Then it is I who must leave. I cannot stay here without you. *No puedo.*"

An entirely different type of panic seized Peter now. This was not the panic of leaving but of being left. He clutched at Ana's hands and pressed them to his lips, even as she tried to pull away from him. Questions rushed out of him.

"What could you possibly mean by that?"

"I leave . . ." she started.

"To London, surely? To Heathridge Hall?" he said, the words very nearly blending together, so quickly they left him.

"I go home," she murmured, her eyes hazy and distant with memory. "*A España.*"

"No, no." Peter's hands moved to her face now, cupping her cheeks, begging her to stay with him in this moment and forever, his mind and movements entirely tortured. "You cannot leave."

"*Pedro,* I need to feel safe. I need a place that is familiar and comfortable for Esperanza and me. And Abbeygate will be neither *sin ti.*"

Abbeygate will be neither without you. Peter had done so much to ensure that Abbeygate offered Ana all the comforts that she required, but he had never considered that *he* might be the comfort she really needed.

"And if you visited your grandmother for a time, would you return?" Peter's voice was brittle, his heart seconds from shattering.

"Will *you* return home?" Ana's voice matched his.

"Of course," the words flew from his lips without hesitation.

"But only when *la armada* allow it, *verdad*?"

"Well, yes . . ." he sputtered.

"Then I must go."

Ana rose to her feet and Peter stood to meet her, although panic and pain made him unsteady.

"I will sell my commission, Ana. I will leave the army."

Ana froze, halting her steps toward her rooms. Finally, the hopelessness and resignation leaked from her eyes as she turned back to Peter. "*De verdad*?"

"Yes. I promise," Peter said, his chest rising and falling quickly. "I only need to return for a short time to see to this matter of San Sebastián. Perhaps a number of months. I wish to see that some sort of justice is brought to pass, even if it only be on our home soil."

Ana groaned and buried her hands in her hair yet again. "*San Sebastián*—it destroy my life. It take my father. Why is *la justicia* so *importante? O San Sebastián?* And why are they more important than our life here? Than me?"

Her words scraped deep into Peter's heart. And he found he could no longer disguise the truth from her. "It's not about justice or the army. It's not even truly about San Sebastián, Ana. It is about you. I care so deeply because they hurt *you*." His voice broke, a groan of agony escaping him. "And I will not survive seeing you hurt so again."

This was what war truly was. War had not allowed him to escape the violence of his father, the cries of his mother. Instead, foolhardy and selfish soldiers had brought that same devastation to him in an entirely new and heartbreaking way. They had violated and forever altered the mother of his child, the creator of his future—the woman that he loved.

He rubbed a hand over his eyes in an effort to block out the tears that threatened to spill down his cheeks and breathed deeply. "I fight for San Sebastián because I fight for you. For us. I will make this right. I will protect you from being put in danger ever again."

He would be worthy of the suffering she'd endured there.

A cold resignation settled across Ana's features now, her forehead smooth of concerned lines, her tears dried. "*Vaya*. If you must," she whispered, her body slumped, defeated.

"And you will not leave?"

"I will wait. For a time."

Peter stepped forward and embraced Ana, pressing a promise of a kiss to her forehead. But all she had endured made her cold and limp in his arms. A moment later, she wandered, her steps unsteady, back to her room. Only once he could see that she had tucked herself securely into bed did Peter shut their adjoining door. Still, soft sobs drifted to him through the cracks beneath the door.

What a great mess he had made of this evening. But his desire to fight for their future was for the better, was it not? He had no question in his mind about his decision to keep Ana from joining him.

Some small portion of translating for the armies had brought Ana fulfillment, he knew. She had seemed alive and vivacious. But perhaps that came more from being seen and appreciated by her father, the parent who had always been too quick to leave her home. When she had witnessed the horrible realities of war stripped bare, Peter had seen that familiar haunted hollowness settle into her body, dulling her eyes and causing her body to curve around itself protectively. Even worse, after she had survived being attacked, she had retreated completely into her own mind, something Peter had never expected from the Ana who had once fed off the liveliness and entertainment of others. Even coming to England had not been an easy journey. She had been surrounded constantly by soldiers in redcoats that reminded her of her attackers.

One night as they were traveling across the sea, Peter awoke to find Ana's bed in their shared cabin empty. He hurried up to the deck, assuming that she was stricken with seasickness yet again. Instead, he found her, silent and motionless, at the rail, staring back across the ocean to an unseen Spain. Peter had held her hand in a rare moment of welcomed contact as she had whispered of longing for family, for safety. And yet Spain could no longer provide her with any of those comforts, leaving her impossibly torn between two unfamiliar worlds. And so Peter had promised himself that he would provide for Ana what he had never been able to provide for Mother, for Matthew, or for himself: a home.

She would never be provided that security again if she joined him. But sometime in the past months, passing as blindingly fast as they had, Peter had realized that *he* needed home too. And not only home with Mother but home with Ana.

Words came to mind that Mother had written to him months ago when he had first shared his plight with her. As always, she had somehow known precisely what he would need to learn in the coming months. She had written, "There will come a point when you must decide that your future is no longer determined by your past—a past which you did not want nor choose—but instead by your decisions, which you will make of your own volition." She had likely been referring more to his past clashes with Father and how they influenced his family relationships. But how fitting those words were now. Finally, Peter could determine his own future.

Chapter 38

July 18, 1814, London, England

Peter felt in his uniform pocket for the well-worn miniature Bible, his fingers brushing the softened leather as he prayed for comfort. Since his visit with Mr. Smith many months ago, he had taken to carrying the book about with him as a source of strength. And how desperately he needed that strength now.

He stepped into the vast, noisy hallway, the tension pulling at his shoulders and the ringing in his ears betraying his discomfort. A wide variety of trimmings, epaulets, and badges designated the variety of officer stations possessed by the soldiers surrounding him. Once, the sight of scarlet coatees, creamy white pantaloons, and tall Hessians brought Peter some sense of comfort, or at least a feeling of belonging that home had never given him. But now the familiar view only made his stomach roil. He could not rid his vision of those same coatees preying on women, crashing through doors, and slumping near-dead in piles across Basque Country.

After the great doors shut behind him and the crowd ceased its milling about, an officer, a major by the looks of it, rose to a pulpit at the front of the room. Harsh, midday light streamed down from the window behind him. But there was no Bible in his hand, no holy robes on his back. This was not to be a sermon of hope and faith and healing, not in the least. And the great irony of the moment was not lost on Peter.

"Welcome to London! We are gladdened by the sight of all of you, particularly after the vigorous battles you all have endured in months past."

A murmur of agreement rippled over the hall.

"First and foremost, we celebrate the deposition of Napoleon and the signed armistice and treaties. Your roles in these events are to be commended to the highest regard."

Cheers rang throughout the hall. Men clapped shoulders and shook hands, and for a moment, there was a sense of unity, of encouragement, that Peter had not felt since Spain.

"Now, there is still a bit of tidying up to do before we move forward with our allies. There has been a great deal of publicity surrounding our little siege in San Sebastián, even to the point of making waves of gossip in the ballrooms of the Ton. We are aware that some of the ungrateful Spanish and Basque have published a number of so-called *libels* to stir up all sorts of rumors surrounding the incident. They claim we burned their city to the ground in an effort to unseat Wellington's hold on their armies."

"Perhaps we should let them see how terribly they fare on their own," a soldier near Peter called out, his gold epaulets badged with a star designating him a major. "What do you say to that, eh, Harrison?" Peter clenched his fists. Was this war simply about defeating Napoleon, no matter the costs to any of the countries they rampaged through?

"We are also displeased by the disorderly manner in which a few of you have conducted yourselves in the aftermath of the siege," the officer—called Harrison, Peter supposed—continued. Finally there would be some larger measure of discipline! Peter rolled back his shoulders and scanned the group, watching for the guilt that would surely shadow their faces.

"There has been a great deal of talk that more civilians were attacked and killed than what we know to have actually occurred. Spain has tried to cast the blame on us, blame that should be rightfully placed on France's shoulders. Undoubtedly, these rumors have grown here in England as well, likely due to your sharing of your own perspectives, as skewed and influenced as they were by exhaustion. Our army physicians can attest that when you are caught in the middle of a battle, particularly one as drawn-out and entirely straining as the Siege of San Sebastián, your mind can start to mislead you. In your overactive imaginations, a few unfortunate casualties of errant bystanders can grow to mythic and horrific proportions, when they were, in fact, quite inevitable."

Peter's gaze returned to the soldiers around him. There was some regret in their eyes. But theirs was an unfeeling passiveness, a resignation that dominated the room in a chilling way. Were they truly adopting these ridiculous excuses?

"And what if those *few* unfortunate casualties were greater in number than you imply?" Peter called, no longer able to stay silent. Anger heated his whole body, causing his uniform to feel restrictive. "Was Major Bailon's death inevitable then?" *Was Ana's assault?*

The officer singled Peter out with a searing gaze and a critical tilt of his chin. "Captain Ashmore, if you had nearly as much wartime experience as Wellington, you would accept that the occurrence of a number of casualties is simply the nature of war. Allow me to bring to your remembrance his thoughts on the matter, having said that these unfortunate occurrences are a consequence of attending the necessity of storming a town."

"An evil consequence," Peter muttered. He had scoured newspapers for any sort of information, and by his best estimation, it had to have been nearly half of the city's remaining population that was killed in the pillaging and plundering. It was no small casualty.

Harrison sniffed, looking down his nose in Peter's direction. "You would be wise to remember that San Sebastián was one battle among many, and that in enlisting, you accepted the possibility of witnessing death around you. This is our lot, and we are fortunate to have come out victorious, despite the cruelty of the French and the vain rebellions of the Spanish."

He then turned to the larger crowd and continued. "And to show our greatest appreciation to the regiments who helped us to break through to the French, we are preparing Battle Honors and a Military General Service Medal. Those of the 52nd will also receive a patch to commemorate a truly commendable example of conduct and exemplary service. We are certain this will help you all to recall the notable feats that were accomplished there, despite any small misfortunes."

So they were, in a way, bribing their men into silence with accolades and honors. Peter would never be able to pin such a badge on his uniform. It would be like proudly displaying a murderer's brand and expecting praise and renown for it. He would not commemorate the foul misdeeds that occurred there, that had led to Ana's attack and Major Bailon's death. Even now, the bloodred color of his uniform felt sickening.

"Many of you have had a period of rest following the variety of sieges and battles you have been involved in as fresh troops were sent in across the ocean. Thanks to Wellington's fine work in invading Southern France earlier this year, we have all been able to enjoy a period of peace. But now you are all being recalled to your duties."

Peter's stomach was a heavy pit of pain. Even with the foresight gifted to him by David and Captain Davies, the words were still a strike to his heart. Could he really leave Ana when she needed him so desperately? Would he sell his commission, as he had promised? Already his mind started to whirl in a panic, wondering how he could possibly provide for the family that was now so entirely dependent upon him for their survival, and in more ways than one. The army had provided him stability and the promise of a future. But now?

"It has been a difficult road, and some of you may question whether you would like to sell your commission. After all, Napoleon is in exile. But consider how abandoning your country would reflect on you, on your family. You will not be hailed a hero in the halls of London for such behavior."

But selling a commission was not the same as desertion! Once again, Peter's gaze went to the soldiers who surrounded him. Officers of some degree, they all were. Nearly all of them were gentlemen and understood the binding nature of honor and reputation. And yet he could see the same doubt and trepidation that he felt shadow some of their faces and draw their shoulders downward. He was not alone in questioning whether he could truly continue in the army after all they had witnessed. The illusion of discipline and honor had long disappeared now. But many of the men surrounding him would continue in their lots, whether motivated by duty to the Crown or the potential to fill their pockets. But those whom Peter pitied most of all were the poor men who felt so haunted, so transformed by life at war, that they doubted if they would ever be able to reenter society, or any degree of normal living, again.

"There is still an important work to do for Crown and country. Our Duke of Wellington has accomplished a great deal, such as the Peace of Paris signing only months ago, of which you are well aware. But much unrest remains, particularly in France and Spain, even as Napoleon is exiled. You will be great tools in ensuring that this period of peace continues."

Peter was all too familiar with the cost of wartime peace. Peace was bloody. It was the ghost of mourning, screaming, suffering. Peace was not quiet. At least it did not start that way. Once, that peace had been enough for him. It had been a sort of comfort compared to the wreckage of his family home. But with Ana María, Peter had found an altogether different sense of peace. A lasting peace, a healing peace. A peace that did not require killing. How would he sacrifice that peace again?

Chapter 39

August 1, 1814, Abbeygate, Surrey Hills, England

LADY ASHMORE AND PETER HAD LEFT FOR LONDON WITHIN NEARLY the same hour, leaving Ana feeling hollow and sending her tumbling, splashing back into the ocean of darkness that had drowned her only weeks before. She had spent the following days entirely on edge. Ana wandered Abbeygate in her dressing gown, as it felt impossible to prepare herself fully for the day when she was entirely certain her entire world was about to shatter to bits around her. She circled past the entryway a few times each hour, checking for letters, waiting for news, straining to hear the sound of hoofbeats. Burnsey was often stationed there, his normally jolly face drawn downward in worry and pity. That only stoked the desperate determination that was burning in Ana's stomach.

She would not remain behind endlessly, waiting for word that Peter had been drawn back to the army by the false promises of glory. She would not sit by idly while all of Surrey Hills whispered about poor Mrs. Ashmore, abandoned again by her duty-bound husband, and all while hardly knowing how to communicate like a civilized person. And she had told Peter as much, had promised him she would wait, but only for a time. If many more weeks passed without his return, Ana would be forced to conclude that despite his protective and caring nature, Peter had determined that his responsibilities to his country were greater than his obligation to her. And why wouldn't he? It was not as if he loved her.

Ana pressed a hand to her face, as if that would quell the tears that wanted so badly to pour out of her. She breathed deeply, desperately, and her throat ached from the tearing emotion that was stifled inside her. Esperanza cooed, her eyes roving around Ana's face, as if searching for the source of unhappiness in her. Her sweet, tiny eyes were cloudy still, both in color and in vision. She had begun to move about her head and gaze as if searching for the source of noises, but she was not so adept at recognizing what she was looking at, from what Ana observed. Still, her cooing increased, and she nuzzled in at Ana's breast, where she was firmly tucked.

"You feel my distress, no? *Lo siento, hijita. Estoy bien.* Nothing is the matter, and if it were, it would not be any fault of yours."

Ana stroked a finger across Esperanza's velvety cheek, the warmth of the contact grounding her again. The nursery was quiet as she rocked, the soothing sounds of nighttime faint outside the window. She would have to act according to Esperanza's needs—and her own. And both of them needed family. If this child was not to have a father present and Ana was not to have a husband, then they would journey to Spain to see her *abuela*. Perhaps someday they would even find *Mamá,* if she had survived the war that ravaged the country.

"We will be well, *mi amor. Te lo prometo.*"

"Ana!" came a yell from the hallway, Elena's bright, open pronunciation bouncing off the walls, echoed by the sound of quick footsteps.

Ana rose to her feet, her heart pounding, "*Qué pasó?*" Esperanza startled at the movement and started to cry, bringing tears to Ana's eyes for more than one reason. She bounced her arms, whispering to the babe.

"Ana!" The maid halted herself at the door, bracing herself against the frame. "Word is arriving, *de Pedro.*"

Ana eased the calming babe into Elena's arms, bunched the skirts of her dressing gown in her hands, and hurried down the hallway and down the stairs.

Burnsey stood at the door. "We heard tell that a soldier approaches on horseback. Likely with notice of Mr. Ashmore."

Without hesitation, Ana disregarded her state of undress, grasped the handle, and heaved open the large, wooden door, ignoring Burnsey's protestations entirely. He was correct, indeed. Off in the distance, beyond the gate and drive, there was a redcoat on horseback. Ana started down the stairs and walked briskly down the gravel path, tears already streaking across her face. This poor, unfortunate soldier hadn't the slightest notion that he was about to determine her entire future and would likely face a very emotional bout of Spanish as a result.

But that was no mere messenger.

As the horse—and Ana's hurried steps—brought the man into closer view, she saw the gold epaulets on his shoulders and badges glinting off his chest. This was an officer. Something terrible had to have occurred for them to send an officer in a messenger's place. Ana broke into a run now, her chest heaving with exertion or emotion, she was not sure which.

At the increase in her movement, the officer urged his horse on to a gallop and ripped the hat off his head. Dark hair escaped its binding, waving in the heavy humidity of the evening. The darkening sky did not aid Ana much in making out his face, but as he drew increasingly closer, his hair, his form, his broad frame looked all too familiar.

She choked on tears and hope, collapsing to her knees as Peter leapt off his horse and ran, closing the remaining distance to her. In one movement, he knelt at her side and swept her onto his lap, into his arms.

"I thought you would never return. *Nunca,*" she sobbed into his crimson jacket.

"But I promised I would, darling. And I would never break a promise to you."

So many times, *Papá* had left her, promising to return soon. So many days Ana had spent searching for *Mamá* in Valencia, convinced that if she could only see her daughter, she would return home. And these past days had filled her with that familiar terror as she walked about Abbeygate, convinced that she and Peter would never share the same space again.

But here he was. Whispering her name, pulling her body closer to his, quelling her trembling with his strong stability, and Ana had never felt so relieved, so safe. Her desperate fingers felt at the rough fabric of his sleeves, clutched at the warmth of his firm arms beneath. Now the panic ebbed out of her in waves as she wet his front with tears, leaving her weak but calmed.

Finally, Ana found her voice and the courage to speak. "When does the *armada* require that you return?" she whispered, proud of how her voice only trembled on the last word.

"Never."

Ana's heart thudded to a stop. "You abandon them?" She pushed back out of his embrace, urgency filling her words as she searched his gaze. "But your mother, your family, their name will be affected, no?"

"No, darling. I sold my commission. Just as I promised."

An aching hope began to grow traitorously in Ana's chest, like an insistent weed in too-wet earth.

"And *San Sebastián*? Did you resolve *todo*?"

The light in Peter's eyes dimmed slightly, and the corners of his mouth pulled downward, his expression sodden with pain and regret. "There is nothing more that can be done, at least not from my former position as a captain."

Ana placed a hand on his cheek, stroking her thumb over the smoothness of his skin and the roughness of his dark whiskers. "*Lo siento mucho, querido.*"

Peter leaned into her touch and scrunched his eyes shut, "I wanted so badly to make something right of all the wrongs that occurred there. Of all the pain and injustice that you wrongfully endured. I felt that if I could not protect you, I could not protect anyone, not even Esperanza, not even our future children."

Ana's chest thrummed with anxious anticipation as she wrapped her hands around Peter's

"But I only discovered that in so many matters of war, my hands are tied. Even if I had been Wellington himself, I doubt there would have been approval given for greater disciplinary actions against our own, or greater measures of recompense and mercy to the Spanish and Basque. Too many view that city, and the many others that were placed under siege in Spain, as a mere part of their conquest and victory over Napoleon. They fail to see how they have destroyed communities, ripped apart families, and altered lives permanently."

Ana remembered seeing joy vanish from *Papá* after having witnessed similar things. He had tried to shield her from such things and ultimately had died in trying to protect her and their countrymen.

Peter took a deep breath, as if to calm himself, and opened his eyes again. "But in focusing for so long on the pain you and so many others endured, I have failed to see that San Sebastián gave me the greatest blessings—blessings I never imagined I would enjoy during this life. It gave me an intelligent, kind, passionate, and beautiful wife, and the most adorable, lovable daughter ever known to man. I regret all that we had to experience there together, my darling. But I will never regret my being there, nor yours. Despite the suffering you endured, San Sebastián brought me you, and you have blessed me with love and healing that I never thought possible. And I will not waste another day sullying our future with the memory of a dark past, preventable as it might have been."

That aching hope throbbed now, in an impossibly physical way, as it grew to fill the cavity of her chest. "*Vas a quedarte conmigo?*" she whispered.

"Yes, love, I am staying with you." Peter's hands cupped Ana's cheeks. "Forever."

Then finally, blessedly, he covered her lips with his. Peter's kisses were slow and soft, trailing across her lips and covering her cheeks, undoing the last of Ana's resolve to keep her emotions at bay. Tears of relief trailed down her cheeks, wetting Peter's face as well. He paused momentarily, concern lining his face as he wiped away her tears. But Ana pulled his hands away and returned his kisses with a new kind of fervor. She moved her lips over his, tangling her hands in his hair. Peter laughed against her lips, clearly pleased with her response, as his hands slid back to that sensitive spot behind her ear and up into her curls. She could spend forever in his embrace, particularly when she was being kissed as intently as she was. This was safety.

This was *love*.

Peter broke away, gasping, but did not move his hands from her. "I will not deny that I have run from difficulties in the past. It was, in all honesty, what drove me to enlist in the army at the beginning. But

Ana, you are not a difficulty. You are the only part of my life that is *not* a difficulty. I would never run from you."

Ana wrapped her arms around his neck, as if she could pull him closer to her. "I no want you to be distant again, not like these past weeks. I cannot bear it. *No puedo.*"

Peter leaned in, bringing Ana's forehead to his. "I have been frightened of hurting you, or of pressuring you. You have endured something so immense as bringing a child to this world, and I did not want to further burden you."

"I missed you—your touch, your wisdom and words. Even your silence. I missed *todo.*" Ana brushed a hand down his shoulder and chest, trying to memorize the feeling of his closeness. "But I also missed me, *mi vida normal.* I lost myself in those days, Peter. *Particularmente* when I think about my parents."

Peter kissed her forehead, her temple. "It pains me to learn of all the difficulties you saw, and while you were still so young. I only wanted to protect you from further pain."

"And you do, more than anyone else. You are my protector, my rescuer. But I need this." She waved a hand between them, indicating the closeness, the openness, the honesty that was difficult to explain.

"As do I. And I promise that we will never lose it again."

"*Te lo prometo también.*" Ana nestled back into Peter's chest and breathed deeply, as if she could absorb the warmth and security that the feeling brought her. He had sacrificed so much for her. He had changed his way of living entirely, particularly now, as he had sold his commission. And while Ana had given him a daughter, a family, she had never truly revealed the most precious gift she could give to him. Not fully, at least. Her pulse thrummed impossibly fast as she whispered into his chest. "*Pedro*?"

"*Sí?*"

She grinned, "*Cómo te amo!*" then threw back her head, laughing and avoiding his gaze. Nervousness was a fire inside her, driving her to make light of the moment in fear of acknowledging the truth of her feelings.

Peter shook his head, tutting. "Is that truly how you are going to confess your feelings to me? When I have waited to hear them for so long?"

Ana protested, hiccupping through her laughter. "*Ay*, *amor*, I said to you I love you in *San Sebastián*. And I believe you did too."

"It is true," Peter said with a chuckle. "But I did not know I meant it then. And I did not have the depth of love for you that I feel now, after all we have endured together, after seeing you become the mother of my child." His voice turned husky and serious. "You are my home. You are my life. Ana María Ashmore, I love you. I love you more than the army, I love you more than my country, I love you more than life itself. I thank God every day that He brought me you."

Ana felt impossibly happy, so intoxicating it was to hear the affirming words she had longed for. She tried to kiss Peter again but could hardly close her lips over the wide smile that split her face. Then she pulled away, breathing deeply to capture some sort of calm to stamp out her nervousness. For so many months, she had dreamed of expressing her feelings for her husband without trepidation, and now it proved much more difficult than she thought to find the words sufficient to do so, particularly in English.

"*Amor*, you have put a siege on *mi corazón*, and I surrendered it to you long, long ago.

"A siege on your heart?" Peter quirked the corner of his mouth. "How entirely appropriate."

"*Sí*," she answered. "And I love you, *con todo mi ser*."

Peter blinked, his brow scrunching as he worked to translate. "With all my being . . . or perhaps, with all that I am?"

Ana laughed. "How your *Español* is improving, my love!" Then she secured his face with her hands and pressed a long, lingering kiss against his forehead. A promise in the form of a *beso*. "*Te amo para siempre, mi vida*."

Chapter 40

August 31, 1814, Abbeygate, Surrey Hills, England

The past month had brought about more transformations and miracles than Peter had ever imagined possible, and it was largely in thanks to his wife. Firstly, the closeness that they now enjoyed was nothing short of heavenly. Ana had finally convinced him that she was ready to share herself completely with him, after reassuring him that she was completely recovered from childbirth. Their trust was healed, and their marriage was true and whole in every sense of the word. Peter doubted he would ever be able to sleep apart from his wife again. The one-year anniversary of their marriage was fast approaching, and they were finally free to show each other how completely and deeply besotted they were with one another.

After recovering from her rather exuberant relief that he had sold his commission, Ana had quickly occupied herself with the business of ensuring the happiness of their future. She had started by busying herself with Peter's career prospects. Together they had dug through his old schoolbooks from his time at Cambridge, and his interest in law had been reignited. There were too many injustices dealt to low-ranking soldiers, particularly after their time of service was concluded, and perhaps as a barrister, Peter could do something about it. With Mother's connections and Matthew's influence, Peter found himself somewhat nervously anticipating the approaching commencement of his education on justice and law in the Inns of Court. He would be interacting with solicitors and barristers, true, but also with his fellow students, and he would likely be at least four years their senior. When Peter had left university to enlist in the army, he had never imagined that he would ever be returning to the studious life, much less with a wife and child in tow.

Ana had also urged him to repair his relationship with Matthew. The circumstances of their marriage and Esperanza's birth had helped him grow closer to his mother than he had ever felt before. It had healed the strain that his years in the service of the Crown had placed upon their relationship. But still, there was a distinct distance—a feeling of cautious formality—between him and Matthew. And there was something he ought to do about it. So he had sent a missive to his brother, and upon receiving a reply, he went to visit him at Heathridge.

Matthew had always carried the weight of his many responsibilities as if they were a natural part of his frame. There was no curving of his shoulders under the burden of his role as earl, no permanent wrinkle at his brow and mouth due to his obvious concern for his mother. Somehow he had handled the difficulties of their lives much more easily and gracefully than Peter had ever been able to manage himself. But when Peter stepped into his brother's study that afternoon, he saw a different man entirely.

The room itself was much changed since Father's time there. The many crystal-housed liquors that had once crowded the desk's corner were cleared away entirely. The constant, suffocating smell of cigar smoke was cleared too—a practice that was frowned upon by Mother, not that Father had given any mind to her. Even the clutter of disorganized estate papers was replaced with several orderly books, stacked neatly, although their pages were visibly well-worn.

But Matthew had seemed to change even more than his surroundings. Instead of having perfect posture, every tall line bleeding confidence, which was the view of Matthew that Peter was accustomed to seeing, he was relaxed. He had one leg crossed over the other, and he was reclined in his seat, his head resting low on the seat's back. And while he was visibly relaxed, there was a rare line of true, deep concern across his forehead.

"Brother, come in," Matthew said, waving his hand as a small smile graced his face.

A moment later, he seemed to find the strength—or motivation—to rise from his chair and gave Peter a hearty, lingering embrace. That sort of touch from a man who looked and sounded so much like Father very nearly caused Peter's legs to tremble. But he clenched his jaw and snapped his feet together into a military pose to prevent the release of emotion.

"I hear congratulations are in order," Peter said, fighting through the waver in his voice.

"Indeed. I am a husband now as well. Mother has successfully seen both of her boys happily married," Matthew chuckled.

"Although she had little to do with my particular arrangement."

"That is not the way I understand it," Matthew said with a knowing glance. "I believe she has done a great deal to support your marriage to Ana throughout this past year. Perhaps in more ways than you know. She has done the same for Isabelle and me. Our own path to marriage has not been as simple as it might appear. But Mother would not rest until we were happily settled."

"I daresay you are correct." Peter nodded. "She is the best of mothers." His heart swelled with gratitude for Mother's attentive compassion. How fortunate they all were to be recipients of her care.

After seeing that Peter was seated comfortably with a glass of cold lemonade in his hand, Matthew leaned forward, wasting no time. "Now, there was something you wished to discuss?"

Peter tilted his head back and forth in an effort to release the tension trapped in his neck.

"Yes. Ana has urged me to see . . . that is, I wished for quite some time to . . ." He shook his head, breathing out an exasperated sigh. "I am not made for these sorts of conversations, it would seem."

"Our wives do a great deal to help us, do they not?" Matthew replied, chuckling. "But I'm afraid you'll need to have out with it yourself, my good man."

Peter rubbed a hand across his neck and squeezed his eyes shut, the words "I am sorry" finally exploding from his mouth in a raw, pain-filled whisper.

The silence that flooded the room after those three words was something Peter had not expected. Truthfully, he had not known what to expect. Would Matthew laugh like when they were young boys and attest that their misunderstandings had been but a small folly? Or did he have some small part of Father in him, and would he rage at Peter, telling him the truth of how wrong he had been to depart when and how he had?

Instead, the silence endured. Finally, Peter cracked an eye open and saw tears rolling down Matthew's face, his expression entirely unabashed.

"Not as sorry as I am," Matthew answered. "No child ought to endure what you and I did. I understand that now more than ever as a husband and a brother by marriage to two young children."

"And I do as well, as a father."

"Yes, of course."

Peter wanted to linger in that moment of understanding and companionship, but there was another issue pulling at his mind and heart.

"I also wish to apologize for the years of my absence," Peter blurted. "It was inexcusable to leave as I did. I had hardly returned from the distraction that was my university studies and, almost immediately, was off again."

"Mother mourned your departure," Matthew said with a nod. "As did I. But nineteen was not an unheard-of age to be seeking your own future, much less in the army. It was an honorable enlistment."

"Not so honorable if you consider that I was running away from home to avoid killing my own father," Peter muttered. "I could not endure him any longer."

A sad sort of smile crossed Matthew's face.

"We could only protect Mother for so long, you and I. And what pained her more than the mottled bruises and scrapes that braceleted her arms was seeing you and me in harm's way—in *his* way. So even though your departure was unexpected and difficult, to be sure, I think in some unexpected way, it was a great relief for her. She knew that if you were on the other side of the sea, he could not get to you."

Peter blinked hard at the tears that formed at the image of his mother, willing to send her son into enemy territory to get him away from her husband. “She is the bravest of mothers,” he managed.

“Indeed, she is,” Matthew said. “And you must know that neither she nor I harbor any ill will against you for leaving. We only wish that you had written more. But now having you back fills that hole that we both have felt for years now.”

“And back for good,” Peter said. “I have sold my commission.”

“Truly?” Matthew’s eyes were wide, his jaw slack in surprise.

Peter nodded in response, then rose from his chair to receive the bear hug brought on by Matthew’s relief and excitement. Once they managed to rein in their emotions somewhat, Peter turned his focus back to his brother.

“Now your happy life at home can begin in earnest,” Matthew said. But what had caused that line of concern to appear in his forehead after all these years?

“I trust that your life at home remains equally happy?” Peter asked.

“Yes, but it is not without sorrow. Isabelle is concerned for her mother, who has fallen ill again. I’m doing all I can to comfort her and her siblings,” Matthew said.

The last memory of regret softened as Peter saw how Matthew’s concern for his new family encompassed him completely. He was trying to care for them and protect them, much as he had always tried to do for Peter, even when Peter had wished that he could be the protector himself.

“You are a good husband and brother. You will be an even better father, I believe.”

“I aspire to be one as caring and attentive as you are.”

After sharing so much raw emotion, the brothers inevitably dropped into a more casual, lighthearted conversation about hunting, horse racing, and Sir David’s prospects, but not before Matthew could bestow upon Peter the official stewardship of Abbeygate. The property was still the Ashmore country seat, but Matthew found himself quite wrapped up in his duties in London and his responsibilities to his new family and had no intention to use it in the future. He desired for Peter exactly what Peter had longed for himself for so many years: a place that was truly home. And now that he would never return to war, Peter had his entire life ahead of him to ensure that Abbeygate became such, even more than it already had.

* * *

The age of three months was perfect, Peter had decided. But he could not deny that every new ability Essie discovered about herself proved to be more exciting than the last. First, the slow, uncontrolled squirming of her arms and legs had adorably fascinated her. And then she had discovered her voice, a voice that was just as musical and enrapturing in its nature as her mother's. Even her squalls of protest were beautiful. She had started to lift her head about and even offered him soft, pink smiles that were surprisingly wet. Every bit of her was enchanting, down to her round fingers and the adorable roll of fat about her ankles and wrists. Best of all, she had her mother's eyes. Peter would never be able to deny her anything if she knew the power of their depths.

Perhaps every age of hers would be his favorite. Peter had never imagined himself so enamored by such a tiny person, particularly one who likely didn't even recognize him yet.

"*Amor?*"

"*Sí?*"

"I believe Esperanza has hunger."

Peter looked down, surprised to see the babe sucking hungrily at his thumb. So lost in reflection he had been, he hadn't even felt it. Or perhaps he was already so accustomed to her new habit.

"Right you are, my dear." Peter crossed the nursery and carefully handed the babe to Ana, who unbuttoned a clever flap on her dress. Within a moment, Essie was attached to her mother and sucking surprisingly violently.

Peter chuckled. "If only we could all dine so quickly and conveniently."

"Convenient for her, perhaps," Ana said with a chuckle. But there was no bitterness or even exhaustion in her voice—only adoration as she brushed the jiggling cheek of their daughter with a gentle finger.

Peter had experienced many transformations in recent days, but he had also seen a great transformation in his wife. Letting go of the fear of abandonment she had carried for so many years had healed her in a way that was strangely visible. Her beautiful face was trusting and open now, her posture relaxed, and her smile genuine and full. Having confidence in her future, even in their love, had made Ana even more beautiful and compassionate than she had ever been before. And Peter found he could hardly resist her. They spent every available moment together walking the grounds, visiting the village, learning Spanish, attending church services, and marveling over the beauty of their growing daughter. And Peter had made a habit of kissing his wife with nearly every breath. The passion of their marriage had returned as all-encompassing and refreshing as a summer rainstorm. He had never dreamed that such a relationship could bring him the wholeness he had always longed for. It was a holy thing to love his wife. It was worship.

Ana still endured moments of fear when panic seized her by the shoulders and froze her mind momentarily, but Peter had been learning how to help her in such moments. Pulling her into a gentle, enduring embrace and reminding her of her present reality often seemed to do the trick, although he was trying to become better at listening to her concerns before offering up a solution, as well-thought-out as it might be.

One of the most important lessons he had begun to understand was that small failures and mistakes were not permanent. Not in his studies, nor in his efforts to care for Abbeygate. And most importantly, not in his relationships with his wife and daughter. He was not perfect by any means and was often less patient or compassionate than he should be. But that did not deem him a failure or dictate that he needed to run away again. Instead, it was merely a reminder that while his love for his wife and daughter was deep, true, and enduring, it still required effort. And when needed, they helped each other make adjustments for the benefit of their family.

"*Amor*, I do believe you are forgetting something," Ana called from her chair in the corner. "*Por qué* today *es tan importante*?"

Speaking of adjustments and corrections, it appeared one was at hand. Peter laughed.

"Why is today important? Well, let me consider. Today is not the anniversary of our wedding, nor is it your birthday, or mine, or Essie's for that matter. It is not Christmas or *Pascua* or *el Día de los Inocentes*.

Now, what could I be forgetting that would be of some importance to us?" He strolled over to his wife and kissed the curly, unruly top of her head, as a smaller head of hair, similarly unruly, finally lolled in a milk-induced dream in her arms.

Ana looked up at him, her ebony eyes wide with feeling, while her lips quirked in a bittersweet smile. "San Sebastián," she whispered.

Peter sighed heavily and lowered himself to the floor at her side. "Right you are, my dear."

"You forgot," Ana said.

But her voice was not thin with pain or criticism or even questioning. Instead, it was soft with some other emotion entirely. Relief, perhaps. Peter reached up for his wife's hand and met her eyes again. Yes, she was relieved. He could see it in the smoothness of her brow and the relaxed tilt of her jaw.

Indeed, he *had* forgotten. There had been months when Peter had believed he would never be able to forget it. The destruction, the horror, the unrestrained and inhumane violence. But now it had been days, perhaps weeks, since the event even crossed his mind. Slowly, he had learned that there was too much evil that occurred in the war for justice to be served on behalf of all of it. No man would ever be able to right all of those wrongs. And that was why there was need for a loving and forgiving God who could offer healing to a broken world.

"Has a year truly passed? And only a year?" he asked as he rubbed a hand across his forehead. "It feels as if that were an entire lifetime ago."

"So much has changed since that time," Ana said. "*We* have changed since that time. A great deal."

Peter nodded and pressed a kiss to her palm. "Maybe we ought to commemorate it somehow. Light some candles, perhaps. In remembrance of your *Papá* and the others who perished there."

"I think that is a lovely notion, *amor*. I would like that very much."

"Very well. Consider it a new family tradition," Peter said, his mind already spinning with ideas. But then the slightest shadow of pain crossed Ana's face. Peter paused his formulating and tightened his grip on Ana's hand. However, it seemed to be more of a reflection of past pain than the true sharpness of lingering, present pain.

"Is there anything else you wish to discuss regarding San Sebastián?"

She rested her head against the back of her chair, closing her eyes. "*En este momento, no.*"

"I propose that we reflect instead upon something of much greater importance. As you said, you and I have changed a great deal since those events. We are married now, of course. You have brought precious, new life into our world and our hearts. I have left the army entirely and find great joy in that decision, something I never could have anticipated."

"And we are in love," Ana said, her tone teasing as she raised her eyes pointedly, as if he had forgotten that as well.

"Most deeply and permanently and *unforgettably* so." Peter smiled as he rose to his feet to better reach his wife's lips. She laughed into his kiss, which only gave him an excuse to kiss her longer and more thoroughly.

"And we found home here," Ana said once he released her, her lips full and cheeks bright with color.

"We made this our home," Peter said, as he pulled his wife to her feet, careful of the slumbering babe in her arms. He led her to the window and wrapped them both in an embrace as they looked out over the gardens and land they treasured.

The name of Abbeygate had never held a special significance for Peter until now. As a young boy, in fact, he hadn't given it any thought at all. But when they had arrived at the manor nearly a year ago, he had only thought of the name in relation to the old stone church that sat some distance behind it, as if the property was a gateway to the church. But now he could see that for him and Ana, Abbeygate had been a gateway to peace, a gateway to God, a gateway to healing. It had become the place of belonging that neither of them had ever imagined they would have.

Abbeygate was, in every essence of the word, a safe haven.

Epilogue

August 31, 1816, San Sebastián, Spain

San Sebastián.

Once, it was a sparkling city that was delicately perched on a hill, at the end of a narrow curve of land that reached out to the turquoise sea like arms eager for an embrace. Once, it was vibrant, beautiful, full of music and culture and faith. Now it was full of ash.

Ana approached the spot where the city gate once stood, hand in hand with Peter, in shock at the emptiness that lay before them. A lonely silence echoed throughout the place. By all appearances, the city had long been abandoned by the few Basque and Spanish that survived the sacking. The remnants of the city were faintly mapped in the form of ash-painted ruins and dusty streets. Pain and sadness still hung heavy in the air, but with them came a sense of hope. Someday, Ana hoped, it would be rebuilt. It was tucked in too beautiful a corner of Basque Country to remain untouched forever, a skeleton of what it once had been. Ana only wished there was some sort of memorial to all the residents who had died there after sacrificing so much to support the Allied armies. She wished to know their names, to know of their lives, as they had been the true pulse of this city.

"Let us pray for them," she whispered, joining her hands with Peter's. Together they kneeled, unconcerned at the ash that would dirty Ana's skirts and Peter's pants at the knees. If offering up a prayer to God was some way that they could help these people, both alive and dead, then having stained clothes was an incredibly small price to pay. And it would be a remembrance of this moment.

Peter wrapped a comforting embrace around her, his lips warm at her temple. Ana leaned into his touch, savoring the strength she drew from it. Theirs was not a visit of happenstance. It was carefully planned, as today marked three years since the burning of the city.

Three years, and seemingly an eternity had passed since then.

Their lives had moved on in ways Ana had never anticipated, bringing blessings that she never could have even hoped for.

Peter had finished his accelerated time at the Inns of Court, had been successful in his call to the bar, had received recommendations from a variety of Matthew's connections of the gentry, and was now a full-fledged barrister. A new type of fulfillment had flooded his life upon realizing that he not only had a way to provide for his family, but he could also advocate for retired or abandoned soldiers who desperately needed help. Of course, working with solicitors and assisting in cases for the Ton also helped to cushion his coffers nicely.

Even with Peter having started his practice as a barrister, the reality of the war with France ending brought a sense of safety and relief to their home that was difficult to put into words. For too many years, the war had torn apart their countries and families and threatened their futures. Ana could sleep more easily, with Peter's deep, slow breathing lulling her into a tranquil rest each night. Even her night terrors of wartime were fading fast, although Peter's still lingered on a particularly loud and stormy night.

Ana had not found *Mamá* nor *Abuelita* in their visits to Spain, although she had found her grandmother's grave in Valencia after much searching. Time had taken them both, it would seem. And after the mixed feelings of mourning and healing had passed, she found a more complete joy in her household roles, both as a hostess and as a mother. She invested a great deal of time and feeling into the quaint and quirky community that surrounded her. And she felt a true sense of trust and belonging in her new family, which provided her with a deep sense of safety and satisfaction. Perhaps most importantly, she was wildly and passionately in love with her husband.

Their love had transformed through the difficulties of their lives and the shifting of their roles as parents, but it had transformed into something even sweeter, even truer, even more enduring. Early in their marriage, Ana had sometimes wished for the enraptured, besotted affection typically shown by a couple newly wedded. But now she understood that she and Peter never could have had such a blissfully ignorant love, not when he had held her battered body and nursed her wounds. Not when he had carried her throughout the past years just as she had carried Esperanza. No, their love always had a profound and enduring depth to it that defied any infatuation she had once longed for. Peter understood her heart and her soul in a manner so healing that she would never be able to put it to words. And that knowledge was irreplaceable.

A true, abiding peace accompanied them now, a reality that Ana had prayed for desperately. In truth, it was a reality she never thought she would experience again after San Sebastián. But now she recognized, as earnestly as did Peter, that in an unforeseen way, San Sebastián had given her the greatest blessing of all: a family. And for that, she would never stop thanking God.

After their first visit to San Sebastián, Ana and Peter started a tradition of lighting a candle in every one of Abbeygate's windows and burning them through the night to commemorate the tragedy that had altered their lives. The candles served as a reminder of the duality of hope and despair, of all that was lost and all that was gained there. And somehow, recognizing that the pain they both had endured there, and in the many years before, made the love that they shared now even sweeter. It was a holy thing. In the small window of Ana's sitting room, she would place three candles. One for *San Sebastián*. One for *Mamá* and *Papá*. And one for their growing family: Peter, Ana, Esperanza, and Mateo.

Both children carried their Spanish legacy and their Ashmore heritage in their names, having been properly baptized as Peter's children at the stone chapel and christened for Ana's sake in a Catholic cathedral during a visit to Spain. Their adorable son, having been named for his uncle, was now starting to learn to toddle about but was still adorably round and rosy-cheeked. Each time he smiled at his parents from where he had flopped on the floor, Peter's crystalline eyes shone up from his small, adorably dimpled face and Ana's curls brushed against his forehead. Ana thanked God each day for her husband and the children he had given her, for Peter had given her both of them. Without Peter, likely neither Ana nor Esperanza would have survived. Without Peter, they would not now have a peaceful home or a blissful family to enjoy. Without Peter, Ana would never know true, selfless, unconditional love. A love that protected. A love that saved. A love that remained.

El Fin (The End)

A Note on San Sebastián and Historical Accuracy

Writing about an event that is somewhat disputed in its accuracy is not a simple task. Uncovering the truth of what occurred in San Sebastián required countless hours of digging through articles, online libraries, old newspapers, and war textbooks. Although the true events of the Siege of San Sebastián were not publicly acknowledged for many years, as we see in this story, there is still much discussion about it today. It has been estimated by historians that over half the town's population was killed in this event, possibly nearing a thousand deaths. The sacking, pillaging, and raping that occurred in this city have been deemed a huge atrocity and one of the worst examples of gross misconduct by the British army in history. Portuguese soldiers may have also been involved.

It is also widely debated as to how Wellington and other army leaders responded to the sacking. There were numerous libels and newspapers published talking about the horrors that happened there, and it seemed that army leaders, Wellington included, tried to deny these accusations, particularly those that testified that the burning of the city had been an intentional, strategic decision. It must be acknowledged that during the Napoleonic War, there was somewhat of a volatile political climate, and surely some of the hushed nature of this and other sieges in Spain was to try to prevent further dangerous conflicts. However, that does not excuse the pillaging and attacking that occurred, which had nothing to do with a strategic necessity and were in apparent disobedience of orders from Wellington.

Town survivors wrote to Wellington and others to acknowledge their victory in the area and to request monetary compensation and assistance for those suffering and in need. They would, after all, need to rebuild not only their sense of community and safety but also their city. Wellington, or perhaps his superiors, refused to carry out such a request. The trial referenced by Peter in chapter 10 did occur and was, in fact, only attended by two women. The rest, it seems, were either dead, seriously incapacitated, or scared to testify of the atrocities they had endured at the hands of the men who were supposed to protect and defend them.

Military General Service Medal

In chapter 38, I wrote about a Military General Service Medal that was given to soldiers who fought in the Siege of San Sebastián. This medal was actually awarded in 1848 denoting service in the Peninsular War, with a special clasp that said "San Sebastián" for those who were present there. The victory was seen as important, historic, and strategic in the eventual overthrow of Napoleon, which is why it was commemorated in such a way. However, that award fails to represent the many Basque and Spanish people who suffered needlessly and mercilessly at the hands of the troops there. Hundreds died after being raped and/or tortured, and after their homes were pillaged, the British set fire to their entire city. This was no normal, expected, or excusable casualty of a battle. There are recorded journals and letters from the soldiers involved documenting just how horrific, inexcusable, and unforgettable the events were that day. Many, it seems, felt as Peter did but were similarly unable to bring any apparent justice to the victims who had suffered there.

Yearly Commemoration of San Sebastián

Each year on August 31, there is a commemoration of the burning of San Sebastián that occurs in the present-day city. Town members and visitors carry torches and candles in a silent procession from church to church and trace the only street that was not destroyed in the burning and subsequent events. People also hold candles and lights on their balconies, an image I tried to replicate in the epilogue of this story. A Catholic mass to the city's patron saint and a reenactment of the sacking also invite those present to reflect on the grave tragedy and injustice of that day. While there is a lot of suffering that is remembered, this event also commemorates the courage of those who, years later, started the rebuilding process to resurrect the spirit and culture of a city so inhumanely lost.

Acknowledgments

WELL, I CERTAINLY CAN'T START THIS ACKNOWLEDGMENT SECTION without highlighting my biggest cheerleader, my husband. He has been patient with me through countless late nights of me being glued to the computer and has heard more sessions of my out-loud brainstorming than he ever agreed to. I love you, babe!

Thank you to my parents and parents-in-law as well as my siblings and siblings-in-law for supporting me on this adventure. It means the world to me!

This story flowed out of me much more quickly than other stories I have written. But I needed a lot of help to work through the many accounts of this debated history to find the story I really wanted to tell. I'm so grateful to my writing group, Brooke Hampton and Sara Cardon, for their help in this over the course of many years. I'm also so grateful to my excellent beta readers, including Marjorie Harris, Kathleen Cummings, Sunny Johnson, Jessie Rich, and Abbie Jensen. Your feedback was invaluable! When it came to the extensive research, I was reliant upon the listed sources as well as assistance from Professor Andrew Roberts, historian Jonathan North, and historian John Lee. My heartfelt thanks go out to the team at Cedar Fort who took a chance on me as a debut author and helped me bring this story to life. I will be forever grateful to you for the help you provided me and the patience you had with my many questions. And I certainly have to thank my new bookstagram and author friends! Thank you, Angela, for keeping me from getting too stressed. A huge thank you to Karen Thornell, Rachel Grow Law, Anneka Walker, and Rachel Kelley Stones for your advice and endorsements. I am so grateful to be connected with such a lovely community. Thank you all for helping to spread the word about my book.

Most of all, I'm grateful to my Father in Heaven, who healed me of some of my own emotional wounds as I explored this story and reflected on my role as a young mother. And I'm eternally grateful to my Savior, who carries the burdens I can't shoulder alone. I know He lives!

Spanish Glossary

abandonada—abandoned

abuela/o(s)—grandma/grandpa/grandparents

actividad—activity

afuera—outside

ahora—now

amor—love

aquí—here

armada—army

arras—coins/money

arreglar—to fix

así—like that

besos—kisses

boda—wedding

buen día—good day

buena suerte—good luck

casa—house

casi llegamos—we're almost there

celebraciones—celebrations

celeste—light blue

chistes—jokes

cielos—heavens

cierra tus ojos—close your eyes

claro—of course / I see

como niños—like children

como siempre—like always

como un beso—like a kiss

completamente enamorada—completely in love

complicado(a)—complicated

con todo mi ser—with all my being

de—of

de hecho—as a matter of fact

de nada—you're welcome / of nothing / no problem

de verdad—truly

desastre—disaster

diferente—different

difícil—difficult

dificuldades—difficulties

dulces—sweets

ellas—they (feminine)

el capitán—the captain

El Día de los Inocentes—the Day of the Innocents

el día—the day

en este momento—in this moment

en la casa—in the house

en mi vida—in my life

entendimiento—understanding

entiendes—you (informal) understand

entiendo—I understand

eso—this

esposo(s)—spouse(s)

estamos juntos—we are together

¿estás bien?—are you well?

está bien—it is well

está siempre—it is always

estoy bien—I am well

estoy lista—I am ready

es nieve—it is snow

es verdad—it is true

familia—family

favorito/a(s)—favorite(s)

felicidad—happiness

futuro—future

gozo—joy

gracias por todo—thank you for everything

gran error—big mistake

hay tanto por hacer para preparar la casa para recibir un bebé—there is so much to do to prepare the house to receive a baby

hermoso/a—beautiful

importante—important

lazo—bow, ribbon, tie, etc.

la justicia—justice

La Navidad—Christmas

la noche—night

la reina—queen

la verdad—the truth

libelo—libel

lo sé—I know

lo siento—I am sorry

luces—lights

luto riguroso—deep mourning

maravilloso—marvelous

más lento por favor—slower, please

mejor—better

me desheredaron—they disinherited me

me encanta—I love it / it enchants me

me falta mucho también—I lack much as well

me gustaría mucho—I would like it very much

me gustaría presentarme—I would like to introduce/present myself

me parece—it seems to me

me vuelvo loca—I'm going crazy

mira—look

mi bebé—my baby

mi hija—my daughter

mi rey—my king

mi vida en—my life in

mi vida normal—my normal life

muchísimas gracias—thank you very much

muy complicado—very complicated

muy diferente—very different

muy rápido—very fast

muy—very

nada—nothing

necesito estar en casa—I need to be home

nieta—niece

no entiendo—I don't understand

no hay—there isn't

no hay problema—no problem

no lo quiero—I don't want

no puedo—I can't

no puedo aguantar más—I can't stand more

no quiero que te vayas—I don't want you to go

no te preocupes—don't worry yourself

nunca—never

obsesionado—obsessed

obvio—obvious

ocho—eight

otra vez—again

pañales—diapers

para mí—for me

particularmente—particularly

perfecto/a—perfect

Pascua—Easter

pero bueno—but okay

piensas—you think

poco tiempo—little time

por fin—at last

por qué—why

por supuesto—of course

porque—because

preciosa/o—precious

precisamente—precisely

qué buenísimo—how great

qué delicioso—how delicious

qué dolor—how painful / what pain

qué error—what error

qué es eso—what is this

qué necesitas—what do you (informal) need

qué pasa?—what happens?

qué pasó?—what happened?

qué romántico—how romantic

querido/a—dear

quizás—maybe

responsabilidades—responsibilities

reyes—kings

ridículo—ridiculous

romántico—romantic

rosario—rosary

se dice así—it is said like this

Señora—Lady/Ma'am

separarme—separate myself

siempre—always

siesta - nap/rest

si está bien—if it is okay

soldados—soldiers

soy—I am

soy una—I am a

tan chistoso—so funny

tan delicioso—so delicious

tan feliz—so happy

tan formal—so formal

tan lejos—so far

tan pronto—as soon as

tan terribles—so terrible

tengo una pregunta—I have a question

terrores—terrors

te amo por siempre—I love you forever

te lo prometo—I promise you it

te necesito—I need you

todavía—still/nonetheless

todo bien—all is well

todo el mundo—all the world

todo eso—all this

todo lo necesario para prepararnos—all that is necessary to prepare us

todos los papeles—all the papers

todos—all

tradiciones—traditions

una bolsa—a bag

un ángel—an angel

un gran hombre—a great man

un poco—a little

un poco tarde—a little late

un ratito—a little bit

vas a quedarte conmigo?—are you going to stay with me?

vaya—go

vaya a tu cama—go to your bed

verdad—truth

vista—view

vuelvo a casa—I return home
ya nos fuimos de allá—we already left there
ya duerme—he/she/it is asleep now
yo también—me too
yo voy—I go

Sources

BritishBattles.com. "Storming of San Sebastian." Accessed November 5, 2025. https://www.britishbattles.com/peninsular-war/storming-of-san-sebastian/.

"The British Rape and Destruction of San Sebastian." The Wild Peak. May 10, 2013. https://thewildpeak.wordpress.com/2013/05/10/the-british-rape-and-destruction-of-san-sebastian/.

Collins, Bruce. Wellington and the Siege of San Sebastian, 1813. Pen and Sword Military, 2018.

Daly, Gavin. Storm and Sack: British Sieges, Violence and the Laws of War in the Napoleonic Era, 1799–1815. Cambridge University Press, 2022.

"The Gentlemanly Professions." Random Bits of Fascination. February 12, 2019. https://randombitsoffascination.com/2019/02/12/gentlemanly-professions/.

Grace, Maria. "Regency Christmas Traditions: Twelfth Night Revelries." Random Bits of Fascination. January 4, 2016. https://randombitsoffascination.com/2016/01/04/regency-christmas-traditions-twelfth-night-revelries/.

Greene, Elena. "An Interesting Condition: Pregnancy and Childbirth During the Regency." Accessed November 5, 2025. http://www.elenagreene.com/regencycb.html.

History.com editors. "Church of England." Accessed November 5, 2025. https://www.history.com/articles/church-of-england.

James, Syrie. "Jane Austen & Regency Christmas Traditions." December 12, 2022. https://syriejames.com/2022/12/12/jane-austen-regency-christmas-traditions/.

Leighton, Mary Elizabeth, and Lisa Surridge. "The Vocabulary of Pregnancy." VictorianWeb.org. May 2, 2023. https://victorianweb.org/science/maternity/uvic/13.html.

Mackenzie, John. "41. Podcast on the Storming of San Sebastian between 11th July and 9th September 1813 in the Peninsular War." britishbattles.com podcast. https://britishbattles.podbean.com/e/41-podcast-on-the-storming-of-san-sebastian-between-11th-july-and-9th-september-1813-in-the-peninsular-war-john-mackenzie-s-britishbattlescom-podcasts/.

Moon, Joshua. Wellington's Two-Front War: The Peninsular Campaigns, at Home and Abroad, 1808–1814. University of Oklahoma Press, 2011.

Muir, Rory. "Commentary Explorer Results." Accessed November 5, 2025. https://lifeofwellington.co.uk/commentary/chapter-32-the-pyrenees-july-september-1813/.

Parkinson, Christian. "The Peninsular War: The Siege of San Sebastian (1813) and the First Ever Creeping Barrage." Posted March 9, 2022, by Redcoat History. YouTube. https://youtu.be/etJ6lmTXkVY?si=-4IEqv1A_tBWq_dt.

"Regency Lingo." Regency Reader. Accessed November 5, 2025. https://regrom.com/regency-lingo/.

"Saint Sebastian Dressed for the Party." Lacunza. Accessed November 5, 2025. https://lacunza.com/en/san-sebastian-vestida-para-la-fiesta/.

"San Sebastian 1813 – 2013." The Wild Peak. July 24, 2013. https://thewildpeak.wordpress.com/2013/07/24/san-sebastian-1813-2013/.

Selin, Shannon. "A 19th-Century Spanish Christmas." Accessed November 5, 2025. https://shannonselin.com/2019/12/19th-century-spanish-christmas/.

"Spain Nobility." FamilySearch.org. August 12, 2024. https://www.familysearch.org/en/wiki/Spain_Nobility.

Wikimedia Foundation. "Arthur Wellesley, 1st Duke of Wellington." Last modified November 5, 2025. https://en.wikipedia.org/wiki/Arthur_Wellesley,_1st_Duke_of_Wellington.

Wikimedia Foundation. "Hidalgo (nobility)." Last modified September 24, 2025. https://en.wikipedia.org/wiki/Hidalgo_(nobility).

Wikimedia Foundation. "History of the Catholic Church in Spain." Last modified October 25, 2025. https://en.wikipedia.org/wiki/History_of_the_Catholic_Church_in_Spain.

Wikimedia Foundation. "Siege of San Sebastián." Last modified November 4, 2025. https://en.wikipedia.org/wiki/Siege_of_San_Sebastián.

About the Author

Jessica has never been able to put a book down late at night, and she notoriously developed the habit of reading Shakespeare in the wee hours of the morning during high school. But her passion for writing started even earlier, when her sixth-grade teacher read her first attempt at historical fiction and told her she should become an author someday. She adored her AP English classes and went on to receive her bachelor's in English literature and creative writing. After serving a Latter-day Saint mission in Argentina, Jessica fell in love with the Spanish language and the history of foreign countries, which helped inspire her first novel. Jessica gets writing motivation by reading daily and constantly watching adaptations of Jane Austen's works. She never goes anywhere without her emotional support Kindle.

Jessica loves crafting, baking, going on walks, playing with her kids, and eating anything that has cream cheese frosting. She lives a real-life love story with her husband, who gives her plenty of inspiration for her stories. Together they are building their happily-ever-after as Utah-born, Midwestern "transplants" in Wisconsin.

Learn more about Jessica and her upcoming projects by connecting with her online!

Instagram: @author.jessica.brousseau
Facebook: Author Jessica Brousseau

Scan to visit

www.authorjessicabrousseau.com